Xuxub Must Die

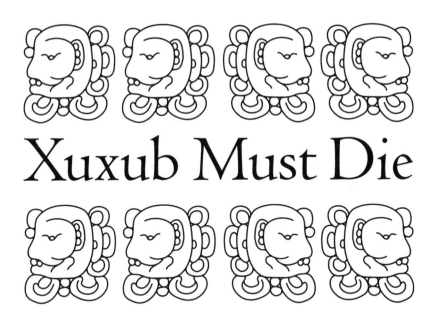

Xuxub Must Die

The Lost Histories of a Murder on the Yucatan

P A U L   S U L L I V A N

UNIVERSITY OF PITTSBURGH PRESS

Published by the University of Pittsburgh Press, Pittsburgh, Pa., 15260
Copyright © 2004, University of Pittsburgh Press
All rights reserved
Manufactured in the United States of America
Printed on acid-free paper
10 9 8 7 6 5 4 3 2 1
ISBN 0-8229-4230-5

Library of Congress Cataloging-in-Publication Data

Sullivan, Paul R.
Xuxub must die : the lost histories of a murder on the Yucatan / Paul
Sullivan.
p. cm.—(Pitt Latin American series)
Includes bibliographical references (p.   ) and index.
ISBN 0-8229-4230-5 (cloth : alk. paper)
1. Mayas—Mexico—Yucatán (State)—History. 2. Peasant
uprisings—Mexico—Yucatán (State) 3. Plantation workers—Crimes
against—Mexico—Yucatán (State) 4. Yucatán (Mexico :
State)—History—19th century. 5. Murder—Mexico—Yucatán (State) 6.
Cen, Bernardino, d. 1875 or 6. 7. Mayas—Wars—Mexico—Yucatán
(State) I. Title. II. Series.
F1435.1.Y89S85 2004
972'.650812—dc22
2003021184

Contents

Xuxub Must Die

Introduction

Terrible Beauty

I WENT WITH MIGUEL, A MAYA FRIEND, LOOKING FOR Xuxub. Cartographers hadn't exerted themselves charting that forsaken corner of Yucatan. You couldn't just find Xuxub on a map.

We came upon the white ruins of a sugar plantation. I thought those might be it, so in Maya I hailed two men laboring on the road. Waving hands they cut me off. They weren't Maya. They came from Veracruz and didn't know the name of that old estate. They had heard, though, that on those walls appeared strange writing which none had yet deciphered.

"Let's go get scolded," Miguel quipped as we went to check it out. I wasn't worried about the trespassing. I sweated the snakes. In the midst of those stout walls, stacks, and sluices, fallen brush lay so thick our feet never touched the ground. Who knew what lurked down there? For a good while we inspected the ruins inside and out but found no inscriptions at all. I guess those fellows from Veracruz had a good laugh on us.

Coming out on the other side we spied a hut nearby. Its elderly owner sat in the shade occupied in some task. They don't get many visitors out there. He dropped what he was doing and watched intently as we approached. In Maya again, this time with success, I declared we sought Xuxub. No, he explained with a hint of a chuckle. Those were not the ruins of Xuxub. That was the plantation San Eusebio, founded early in the twentieth century but soon abandoned when the revolution arrived to free its slaves. (How long had he sat there, waiting for someone to ask?)

The ruins of the Xuxub plantation lay ten kilometers further east. The fellow used to hike there through the forest, so he knew. But a recent hurricane had littered the ground with trees and obliterated the trail. Such was his excuse for declining to lead us there. He said we'd have to travel by launch along the coast and through the mangroves to reach Xuxub, if that's where we wanted to go.

Foreigners visit Yucatan for temples and pyramids, beaches and blue

water. Just a mile back down the road stood ancient structures, likely once
part of the largest Maya town on the north coast of Yucatan and a major
port for coastal trade before the arrival of the Spaniards. But I had not
come drawn to spectacles of lost civilization. Remains of more recent vin-
tage attracted me. On the coast at Chiquila we met two brothers who
could take us. They didn't need to ask why we'd go out there.

Almost the only stories you'll hear of Xuxub are told in Maya, in villages like that from which my companion came. What happened there
once reverberated across all of Yucatan. It made front-page news in New
York, too. Then memory failed. Time alone was not the culprit. Keepers of
history encouraged us to forget. What happened there was too painful,
awkward, controversial. A few pages of chronicle were rewritten, and
Xuxub vanished. Almost.

I'd first heard of Xuxub a decade before when as an anthropologist I
lived among Mayas in Quintana Roo. The tale was brief, but a little history can go a long way. While working on another story, I chanced upon a
State Department file concerning the murder of an American at Xuxub. It
had to be the same known to my Maya friends. The name (*shooshoob*,
"whistling") is too rare. A fellow American lived and died out there, long
before archeology and anthropology, tourism, sport fishing, scuba diving,
and cave exploration drew tens of thousands of my countrymen to the
shores of the Yucatan. What twisted path brought this working man to
Xuxub and to his encounter with the predecessors of my friend Miguel?
What happened to him there?

Those weren't questions that Mayas ever pondered. It's enough that
the American was white like their enemies and played a destined part in
their history. Others who once wrote and talked about Xuxub took little
more interest in the man. He was just another gringo, come like so many
others to make a buck, a minor example of aggressive, brazen, often insulting foreign capitalists whose grip upon the people and economy of
Mexico grew stronger by the year. His death represented a slight, but
hardly tragic (maybe even welcomed), receding of that foreign tide. In yet
other hands, those of attorneys, jurists, and diplomats, the dead American
became a symbol of any honest, hardworking citizen whose rights are brutally trampled in a foreign land, for which offense, no matter how trivial in
the grander scheme of things, nations must account.

Of course, whatever happened to that American didn't happen to the
shadow puppet that he became in death. It happened to a man who had a

full life. I thought to understand it all, I'd uncover what that life had been. So, too, the lives of others who built Xuxub up and tore it down, most of whom perished there.

Xuxub struck a deep chord in folks like Miguel, descendants of Indians who waged a long war against their white oppressors and who for decades enjoyed hard-won independence in the deep forests of the Caribbean littoral. They lost that independence only in the time of Miguel's grandparents, and from that elder generation Miguel and his cohorts learned many stories of the time of war and sacrifice. To the tale of Xuxub they return again and again, at least when I'm around to listen, as though that story best captures who they think they are and how they became that way, their greatness and their flaws, and where they might be headed, for better or for worse.

Yet the cherished tale as it's told by Miguel and other Mayas doesn't jibe with stories we've been telling ever since they fought that war. The first and bitterly hostile generation of historians understood Maya rebels simply as enemies of civilization; Indians kept in darkness for centuries by a jealous Catholic church, confused when a new era of enlightenment offered them new freedoms as citizens of Mexico. Egged on by white opportunists and ambitious leaders of their own, they waged unjust and futile war against the inexorable march of progress. It was a war of evil against good, and evil wore an Indian mask. In such a history the tale of Xuxub, should it be told, would strike a discordant note. What happened there obscured boundaries of good and evil, of barbarity and civilization. The story of Xuxub would tarnish the shining image of progress that white authors so cherished and championed. In modern times more sympathetic chroniclers rehabilitated the Maya rebels and on paper marshaled them to fight the battles we wished they had. We recast Maya warriors as peasant insurgents fighting the kind of war of national liberation with which half of the twentieth century made us so familiar. We cast them as ethnic militants struggling to preserve their unique culture and identity, once we had lost ours in the bland commercial sameness of postmodern times. We championed them as social revolutionaries battling (our) encroaching western capitalism so that they could preserve their primitive egalitarianism and harmonious relationship to nature. Or, in good Mexican tradition, we admired them as agrarian activists who killed only to save their land and their simple but balanced farming way of life. Perhaps one day we'll yet marshal those dead rebels to the cause of environmental-

ism, or some other -ism of our choosing. In short, where enemy historians
had cast them as evil, we embraced the Maya and viewed them only as
good, and having done so had no use for a story like Xuxub, in which good
and evil seem so inextricably entwined, and in which the causes and motives of men are so disputable.

In any event, that's not how Miguel, his people, and his predecessors
viewed themselves—as warriors for our notions of evil or for good.
They've long understood themselves to be, as they say, "just humans," children of God, the same as their enemies. As for why they fought that war,
they cite no cause for which they killed, only causes that drove them to it.
They were raped and beaten, cheated and starved, killed with impunity,
until they turned to killing because they had no other choice and nothing
more to lose. They killed the whites and died by droves themselves and all
the while inched closer to that God who too had suffered and been cruci-
fied and who returned to the forest to help his Maya children in their
struggle. They didn't fight for a cause. They fought simply to live and because it seemed God willed it, and no one dared to defy God.

For now the fighting is over; times have changed. Miguel and his
neighbors still organize themselves in military-style companies ruled by
officers like Miguel himself. They used to fight and pray. Now they just
pray, keep the God house up, make sacrifices for rain and health and favor,
and await with some expectation the return of war in the Final Days.
Times have changed, and when they reckon just when that change began,
Xuxub comes quickly to mind. What happened there altered the course of
their history, at least as they tell it. At Xuxub they broke ranks with God
momentarily, and defeat followed as He said it would. They pay the price
to this very day, or so some of them see it. They're only human, and at
Xuxub the flaws of humans had great consequence.

The story I'll tell about Xuxub isn't precisely theirs, but I hope for
once in this written tale of war Miguel and his friends will at least recognize themselves. At Xuxub cruel deeds were done, some by Mayas like
Miguel. Telling this story might make them seem blindly cruel, even barbaric, as their white oppressors so often claimed. It shouldn't, though.
Maya rebels weren't barbaric. War was barbaric, and men, Mayas included, did terrible things to the children of God. Their humanity included a capacity for evil. Deny that capacity, and one denies their
humanity. Xuxub as a Maya parable, a revelation of humanity—that's
why I started on the trail. From the ruins of Xuxub, I later learned, other

people had drawn quite different lessons about themselves and their world.

From Chiquila, our only hope of getting to Xuxub was if those two brothers would take us in their boat. But the eldest hemmed and hawed. If they went, they'd lose half a day's work. Maybe a whole day. It was a long way out to Xuxub. Curiosity drew men and children close as Fidencio made up his mind. "Well, what do you think?" I finally asked. He wordlessly splayed two fingers against his chest. The price was steep, two hundred dollars, but I quickly said OK.

We were still standing on the plaza when the grim-faced mayor strode up. Strangers arriving with a queer request prompted someone to fetch authority. I explained I wanted to go to Xuxub. The news didn't please him. He consented, though, comforted to hear we would leave them the next day. Chiquila is a fishing village and parking lot for the ferry to Holbox Island. A few stores, small masonry houses, and a church surround the plaza. Pole and thatch dwellings string down the beach, and a long pier juts over the water. All that is sandwiched between the swamp and a broad lagoon. Dead by day, it bustles after dark with vehicles coming and going. Maybe they just come to meet a late ferry or buy the day's catch. But that distant corner of the Yucatan Peninsula, so close to the sea and so far from everywhere else, has been a favored haunt for pirates, later for smugglers, fugitives, and anyone else needing to enter and leave the country discreetly. Whatever they had going for themselves in Chiquila, they seemed not to want strangers hanging around long.

Before daybreak we went out to the pier, even as Fidencio and his brother motored the launch around. They'd brought shotguns. Miguel regretted not bringing his own, but we got in anyway and set out for Xuxub. For twenty or thirty minutes the launch cruised full throttle eastward off the southern shore of the briny lagoon. Fidencio manned the outboard astern, while his brother, perched on the bow, watched for rocks or shallows or floating debris, pointing out here and there the curious eyes of fresh water that bubbled up from below. Guided by a solitary coconut tree standing on a low spit of beach, suddenly Fidencio swung the boat toward shore and into the hidden mouth of the Xuxub River.

Back when their father was still alive he had often boated out to farm and hunt around Xuxub. Each time he went, he'd prune the mangroves, slashing here and there with his machete wherever the bush threatened to choke off the narrow passage. The spirit of that old man had so entwined itself with the thickets that when he died, the mangrove languished overnight. Since then it had returned, lush as ever, and it slowed our progress to a crawl.

Eventually the water grew so shallow that Fidencio's brother had to pole us the final yards, until a drought-thirsty river could carry us no further. We jumped out where a low bridge once spanned the way. By then I realized the folly of our trip. Now that I was there, I knew little better than before just where Xuxub lay. We'd traveled east, then south, then so many turns later through the mangroves, I could not say precisely where we were. Only that we were at Xuxub. I should have taken this as a sign. Each of my efforts to decipher what really happened there would bring me to the same point—amidst truths without sound bearings.

Just where was Xuxub? It was a no-place, really. No one ever happily called it home. No one really belonged there. People came there, or were thrown together, in one of those odd, often fleeting, sometimes bloody encounters across national and ethnic divides. Saint Anthony stood nominally as protector over the place, and once a year with prayer, drink, music, dance, and fireworks they'd fete that icon of charity—"go and sell that thou hast, and give to the poor, and thou shalt have treasure in heaven." Yet over Xuxub every other day reigned money, and to that men sacrificed tolerance and mutual respect, dignity and truth, and, finally, human lives.

Fidencio and his brother forged ahead. They slashed at the emerald thicket of fronds and saplings as mosquitoes, our constant, buzzing companions, welcomed us into that forsaken corner of the world. At first the guides fumbled for their bearings. It all looked different from the last time they were there. The hurricane had knocked down many trees, and then sunlight hitting the forest floor ignited blasts of new growth. As they hacked on, however, a stack came into view. There once stood the rum distillery. All of it had long since crumbled but that chimney, held erect by an ancient tree, as though nature itself remembered yet what had happened there.

Further on Fidencio uncovered another structure—four masonry walls, no roof, no door, no windows. Some sort of storage tank. Elsewhere in the rank tangle near the river's edge one could still spy parts of the fine, tiled floor of the plantation's big house. That's what they told us, anyway. Most else had vanished long ago. The bodies and the blood, the echoes of music and screams. Mosquitoes taunted us to move on, so we did. Little more than an hour after landing at Xuxub, we boarded the launch and drifted downriver again.

What happened at Xuxub once echoed far and wide. Rival city newspapers trumpeted one explanation or another for the killings there, and diplomats tussled over who to blame. More than one U.S. president and several secretaries of state handled plaintive missives from the aggrieved. The case even wormed its way into compendiums of international law.

The killing took little more than a day, but angry pens shed ink for decades to come, until they finally stilled. Then only the talk was left, and the talk goes on. Everyone knew from the start who did the killing. But why did it happen? What sinuous chain of human events, passions, hopes, and frailties had caused Xuxub to die? That question begged. The answers seemed simple, though each contained the germ of a different vision of the world. Each attempt to answer the question, *Why?* evoked an alternative world in which Xuxub and its people had, of course, to perish. Neighbors then lived in such different worlds. So too, today, when they speak of what happened there. Each story told starts in a different place and leads you down one trail or another until you reach Xuxub. Any trail you follow will get you there, but leave you with a different notion about why Xuxub must die.

The event still fresh, storytellers chose their paths well. Some had lost kin there, some property, some lost prospects and gained a grievance or a right to boast, or sullen satisfaction to share about vengeance and the like. They were partisan and fashioned tales to lure others to their cause. Until, at last, blood debts were paid, money changed hands, some history was rewritten, and Xuxub could be buried deep where none might chance upon it.

Why now dig it up again? Partly to wonder at the spectacle of it all, at how everything can come together to make for such a very bad day. It's like watching flames consume what man has built, illuminating a dark sky. Terrible, but not without its beauty, too. So with the story of Xuxub.

There's the spectacle, too, of intelligent gentlemen deploying venerable texts and skill at rational disputation in vain attempts to agree upon what happened and why. Attorneys, judges, and the law could extinguish lives or spare them but never find the truth behind it all. Representatives of sister republics appealing to august principles—the rights and duties of man and nations—could find no common ground in equity or justice, as long and hard as they tried. Truth, it seems, must yield to interest, power, and prejudice.

Why dig it up again? A kind of duty inclines me to. Mayas remember. Their white neighbors have forgotten. We've forgotten, even though what happened at Xuxub for one brief moment linked us all. What happened at that little no-place in the mangroves dashed hopes in a suburb of New York, raised passions and rhetoric in Washington and Mexico City, and eased fear on a far frontier of the British Empire. Close by, many heralded Xuxub as an extraordinary triumph for civilization and humanity. Others just as grandly lamented what happened as a rupture between man and God. Yet only Mayas now remember, choose to remember. And the rest of us? Is there nothing of Xuxub worth remembering, worth preserving, besides a gravestone in New Jersey, a skull in a museum in Yucatan, some meager ruins half-lost in the mangroves? Listening once more to the story of Xuxub, we might recover something lost, something we should recall.

Before Miguel and I set out to find Xuxub, Miguel's aged superior lamented the forgetting, even among the Maya. Years before, he said, their priests still knew the history of older times. They could tell the stories. From them one learned much. But it's not that way anymore. They don't know or won't tell, and slowly people are forgetting. People have their own thoughts now. There are so many thoughts, so many views now, but we don't know, he concluded, which ones are *true*.

About Xuxub I thought at least I'd find the truth. No one had ever gotten to the bottom of it all, sifted through the evidence to tell what really happened there and why. One before had actually tried. A young American consul in Yucatan followed trails as far as he could before fleeing for places more familiar. Afterward many others offered their explanations for the mayhem at Xuxub. But which was true? Miguel and his neighbors would like to know. So too maybe that legion of my countrymen tourists, treading well-worn paths to the beach or pyramids not so very far from Xuxub, would be interested in the fate of one who came before them to this far corner of Mexico.

Before reading on, know this. I never did get to the bottom of it all, or find one true account to share with others. At best I reached a place where one can watch it all, a calm in the eye of the storm of death and debate that once raged over Xuxub. And of those different stories once told about Xuxub, which is really true? That's not for me to say. In any event, when you get to the end, you'll know as much as I. Let then each reader judge.

10 October

So late in the season they might count themselves lucky. No hurricane would hit the coast of Yucatan that year. Rain might still fall. One hoped for such brief respite from the heat. But they'd be spared that strongest of storms, what Mayas called *chac ikal*. They carried on with their tasks that morning in October. Some harvested corn, others prepared to plant fresh ground with sugarcane, confident that nature would tolerate man a while longer on that small plantation wedged between the red mangrove walls of the northern coast and endless savannas and forests of the south and east.

Two years before nature had punished them for their hubris. One September day pale blue skies quickly blackened. The wind began to blow, then to howl, then to rage. Rain started falling, and people quickly took to their houses. For the next five days gales raked the land. A surging sea broke through the mangroves and ebbed ankle-deep. The angry elements carried off the homes of plantation laborers and the sheds for storing corn and sugar. Uprooted crops bobbed on the water and tumbled trees blocked passage for miles in every direction. Two low bridges over the normally placid, black, serpentine river disappeared, and all that men and women had labored to build or produce over the last year at Xuxub was gone. Only the people remained to start again, if their master told them to. He was still new to Yucatan and could believe, as he wrote his wife just after the blow, "it cannot be posable to have such gales every year, and the prospects is all good."

They built their houses and planted field of cane again, and two years later the skies remained clear and the crop looked to be the best ever. If any saw a storm coming, none told the master.[a]

One

Promises of Quiet

THE NEW CONSUL WAS YOUNG, EAGER, INEXPERIENCED, and far from all he knew, posted to defend his nation's interests in a distant corner of Mexico. If he survived his first assignment abroad, he might aspire to a position in more cultured surroundings. Six months shy of his twenty-first year, Alphonse Lespinasse landed at the Mexican port of Progreso and assumed his office as the consul of the United States in Merida, Yucatan.

Born on Long Island, Lespinasse heralded from Manhattan where he'd attended Fort Washington Institute. He applied for his first real job simply by writing a letter to the secretary of state in October of 1874, seeking the vacant position in Yucatan. He had never visited Mexico, but he was well educated and knew Spanish. Of course connections, not qualifications, made the difference. A score of New York merchants engaged in Mexican commerce supported his candidacy, and Lespinasse was a protégé of Charles O'Conor, national political figure and one of the most prominent attorneys in the country. As a prosecutor of New York's Boss Tweed, O'Conor was still trying to recover the public's looted money when he paused to support Lespinasse's bid for a start in the consular service. Even that bevy of New York merchants and a highly respected attorney, however, couldn't clinch the post for Lespinasse. He needed the backing, too, of three key members of the corrupt New York Republican patronage machine—Thomas Murphy, former collector of the scandal-ridden Port of New York Customs House; the current collector of the port, Chester Arthur (whom years later an assassin would make president of the United States); and George Bliss, a federal attorney in New York who had a suspicious knack for blowing federal corruption cases. They got Lespinasse the job.[1]

The Yucatan post was hardly a plum. The pay was poor. No other nation had a full consulate there. Over the previous twenty years the position of U.S. consul had been vacant for months or years at a time. When it was filled, the consul was usually a peninsular—Mexicans naturalized as Americans but otherwise long-term residents of Yucatan. The most recent occupant had hung on just seventeen months. Six months after he quit Lespinasse arrived to pick things up in December of 1874.[2]

Few Americans lived in Yucatan. Only seven registered with the consulate and only three were native Americans, that is to say, really foreigners in that place.[3] U.S. consuls in places like Merida mostly busied themselves filing reports on port commerce, assisting distressed or abandoned American seamen (giving them vouchers for passage home), renewing passports, and the like. They would also, if the case seemed to warrant, assist American businessmen or skippers in conflicts with Mexican authorities, especially over import duties or the seizure of cargoes or vessels.

Foreigners hardly flocked to that corner of Mexico. The Yucatan Peninsula had no mines of precious metals so coveted elsewhere. It had few factories, only dreams of railroads to come, and most of its farms produced little beyond what locals would consume. The country was still only slowly recovering from its share and more of the revolts and civil wars that had afflicted the whole Mexican republic. A catastrophic uprising of the peninsula's Maya Indians back in 1847 cut population almost by a third and destroyed much of the state. (In the desperate first months of that uprising, Yucatan offered itself to the United States, if only Americans would come to save them. A Congress already distracted by growing sectional tension between slave and free states declined the offer.) Once Yucatecans had largely suppressed the revolt and pushed remaining rebel Indians into distant forested recesses of the peninsula, whites returned to battling one another over politics and the spoils of government, until the French arrived to impose an imperial peace in Mexico. Yucatecans of all political stripes largely tolerated the imperialists, and for a while Yucatan enjoyed some relative tranquility and order. Once French troops began withdrawing from central Mexico, Yucatecans rose up and drove their imperialists out, too. Then back to fighting one another. For years Yucatan attracted some defeated American Confederates, a few intrepid archeologists and tourists come to see the Maya pyramids and temples, and hardly anybody else.

By the time Lespinasse assumed his post there things were actually looking up. The state was enjoying a rare period of prosperity, thanks to rising foreign demand for its principal export, henequen fiber for rope and

The Yucatan Peninsula

twine. Some locals busily converted their cattle haciendas to plantations of henequen and installed steam power to speed the time-consuming task of stripping fiber from henequen leaves. As they did so Yucatan exported more and more. A nascent sugar industry, destroyed back during the Indian uprising, rose from the ashes, too. Abandoned sugar estates were resettled and restocked, and new mills, boilers, and stills were installed.

Yucatecans built a new port to handle increasing exports, railroads were poised to move off the drawing board, and plans circulated to stimulate all the productive energies of the country.[4] American merchants expected to profit directly from Yucatan's awakening, and they sent an energetic young Lespinasse to watch over their growing interests there.

Yucatan's new port Progreso ranked middle among nine Mexican gulf ports, well behind the busy harbors of Veracruz or Matamoros.[5] But it was a new port, after all, and the exports of Yucatan were expected to grow substantially, especially with the United States. The New York merchants who backed Lespinasse expressed as much in their petition to the secretary of state. Talk like that about the boundless potential of a little-known place animated Lespinasse, too.

All told, it was not a bad place for a green twenty-year-old to get his start. Merida was neither a trouble spot in U.S.-Mexican relations (unlike posts closer to the northern border), nor an especially unhealthy place, usually. If Lespinasse did his job diligently, in a few years he'd move on to better posts in Latin America or even Europe. After acclimating himself a bit to his new surroundings, Lespinasse settled into his humble consular office—one room, one desk, one bookcase, two tables. Among his first official acts, Lespinasse requested Washington send new stationery and an American flag. He was still waiting for both nine months later when expatriate Robert Stephens walked in and turned Lespinasse's career on its head.[6]

Robert L. Stephens was co-owner and manager of a sugar estate called Xuxub out on the eastern frontier of Yucatan. He had hoped to be elsewhere at forty-four, already, he lamented, gray as a badger and bent like his aged father. At least he wouldn't have to stay there much longer, or so he hoped.

Stephens had little in common with the young American consul, except that both called home the banks of the Hudson River. Stephens came from Hoboken. His father had lived and labored as a gardener alongside other Irish immigrants on the great Stevens estate of that town.[7] In the early 1800s the Stevens marketed parts of their Hoboken fields in small lots to crowded Manhattanites, advertising lower taxes, no yellow fever, and a cheap ferry ride each day to work in the city. Of course Stevens owned the ferry. They hired immigrant laborers to build a quaint mansion at Castle Point, replant orchards neglected since the revolution, lay cobbled promenades, and prepare three or four acres as a bucolic getaway for city families which they dubbed the Elysian Fields.[8] They even laid out a baseball diamond, soon to become the home field for the Knickerbocker Base Ball Club of New York.[9]

It succeeded fabulously, for a while. Ten thousand Manhattanites crossed on warm summer Sundays to stroll the river walk, peek into Sibyl's cave and pay a penny for a glass of its spring water, amble through gardens and orchards, take a spin on the Stevens railroad amusement, visit the souvenir shop, view wax sculptures, watch baseball, or simply picnic on the fields. Jobs there were for the son of a Stevens laborer, nor did it hurt that James Stephens, who then lived in a house at the northeast corner of the Elysian Fields, named his son after the principal figure thereabouts, Robert L. Stevens, and asked the famous inventor and developer to be the child's godfather.[10] But young Robert Stephens had no lust to serve like his father as a park attendant or gardener, nor in any other capacity on the Stevens' suburban plantation. He shied too from labor in the manufactories of neighboring Jersey City and from mean toil with the rabble of Irish famine refugees then cutting railway tunnels through the nearby Bergen Hills. Instead, Robert signed on to a surveying expedition of the southern Atlantic coast. The work taught him drafting and engineering skills, and the voyage turned Robert's eye to southern lands, the Latin republics in which his family showed some interest. His father's dwelling on the edge of the Elysian Fields was known to all as the "Bolivar House," after the by then world famous and highly popular liberator of the young republics of South America.[11]

At eighteen Robert wed a kindred spirit from the Bowery, Mary Donohue, child of Irish immigrants, too, and soon both boarded a steamer bound not yet to Mexico, but rather to the island of Cuba. Although leaving home, Robert and Mary were hardly mimicking their immigrant parents. Their fathers and mothers, fortunate though they were to have had the means to emigrate from Ireland, had left that green isle with reluctance. Tens of thousands of pre-famine immigrants greeted arrival in North America as a deliverance from loathsome landlords, from the avaricious English, and from the inexorably deepening misery that some already foresaw could only culminate in catastrophe. Yet sorrow tempered their joy. They'd rather have stayed home and not crossed the North Atlantic in the holds of rickety timber ships. They'd rather that Ireland were free and prosperous, or that at least a man there could feed and shelter his family as just reward for honest labor. Thousands of Irish immigrants like the parents of Robert and Mary forever bore the bitterness of being exiles and martyrs on foreign soil.[12]

Robert Stephens and his wife were different. They could have stayed at home. Their leaving was no flight; they were not exiles or martyrs. They ventured far from home as adventurers, pioneers, even heroes. They struck out for unfamiliar lands not just to make a living, but to play their small part in the grand march of progress, carrying their skills, their dignity as working people, and their American values to deploy in the improvement of a foreign place.

In wars of liberation decades before, Spain had lost most of its once-vast colonial empire. Cuba had remained loyal, however, and by the 1850s witnessed a feverish expansion of its sugar industry. Machinery built in the U.S. or England drove that expansion, and to install and maintain the mills and boilers, Cubans hired American and British machinists and engineers. Robert Stephens went to Cuba as one of a legion of such skilled men who kept boilers hot and wheels turning on virtually every island plantation and on the railroads over which their product moved.[13]

Machinists earned good pay in Cuba, but Robert Stephens aspired to more, and over almost two decades on the island he graduated from improving sugar estates to managing a small one around Nuevitas, a small port on the north-central coast. His wife bore him two daughters there, one of whom when grown married a local cigar maker. The whole family might well have settled permanently in Cuba were it not for the vortex of revolutionary violence and repression that soon engulfed all on the island.

Revolution had been brewing for decades, as increasing numbers of Cubans yearned for their independence from Spain. The cause was popular among Americans, too, and some joined the ranks while others cheered it on from stateside. Some of those Americans dreamed of a greater American union and believed that with independence, Cuba would seek admission. For others, many of recent immigrant origin, the Cuban struggle resonated with their own dreams of freedom for their homelands. That longing was especially intense with the Irish. They swelled the ranks of those thousands—no aristocrats, monopolists, or Wall Street types present, according to one speaker—who one night gathered under the flag of Cuban independence in a bonfire-lit square of Jersey City. Fifty-two cannon shots saluted fifty-two captured American volunteers recently executed by the Spaniards, and the crowd cheered to hear that it was "the right and the duty of the citizens of the free and enlightened republic of the United States to sympathize with and aid every effort of the people of any country under despotic sway to free themselves from the curse of despotism." To help the people of Cuba struggling for their independence was even a special duty of the men of New Jersey, "who have ever responded to the cry of the oppressed of whatever land."[14]

Robert Stephens hadn't gone to Cuba to fight for its independence, but he could not escape the times in which he lived, the crosscurrents of conflicting aspirations that animated men repeatedly to arms, especially out around Nuevitas, a hotbed of resentment against the Spaniards. When in October 1868 a small band of Cuban revolutionaries issued yet another declaration of independence, the district in which Nuevitas lay quickly became the main theater of the contest. Small bands of revolutionaries enjoyed early successes against Spanish garrisons, but the struggle rapidly stalemated and turned maddeningly brutal.

It was a very dangerous place for Americans to linger, and more than one railroad man or machinist like Robert Stephens rued having ever left home.[15] But the predicament of Robert Stephens was especially delicate. He was an intimate friend of one of the revolutionary leaders of the district, Napoleon Arango, for whom, it seems, Stephens worked.[16] Arango and his brothers had impeccable revolutionary credentials, but they weren't happy to be fighting just now.[17] Before the declaration that started the war, Arango had tried to convince his colleagues they had not prepared well enough to defeat the forces that Spain would send against them. He also feared the effect that war and independence would have upon social order in Cuba, which is to say, upon the slaves. According to Arango, Cuba was not ready to be sole master of its destiny or to abolish slavery. Despite their views, when the new revolt began the Arango brothers freed their slaves and accepted commissions in the insurrection—Napoleon as "general in the Army of National Liberation," and his brother Augusto as department chief. However, while they fought for the revolution, they also maneuvered to provoke a rapid, negotiated settlement that would bring Cuba substantial reforms and autonomy, but not a complete break with the mother country.[18] The gambit failed miserably. Spanish soldiers treacherously murdered Augusto when he arrived to negotiate with their peace commissioners, and Napoleon's rebel colleagues turned on him and charged him with treason. When rebels seized Napoleon, Robert Stephens was by his side and loudly protested his innocence. So they grabbed Robert Stephens, too.[19]

A revolutionary tribunal acquitted Napoleon Arango and released him along with his loudmouthed American friend. Meanwhile, however, with the arrival of Spanish reinforcements in the district, the war began to turn decisively against the rebellion there. Both sides took to burning as much as they could until the district lay in ruins.[20] Spaniards attacked El Destino, Arango's plantation near Las Minas, and later almost managed to capture Napoleon's family. Soon after, Napoleon was offered the post of rebel commander-in-chief. He declined the honor. He still opposed this war, and despite the murder of his brother, destruction of his estate, and persecution of his family, Napoleon took the bold and desperate step of defecting to the enemy. From the Spanish side he then pleaded with his former colleagues to lay down their arms and go home. Some did, others tried but were shot by their rebel colleagues, and one hundred thousand deaths later, the Cuban revolution ended in failure.[21]

Before his friend Napoleon turned, Robert Stephens and his family (including their Cuban son-in-law) abandoned their Cuban homes and sailed for the States. Apart from a stint during the Civil War, when Robert Stephens helped install machinery in Union gunboats at New York's Novelty Iron Works, he and his family had spent little time in Hoboken over the previous twenty years.[22] The town had changed almost beyond recognition. It was now a crowded place, its population ballooning from some twenty-six hundred to over thirteen thousand. The waterfronts of Hoboken and neighboring Jersey City bustled with trans-Atlantic and Latin American arrivals and departures, and the streets near the wharves hosted dozens of hotels to cater to the crowds moving through the port. Matthiesen and Wiecher Sugar Refining Company, the largest sugar refinery in the United States, rose in Jersey City, so over the docks and neighboring streets flowed sweeteners from the south and from Europe, as well.[23]

Robert Stephens's father had retired from gardening for the wealthy and opened an alehouse on the fringe of the Elysian Fields.[24] When Robert returned, they all moved to the escarpment overlooking Hoboken and the Hudson. They bought house lots in West Hoboken, a swampy one-street village of immigrants where a humble man could at least be master of his home.[25]

If Robert Stephens planned to settle down there, fate soon tempted him southward again, this time to the peninsula of Yucatan. For years the politicians and businessmen of the Mexican state of Yucatan had discussed and debated, and finally planned, construction of a new port to accommodate their growing exports, especially henequen fiber. Their principal port since colonial times, Sisal, was too shallow and inconvenient to handle expanded trade, and by 1871 they were ready to commence construction of facilities at a new port called Progreso. The architect of that project, the locally revered engineer Juan Miguel Castro, contacted the New York firm of Moller and Thebaud to seek their assistance in hiring an engineer to supervise erection of the main pier. Moller and Thebaud, in turn, picked Robert Stephens for the job.[26]

Stephens sailed for Yucatan and was on the job by May. Eight months later the new port had a pier. The wooden dock ended up too short, standing dry at low tide, but that would have to do. Before he could head home again, Stephens found his other talents in demand. One of the wealthy plantation families of Yucatan had the contract to supply lumber for the pier. When the job was done they hired Stephens to install sugar-milling and refining equipment on one of their estates far east of the capital. It was out there that Robert Stephens succumbed to the siren's song of Yucatan's elite.[27]

The political and economic leaders of Yucatan had long believed that the main obstacle to economic development of their corner of the world was the Indian population, still numerically predominant and locked into inefficient corn farming in small communities throughout the peninsula. Maya Indians raised almost everything the city- and town-dwellers of Yucatan ate, and this became even truer as white-owned haciendas abandoned cattle and corn to grow henequen for American twine factories. Yet whites held little hope that Indians with poor land, little credit, and scant incentive would ever get with the times and produce exportable products or even keep up with the rising food needs of an expanding urban population. Instead, the wise pronounced, Yucatan must lure European or North American colonists. The main commercial newspaper in Merida waxed eloquent, assuring that: "the influence of foreigners civilizes people, banishes prejudices, perfects industry, agriculture and the arts, develops commerce and propagates abundance and the celestial benedictions. Where there are no foreigners, all appears to stagnate; without life and movement, everything diminishes, and degrades itself and life comes to be impossible in that corrupt, intolerant and miserable society."[28] Yucatan's leaders had already gotten some 250 Germans to cross the Atlantic and establish a farming colony on the peninsula, and some Cubans fleeing their own war had come over as well. Perhaps still more from other nations could be enticed. Men like Robert Stephens.

Working out east, Robert Stephens noticed a small sugar estate up for sale. Mauricio Palmero, a small-time cattle rancher and merchant, had founded Xuxub in the wilderness just two or three years earlier. He had thirty workers and their families there cultivating corn and sugarcane. The little place prospered, but failing health and a messy divorce forced him to liquidate. Just as Stephens showed up there, Palmero was desperately seeking a buyer for Xuxub. Stephens didn't have that kind of money, but he knew how to run a plantation. If someone would stake him the price, he'd make a go of it on the eastern frontier of Yucatan. Stephens didn't have to look very hard.[29]

The Aznars were one of the wealthiest and most prominent families of Yucatan. The Aznar brothers were all city merchants, hacienda owners, and attorneys, born of the old wealth of Yucatan. Their grandfather had been captain general and governor of Yucatan and later viceroy of New Granada under Spanish rule. Their father was a lieutenant colonel in the Spanish colonial army, and he inherited military command over Yucatan when Mexico won its independence.[30] Two of the Aznar brothers, Ramón and Tomás, ran a large sugar plantation, Salsipuedes, on the western frontier of the Yucatan peninsula. When Tomás died Ramón tried to hold on, but the Mexican army, trying to dislodge French imperialists from the peninsula of Yucatan, sapped the estate of goods and workers and Ramón had to sell it for what little he could get.[31] Ramón Aznar then dedicated himself to his other line of work—importing foreign merchandise and selling it retail from his large store in Merida. From Liverpool or New York Ramón ordered furniture, kitchenware, cloth and clothing, English beer, wine, flour, farm machinery, hardware, and, from New Orleans, lumber. He also plied domestic products—including sugar and rum from farms in the east of the state. From time to time he enticed the buying public with newspaper advertisements announcing newly arrived shipments, "Fabulously Low Prices!" and once in a while a "Great Sale That Will Cause General Surprise!" Whether the sales caused surprise or not, Ramón enjoyed success and became one of the wealthier men in Yucatan. He participated in a modest share as well of the civic and charitable duties that his station required.[32]

Buying an estate was out of the question for a working man like Stephens. For a vigorous and rising entrepreneur like Ramón Aznar, it was sport. Aznar already knew about Xuxub. His lawyer brother represented Palmero's ex-wife in her lawsuit for support, and the vexed owner of Xuxub had asked Aznar to buy him out. But Ramón Aznar had just bought an old-style hacienda in western Yucatan complete with a grand, colonnaded main house, a small church, two wells, and some thirteen thousand acres of farmland, pasture, and scrub forest on which his workers tended eight hundred head of cattle. Buying another estate on the far eastern frontier of the state then seemed poor timing to Ramón Aznar.[33] The location was good, with soils appropriate for sugar cultivation and easy access to the sea through the Xuxub River. So far out in the boondocks one could easily evade state taxes on alcohol. No need to recruit workers, as the old ones would stay in place. Still, Aznar had his hands full with his store and the new cattle hacienda that he hoped to convert to henequen. So Aznar turned Palmero down. The appearance of Robert Stephens changed Aznar's calculations. On the verge of returning home again, Stephens made a deal with Ramón Aznar. Aznar would put up the money to purchase San Antonio Xuxub: six thousand pesos. Stephens would live there and manage operations for the next ten years. At the end of that time they would sell the place and split the gain.[34] Before starting this newest chapter of his life Stephens scarcely had time to sail back to Hoboken and explain all to his wife and mother—his father had just died. Stephens took a few days to put affairs in order and then sailed back again to assume his new duties at Xuxub the first week of July.[35]

It was a long way from Hoboken to Xuxub. To get there you took the New York and Mexican Mail Steamer to Havana. It took six days to reach the Cuban capital. From there, you sailed for the Mexican mainland on a Veracruz-bound steamer, which touched twice a month at Yucatan's new port of Progreso. The only practical way to then get out to Xuxub, some two hundred miles to the east, was to hire passage on one or another of the sailing vessels that irregularly plied the waters off the north coast of Yucatan, touching near numerous villages, hamlets, or desolate loading sites along the way. Some carried their passengers, cargo, and the mail as far as the islands of Isla Mujeres and Cozumel on the Caribbean side of the peninsula, or even to Belize City, capital of British Honduras, and then returned laden with peninsular products for markets in Merida, Mexico, or abroad.

From Merida's new port of Progreso it took two or three days to reach the stop closest to Xuxub. The speck of a coastal settlement called Puntachen had one "street" running parallel to the beach, along which straggled the pole and thatch houses of its hundred or so inhabitants. It had no school, no formal cemetery, no plaza, no jail, nothing, yet it counted as the seat of civil and military authority on that part of the frontier.[36] Three more hours by canoe took you to Xuxub. You headed east along the south coast of Conil Lagoon, a wide, shallow bay teeming with sharks in the spawning time.[37] Here and there along the southern coast of the bay small streams wended through the mangroves and swamps, sometimes opening into small lagoons, only to narrow again, threatening even to disappear altogether as mangrove brushed the sides of canoes and lashed at their sweltering passengers. After ascending one such tree-walled stream a low wood-plank bridge halted progress at the plantation San Antonio Xuxub.

For sure it was not Cuba. Had war not erupted in Cuba, or if Stephens had good-paying work back in New York, he wouldn't have ventured out there. His first year was especially hard. His wife and youngest daughter could not join him until he fixed up the place and made it fit for them, and he felt the isolation sorely. Not that he was alone. Some thirty families lived on the plantation, many of them Maya Indians who had labored for the previous owner and who continued on under new management. But Stephens would hardly call Mayas company, and he once wrote to his wife that "this soletery life is horable, and more so when you have no sevelised person to tell your troubles or one to sympethise with you." He

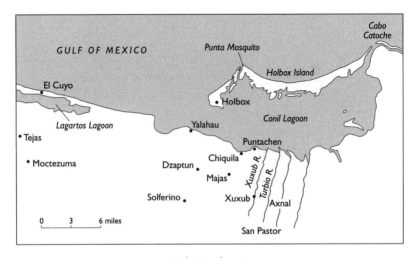

The Northeast

had it in mind to hire a good Cuban overseer once the plantation started making enough money. That would relieve him of many of the cares of managing laborers and provide him with some of the civilized companionship he so missed.[38]

Stephens made rapid progress whipping the 769-acre estate into shape. He built a new house for his family on a small island formed by mangrove and the bending river. There stood also the rum distillery. On the other side of the river shacks housing laborers and their families ringed a dirt plaza lightly shaded by coconut trees. Nearby were a mule-driven grinding mill; the sugarhouse with its stack, furnace, and train of kettles for boiling down cane juice; and storage houses for corn, sugar, and barrels of estate liquor. Still further beyond spread the cane and corn, and corrals for horses and cattle. Beyond those lay the great savanna. Beyond the savanna—Stephens had little idea what lay beyond, except forest and hostile Indians for countless leagues southward up to the border with British Honduras.

Stephens's efforts at Xuxub paid off. Laborers grew corn for their sustenance and that of their employer, but sugarcane was the main concern. From cane they made sweetener and rum. The high-quality spirits sold well in Merida. The fields of cane advanced from one year to the next, as laborers opened new ground between mangrove and savanna, until the harvest exceeded their capacity to mill and distill, let alone to transport the products back to Merida. By scrimping on expenses at Xuxub, Stephens could periodically remit some of the money Aznar gave him to his wife back in the States. He would even ship her demijohns of the estate rum from time to time, "as it will help to keep out the colde and is very handy to have in the house in case of sickness, for every boddy says it is the best that they have ever tasted."[39]

Toward the end of his first year at Xuxub Stephens finally hired an overseer. Not the Cuban he wanted, but someone to help out nonetheless. Hiring the man gave Stephens the chance to sail home to see his family in May of 1873.[40] Robert Stephens hoped to venture home again later in that year, but a September hurricane wreaked havoc on the estate and set Stephens and Aznar back several thousand dollars. With so much now to do because of the storm, Stephens contented himself with a short trip to Belize City in British Honduras. He went to buy a small schooner to employ carrying Xuxub products to Progreso, thereby eliminating some five or six hundred dollars of freight costs every year. From Belize City

Stephens also planned to send his wife three hundred dollars or so that he had saved up.[41]

By 1875 all was looking up again. Stephens's wife and younger daughter finally joined him at Xuxub, and Stephens hired another assistant, a fellow Irish-American from New York, Joseph Byrne, who could keep accounts and handle sundry other administrative duties on the estate. They expected a good sugar crop, despite the drought that had worried them earlier. They thought they'd clear nine thousand dollars that year. Soon, they hoped, the plantation could yield an annual profit of some twenty thousand dollars or so—all that on an initial investment of six thousand to buy the property and about fourteen hundred in capital improvements and expenses over the last three years. If they sold the property then and there, they might get thirty thousand dollars for it.[42]

The skies remained clear that October of 1875. Hurricanes would not strike every year, as Stephens reasoned. Seven more good harvests and he could retire in comfort back across the Hudson from New York. How sweet the promises of quiet seemed.

There was only one problem—and it was that which led the otherwise self-reliant Stephens to seek help from young consul Lespinasse. Stephens's neighbors, the Urcelays, were trying to kill him in a way so devious it took some time to explain.

11 October

A fisherman made his way up the Turbio River from Conil Lagoon. He looked for a tree that would yield a good pole to secure the sail of his small boat. He knew the area well. Ramón Gasca lived on the island of Holbox, though sometimes he stayed on the mainland at Puntachen. He had worked fourteen years off and on for the Urcelays. He knew Stephens well, too. He knew the places and people around there as well as anyone else. So it did not take him long to realize something was amiss when he found two logs lying across the narrow stream and footprints all over in the damp earth on both sides. The footprints of many men who must only recently have crossed. The normally clear water was still murky from the mud that misplaced steps had stirred. Some sort of trail through the bush appeared to have opened in the direction of the Xuxub plantation. Gasca forgot about the mast he needed and hurried back to Puntachen.

It was almost noon when Gasca arrived in the village. He headed straight to tell the National Guard commander what he had found. As far as Gasca was concerned, it could only mean one thing. An Indian raiding party had arrived. Xuxub, the nearest establishment to the Río Turbio, was in danger. They had to act quickly to warn people there.

Commander Montilla brushed off the frightened fisherman. There was nothing going on. Gasca asked at least that some men be sent to reconnoiter. Not only might Xuxub be in danger, but Puntachen itself, or men working in cornfields thereabouts. The raiders could strike anywhere or every-where. Montilla told him to forget about it and warned him not to tell a soul about what he had seen. The fisherman was no fool. He had been around long enough to know what Montilla could do. He was not going to cross Montilla by going himself to warn the people of Xuxub. Instead Gasca set sail for home and the safety of the island of Holbox.[a]

Two

A Dangerous Path

IS NEIGHBORS WERE PLOTTING TO KILL HIM, Stephens told consul Lespinasse. Not murder him outright, but destroy him all the same by the most devious means that such power and envy could conjure. Just ten days earlier, on 18 June, according to the aggrieved American:

there passed through my estate an armed force of men headed by the Judge and Commissary of Punta Chen, and on their march through my land they took down my fences and left them open so as to let in the cattle and horses into my sugar-cane fields and corn fields and destroyed a large quantity of both cane and corn.

When they got to the end of my road, they opened a new pass through the woods and brush as far as the Savanna where the Savage indians come in the dry weather to get water when they are out on their hunting expeditions.

On their return through my estate they sounded their Bugles for an attack of machete and an attack of bayonet and several other charges to such an extent that my servants became afraid thinking it was the savages who were coming to attack the ranch. Not satisfied with the damage they had done on the Sugar estate, they committed another in the house of my fisherman who provides the estate with fish, they stole all the lead off from his nets and committed all kinds of excesses in his house, such as using it for a privy and making indecent use of his cooking wares for chambers and trying all kinds of indecencies so as to provoke me into hostilities with them such as hallooing that they have never seen the color of american blood, but hoped to soon have the pleasure of seeing what color it was.[1]

The principal culprit, Stephens claimed, was twenty-two-year-old Baltazar Montilla, mayor at Puntachen and commander of the local national guard. Besides Montilla only one other man, a lieutenant, was enlisted in the guard out there, but in times of danger Montilla could call upon local men to take up arms against rebellious Indians, bandits, revolutionaries, and the like.

He'd only been on the job a few months, but he rapidly exercised his military prerogatives on that otherwise calm frontier.[2] In mid-May someone spied smoke rising from the savanna to the east. Montilla dispatched thirteen men to investigate on the pretext that hostile Indians might be about. Nine days later the weary party straggled on to a Caribbean beach. They'd found nothing along the way, Montilla reported to the governor. In that report Montilla omitted to mention, however, a curious detour he had his men take. Rather than head directly to the savanna from which smoke once rose, he sent his armed party south along the Turbio River and through the lands of Stephens's Xuxub.[3]

That, however, was not the incursion about which Robert Stephens complained. The first group of men Montilla sent out got cold feet and wouldn't linger long in so-called enemy territory. So Montilla assembled a larger party. He asked Stephens to contribute fifteen or so of his men, but Stephens declined, since none of his workers would volunteer, and he wouldn't force any to go. Besides, Stephens said, they shouldn't go bothering Indians out in their own territory where they do no harm to anyone. Stephens said he doubted that the government even knew or approved of what Montilla was doing.[4]

As Montilla later informed the governor, on 16 June he led a force out of Puntachen consisting of forty loyal Indians from Kantunilkin, workers from a nearby sugar plantation called Solferino, and Justice of the Peace Morales and Lieutenant Fernández of Puntachen. They headed south and soon located the spot from which smoke had risen weeks before—a patch of burned savanna. Montilla had his men carefully search the area for signs of rebel Indians—a large number of footprints, for example. They found nothing, and Montilla's guide speculated that a fugitive worker from a local plantation had set that fire.

Montilla ordered his men back to their homes, he later reported to the governor. In fact the excursion had not been so dull and pointless as Montilla made it seem. When Montilla and his men set out on 16 June, they followed much the same route as the earlier party. They proceeded by boat up the south coast of Conil Lagoon as far as a spit of land called Puntatunich, a few miles from Xuxub. From there they marched south, finally en-tering into lands of Xuxub. They walked down the San Pastor road, which led to an abandoned farm of that name south of Xuxub, and on through the savanna to San Ignacio and the old Indian watering hole that Stephens had mentioned. Stephens said that they opened a road on their way out there. Actually, it was just the reverse. Montilla ordered his men to use their machetes to hack a trail open from the well *back* to Xuxub. It was hard work under a June sun, and seemingly without purpose, but at least some of the men did as they were told. In his complaint to the American consul, Stephens forgot to mention how angrily he confronted Montilla when they arrived back at Xuxub; how he said he should have them all bound and sent for punishment in Merida for having trespassed as they did. That's what provoked Montilla to respond that if Stephens felt himself capable, he should go ahead and try. Mary and Joseph Byrne defused the crisis by drawing Stephens back into the house, letting Montilla and his little army continue peaceably on their way.[5]

Stephens might have let the incident pass. Maybe he would have gotten over it. But when he discovered that Montilla had cut a road from that watering place in the savanna right up to his property, it all became suddenly clear. They were trying to kill him by getting the hostile Indians to come down that road and slaughter them all at Xuxub. And one of Stephens's workers was missing. Where had he gone?

Montilla had it in for Stephens, but he wasn't acting alone. Montilla, by the way, was just the man's most recent name. In repeated flights from justice out in western Yucatan he'd added and dropped names as circumstances required. Just three years earlier he'd escaped from the House of Detention in Merida where he was serving time for theft, or fencing stolen goods, or something of that sort. Some whispered he'd been in for murder. Whatever Montilla was up to, Stephens explained to the American consul, he was only acting as the tool of the wealthy and powerful Urcelays, who owned the adjacent sugar plantation, Solferino. As district political chief, one of those Urcelays had put the fugitive Montilla in his post in Puntachen, and thereafter they ensured he'd do their bidding by supplementing his poor salary with private payments. Montilla harassed Xuxub and his opened that dangerous road at the orders of the Urcelays, of that Stephens was sure and he could explain it all to a doubting green consul like Lespinasse.[6]

The Urcelays were rising stars of Yucatan's commercial, landed, and political elite. Much old wealth on the peninsula had been torched in civil

war and the Indian rebellion, or ground under by desperate, ruinous taxa-
tion to meet endless military needs and emergencies. Many hacienda
owners and merchants, in debt or mortgaged to others, found it impossible to recover from the calamities. To replace those who had perished, a
host of young men with money, connections, and an entrepreneurial spirit
came of age ready to step in—men like the Urcelay brothers—Juan Antonio, Manuel, Nicolás, and Andrés.[7]

There was more than a little irony in that. The progressive ideals of
such men, put into practice with abandon, had largely been responsible for
sparking the devastating Indian rebellion. During the colonial period,
though many Spaniards owned estates, they didn't aim to get wealthy as
farmers. Rather, wealth flowed from exploitation of the Indians who paid
tribute and religious taxes, or who were forced to sell wax, cotton, and
other products of their making to whites at below market prices.
Spaniards did establish modest cattle ranches close to their urban markets
in order to satisfy their taste for beef, and to do that they acquired most of
the Indian lands nearby. But Indians often willingly sold land made sur-
plus by the drastic post-conquest decline in their numbers, while further
inland from Spanish settlements there was little need or impetus to en-
croach on Maya forests.

That changed, however. By late colonial times Indian numbers had re-
bounded, and the non-Indian population of towns and cities had grown
markedly as well. The prices of staples had multiplied, and increasingly
whites saw that there was money to be made in satisfying local demand for
agricultural produce and even in exporting surpluses abroad. Expansion
of commercial agriculture would have been hampered by continued Indian possession, as communities rather than individuals, of so much land
and forest under colonial-era statutes. Progressive thinkers bemoaned
such anachronisms and argued that communities should not hold land,
only individuals; that land should be bought and sold freely, so that it
would end up in the hands of those most capable of cultivating and improving it; that the nation needed to create a class of capable, small farmers who'd produce not only for their meager subsistence (as Indians
seemed inclined to do) but who'd produce surpluses for market and export, too. Finally, many of those who dreamed of prosperous, commercial
agricultural establishments bringing wealth and progress to the peninsula
of Yucatan also well understood that someone would have to labor on
those plantations, and so long as Indians could support themselves on

their own lands, they were unlikely to toil for whites. This was seen as yet another reason why, if possible, the Mayas should be separated from the natural resources which seemed to afford lives of idleness and leisure.

Independence from Spain brought the opportunity to effect those changes, and almost overnight a new elite passed laws stripping Indian communities of most of the land they still held. Those lands and forests seemed abandoned and unused to whites. Indians understood better. Those were their fields in long fallow, so necessary in the thin-soiled tropics. Those were the forests from which they gathered essential firewood and wild plants. There they hunted deer, peccary, coatimundi, and birds, and from scarce water holes scattered about they drew fresh water. Upon those "unused" lands Indians depended for their very existence. Declared public domain by new governments, those lands and forests were sold away, mostly to wealthy whites. (Some were given to soldiers who fought in one or more of Yucatan's numerous revolutions—conflicts with Campeche or Mexico—and many of those soldiers turned around and sold the land to wealthy whites.) In just two decades over two million acres were taken from Indian hands and transferred to Yucatan's elite who eagerly planned to establish sugar plantations, large cattle ranches, cotton plantations, tobacco plantations. The plans were endless, but Indian patience had grown short, and soon their wrath destroyed most of what agrarian entrepreneurs managed to build on such stolen resources.[8]

With rebel Indians pushed back to eastern forests, commercial estates sprouted again in much of Yucatan, and by the time the Urcelay brothers came upon the scene, there were about a thousand haciendas in Yucatan. They weren't large by Mexican standards, but put in some machines and raise a crop with strong foreign demand and they could be very lucrative. The elite of Yucatan's middling towns owned many of those properties. Such people might also own a country store, a few house lots in the village or town, and not much else. Owning haciendas did not mean they were rich, only that they were well established in their little rural domains. Men like the Urcelays were different. Yucatan's city-based elite had bigger plans and higher aspirations. For them the entire state was a field of action, and national and international markets were as important as the local. They were merchants, lawyers, government officials, importers. They lived in Merida, traveled on business to central Mexico or abroad, and only visited their rural estates from time to time. Many of them knew little about farming at all, but could discern where future riches were to be found, and with money and experienced administrators, they converted their old cattle and corn haciendas into modern plantations of henequen or sugar.

Producing crops for sale was only half the game. Politics was the other half. Fortunes wilted if judges issued adverse decisions in land or labor disputes, if rivals or enemies won choice federal concessions (for logging, or for building railroads or port facilities), if local authorities failed to cooperate in coercing labor or intimidating rivals in the countryside. So keeping one eye on their estates and businesses, men like the Urcelays grappled for political power.

The dozens of families who counted for anything in Yucatan congealed into rival political camps. Each might, at times, espouse a political philosophy, but they really existed not to advance principles or ideologies, but, rather, to secure and retain government posts and government beneficence for their families and friends. The Urcelays learned well how to play that rough and tumble game. They bought up old properties, corralled enough labor to work them, raised capital to expand and mechanize, nudged rivals and competitors aside or allied with them for mutual benefit, and jockeyed to keep their friends in power and their enemies out. Over time, the elite of once prostrate Yucatan grew as rich and ostentatious as any in Mexico, and among the most narrowly concentrated. Only thirty or forty families reigned supreme in economics and politics at the dawn of the twentieth century. The Urcelays stood among those who made the cut.[9]

Ranging across only seven years in age, when the four Urcelay brothers started building their fortunes back in the 1860s, each focused on a different economic or political niche. Juan Antonio was the wholesale merchant and importer, though he dabbled too in cattle ranching and cordage manufacturing. Manuel and his younger brother Andrés bought up haciendas around the capital and sought federal grants to even greater extensions of so-called ownerless tracts, on which they set their laborers to raising cattle, corn, cotton, and henequen.

While Andrés stayed focused on opportunities near the capital, Manuel sought still newer fields to exploit. Many then thought that the northeast coast of the Yucatan Peninsula offered marvelous possibilities for gain, especially the region from the coastal village of San Fernando to the tip at Cabo Catoche. According to one glowing report, not only did the region brim with wild plants like indigo, vanilla, and logwood—all useful for industry—but within two or three leagues of the sea, fertile soil lay waiting for the bold to found plantations of tobacco, sugarcane, and cotton. Especially sugarcane. The Indian rebellion annihilated a flourishing sugar industry in the interior of the state, where soil was deep and rain plentiful. The industry recovered only slowly. So scarce was sugar in Merida markets during the early 1860s that the government toyed with permitting foreign imports. Imports or not, prices were likely to rise more, and if sugar producers could stave off foreign competition, they might reap very handsome returns. Manuel would gamble on sugar.[10]

Manuel's brother Nicolás knew that coast well. He'd once commanded armed sloops on those waters and later married and settled near there. Nicolás became a major purchaser of salt scraped from coastal pans all along the north coast. He'd ship it to Merida where his brother Juan Antonio would re-export much of it. Nicolás's many forays all along the northern coast of Yucatan brought powerfully to his attention the rich potential of that region still largely abandoned by the prewar generation.[11] It made sense then that he should spearhead the Urcelays' move onto the eastern frontier, acquiring a 4,500-acre cattle ranch called Majas.[12] His father-in-law started up a ranch out that way, too, where trees planted by a lost generation still bore fruit worth picking.[13] Seeking a strong foothold further inland from the coast, Manuel and his brother Andrés petitioned the federal government for title to a large tract of land around an abandoned and ruined village called Labcah. There they proposed to found a sugar plantation they'd call Solferino.[14]

They received the grant despite opposition from some locals who had hoped that once the Indian wars were completely extinguished, old Labcah could become a large and thriving frontier town, not some rich man's private estate.[15] The Urcelays commenced erecting Solferino and convincing about sixty workers to settle there, most with families. The workers lived crowded in pole-and-thatch dwellings. Some had to double up. For his own family Manuel built a good three-story stucco house. Before the family could move in, however, Manuel's wife died in childbirth, leaving him with five children, all under ten years of age. Thereafter he'd continue living with the children in the city of Merida and only commute periodically to check on operations at Solferino.[16]

With the enterprise at Solferino well underway, the Urcelays hired Robert Stephens to install a modern horizontal steam-driven mill there and new equipment for processing sugar and distilling alcohol. That, inadvertently, was the start of their trouble with the American. When the

Urcelays imported expensive new sugar-making equipment for Solferino, Stephens was just finishing up his work on the Progreso docks. They hired the experienced mechanic to get everything up and running in time for the spring harvest. But late in January the equipment still sat in a warehouse in Progreso, and time was growing short. Andrés Urcelay hired a boat, the *Fulita*, to move the equipment from Progreso to Puntachen. From there laborers and beasts would lug it overland to the Solferino plantation. At Progreso Stephens arranged with the boat owner to load the cargo on 27 January, but when the day came, no hands appeared to lift the heavy parts. They'd have to wait a day and try again. Early the next morning Stephens ordered the *Fulita* brought alongside the dock, but the boat's handler balked. The weather was turning. One of those winter storms was brewing, a "norther," the bane of coastal mariners. They'd need half a day to load the cargo, and by then the weather would have soured. So instead the skipper got conveniently drunk, slipped away, and returned no more.

At midday an angry and shouting Stephens ordered hands to get the precious cargo out of the warehouse and onto the pier, boat or no boat. Meanwhile the vessel's owner searched for another captain. By one-thirty in the afternoon someone found a sober boatman, and the air crackled with shouts from Robert Stephens, urging his loaders to hurry. With half the cargo on the boat and half still on the pier, the wind kicked up. The new skipper told Stephens they'd have to stop and unload everything, but Stephens paid him no heed. He, Robert Stephens, agent of the Urcelays, was in charge, and he said the work must proceed.

They finished loading as the vessel's frantic owner marched off to file a protest with the captain of the port of Progreso, who summoned Stephens and ordered him to unload. Stephens refused. If the boat had been loaded on schedule, they'd be on their way already. He was not going to lose any more time by unloading now. They could depart soon and reach the shelter of Dzilam Puerto before the worst of the storm arrived.

Had Stephens been in Yucatan longer, he'd know what happens when a strong north wind blows down upon that coast. On the night of 28 January, before they could depart, the wind shifted, blew strong out of the northwest, and claimed its prize, smashing the *Fulita* to bits against the new pier and dumping the Urcelays' cargo into shallow brine.

It took them a week, and sweat, hoists, and winches, to salvage most of the equipment. They could not retrieve all of it, nor had they time anymore to install it at Solferino before the cutting of the cane. The owner of the *Fulita* sued the Urcelays for the loss of his boat. The Urcelays sued him for the loss of equipment and the waste of the spring harvest, ten thousand dollars worth of sugar and liquor they were never able to make. Stephens did finally get the turbines, mills, and sugar pans set up at the Solferino plantation. Whether they worked properly or not was a matter of some dispute. Still angry over mishap of the *Fulita* or dissatisfied with the installation, the Urcelays gave Stephens only half his promised pay.[17]

They didn't like Stephens after that, and they envied his success at Xuxub. That's why the Urcelays were out to get him. But that wasn't all, Stephens confided to the young consul. They hated him also because he was so well regarded by the laborers and little people of the frontier, who felt abused by the Urcelays. No sooner had the Urcelays started out there when workers on Nicolás's Majas estate complained they'd been reduced to servitude, forced to work against their will. Officials did nothing. A few years later a group of workers from Solferino fled into the arms of authorities, alleging that they, too, were being forced to work for nothing. They asked officials to release them from the grasp of the Urcelays, to let them work elsewhere, or even join the frontier defense corps (which otherwise people avoided at all cost). That group fared better than the first. While authorities pondered their fate, they just took off for parts unknown.[18] Stephens, on the contrary, was well liked by his workers, especially by those who had been with him longest. They found the American to be charitable and generous, and he shielded them from onerous and dangerous military service. In a word, he set a standard that the Urcelays could not meet. At least one of the abused souls who fled the Urcelays' employ took shelter at Xuxub and labored on happily for the American Robert Stephens.[19]

Stephens was popular off the plantation, too. Small farmers, ranchers, and fishermen on that frontier who felt abused by local authorities at Puntachen often recruited Stephens to assist. From the time Solferino was established, locals complained that the Urcelays usurped land they had been farming for twenty years. On top of that the Urcelays grabbed still more terrain when they united Majas and Solferino. While locals may have had similar complaints when Palmero established Xuxub, the Urcelays represented the greater threat to independent cultivators in the northeast.[20]

Stephens also got along well with the local Indians. That alarmed the Urcelays. The two hundred or so armed men of the nearby Maya village of

Kantunilkin were survivors of Yucatan's brutal campaign to crush rebellious Indians in the northeast. Almost two decades earlier, while still able to launch damaging raids against frontier communities and estates, the rebel Indians of the northeast sued for peace. They asked for little. They wanted amnesty. They wanted to settle together around the abandoned hacienda of Kantunilkin and have for farming and hunting the territory around it for eight leagues in all directions. And they wanted their women back, those who had been captured by government forces and sent into servitude elsewhere. In return for that they would swear allegiance to Yucatan, against whom they'd already warred for a decade.[21] Those Indians got all they wanted, and more. Yucatan granted them autonomy so long as the government continued to battle larger groups of rebel Indians elsewhere on the peninsula. Once those rebels were crushed, they'd exert more direct control over the peaceful Indians. But the campaign against other rebel Indians went very badly for Yucatan, war dragged on year after year, and peaceful Indians like those of Kantunilkin were left largely to their own devices.

For the Urcelays at Solferino, that was a problem. The land the Indians of Kantunilkin claimed included land the Urcelays wanted for their own. As early as 1868 the Indians complained that Nicolás Urcelay was putting cattle on their property, and they protested when the Urcelays received title to Labcah and established Solferino on the site. Still armed, still organized in old military units, and subject to almost no outside authority at all, the Indians of Kantunilkin might yet turn from protest to direct action against the Urcelays.[22]

The Urcelays got a break when still hostile Indians raided their peaceful counterparts in July of 1872, burning Kantunilkin to the ground and exhorting their chastised brethren to rejoin the war against the whites. To avenge Kantunilkin, Andrés Urcelay himself rushed east the governor's orders to launch a retaliatory raid. While Andrés led volunteers from the Tizimin area to Kantunilkin, Nicolás Urcelay led his own armed workers there. Uniting those forces with a contingent of fighting men from Kantunilkin, Nicolás Urcelay led them, 106 in all, south and east to wreak vengeance where they could. They returned victorious eighteen days later, having found the rebel canton responsible for the attack on Kantunilkin, killed its commander, driven its inhabitants into the forest, and burned its church and eighty houses to the ground.[23]

How long would that brutal demonstration of goodwill keep peaceful

Indians allied with whites? Frontier whites worried that their Indian neighbors might yet respond to the call of rebel brethren. If they did, for sure the Urcelays would be among the first targets of their wrath. For the worriers the summer of 1873 provided a real scare. After a couple of quiet years back in the capital, politics again descended into revolt and anarchy. Out east at Valladolid, military officials decided to support their men for governor and vice governor by arming Indians around the town and preparing them to battle political enemies. With promises of rewards if their revolt triumphed, with threats of whipping if they did not comply, they induced former rebel Maya living peacefully around the city to take the guns offered and attack haciendas and garrisons. Federal and Yucatecan troops responded urgently, before this little political revolt could evolve, as it had once before, into a racial conflagration. In a daylong battle they defeated the rebels, six hundred strong, though the east remained uneasy for months afterward. The Indians of Kantunilkin had not joined in, but the Urcelays angrily noted that the American Robert Stephens had been counseling those Indians—trying to stir them up, it seemed, and turn them against their other white neighbors. Stephens didn't tell his American consul about that, and nothing more was ever revealed about just what had gone on.[24] It was just one more reason, though, for the Urcelays to decide that that American had to go.

But these were not reasons enough to try and destroy Xuxub. The reason for that was beyond even Stephens's ken. Forests of the eastern frontier were up for grabs because old owners had abandoned their land at the outset of the Indian rebellion. When over a decade later peace was restored, few returned to their parcels. Many, perhaps most, were dead. Others had started over somewhere else and chose not to trust in the peacefulness of Indians out there. A Catalan immigrant settled with his Yucatecan wife at an abandoned hacienda called Dzaptun, brought forty laborers in and started to raise corn, cattle, and sugarcane, and distill rum. Another man from the town of Tizimin took over an old ranch near the coast of Lagartos Lagoon and brought in workers to raise corn and cane, to cut wood for construction, and to harvest a dyestuff called logwood that in colonial times had colored the cloth of Europe and America. And then came the Urcelays to establish themselves at Majas and Solferino. There were no other claimants to abandoned frontier lands that could block the Urcelays from expanding wherever they wanted, except for that man Palmero who founded little Xuxub, and they could deal with him.[25]

Then that thorn-in-their-side American went and pricked the interest of Ramón Aznar, a man their equal in wealth and connections. The Aznars had a long moribund interest in that eastern frontier. Before the Indian uprising, Ramón's brother Tomás had owned and operated a ranch out there called Axnal. On that six-thousand-acre estate he and his laborers grew sugarcane, corn, cotton, and fabricated sugar and rum. They cut logwood and loaded it directly onto American schooners touching at Río Lagartos. Just three years before the Indian uprising and the devastation that followed, Tomás acquired another large property in the east, fifteen hundred acres surrounding a good well and laying along Conil Lagoon. Time was running out, however. As Tomás prophetically commented in his 1847 New Year's greeting to his brother back in Merida, "from what I understand this year will be good for everything except for progress and advancement." Within months the Indians had rebelled and most all lay in ruins across the peninsula of Yucatan.[26]

Since the outbreak the Aznars had cultivated other lands and other pursuits, and none displayed interest in returning to the eastern frontier. Eventually they'd lose their claim to new settlers out there or they'd sell out cheap. So the Urcelays must have hoped. Then Robert Stephens stirred things up. He convinced Aznar to buy Xuxub and bankroll its expansion, and he renewed the rich man's interest in old properties further east. If the Aznars really established themselves out there again, they'd fence the Urcelays off from what seemed unbounded opportunity. The fences were already going up. The Urcelays would have to find a way quickly to tear them down.

It took them a while to figure out how, but they did. That's what Stephens told his young consul. They'd already put a plan in motion, a plan that was simple but devious. Of course the Urcelays didn't want anything traced back to them. First Andrés Urcelay got himself appointed head of the Merida district. He'd already served two years as alderman of the city council there when a new governor gave him the nod for district chief. In that post Urcelay would wield almost dictatorial civil and military powers over his district. During two-year terms, the chiefs of each of Yucatan's fifteen districts named, supervised, and if need be, dismissed local-level civil and military officials charged with dispensing justice, collecting taxes, maintaining militias, and gathering intelligence. Along the frontier, district chiefs shared command of local defenses, could order the requisition of goods from local merchants to supply troops, and interrogated and held suspected rebel Indians. Everywhere district chiefs could sometimes act as judges in criminal matters. They heard evidence, determined guilt, and meted out punishment, whether it was imprisonment, flogging, or death. As a direct extension of the power and authority of a governor into the countryside, district chiefs could act beyond the scope of other branches of government, concentrating and deploying a range of powers that not even the governor himself enjoyed. When it came to bending political power to serve private interests, you could hardly do better than to have a family member or friend as chief of the district.[27]

But Xuxub, Solferino, and those eastern lands weren't part of the Merida district, so how could Andrés Urcelay make his power felt out there? Easy, Stephens explained to the American consul. Urcelay had jurisdiction over that eastern frontier shifted to his district hundreds of miles away. Authority over the sparsely settled northeast had been bouncing around for years anyway between the town of Tizimin, the island of Cozumel, the old port of Sisal, and back to Tizimin, depending upon who seemed most able to keep an eye on the newly pacified Indians of Kantunilkin and assert some modicum of law in the boondocks. As the frontier started to flower again, most of the major investors lived far away in the capital—people like the Urcelays and the Aznars. Sooner or later they'd want to have the all-important political authority over the northeast exercised directly from the capital. So in March 1875 the northeast was transferred to the capital district, presided over (for several months already) by Andrés Urcelay.[28]

One of the first things Urcelay did for his district, of course, was to appoint the outlaw Baltazar Montilla as the principal authority there and to order him to undertake those odd military expeditions through the land of the Xuxub estate. Any doubt about their purpose vanished as Montilla's men cut a path from that water source in the savanna all the way back to Xuxub. They might as well have staked a sign directing hostile Indians to the nearest property they could plunder.

Sober reflection should have assuaged such fear of Indian barbarities. True, Montilla's "road" put Xuxub at some risk, but the risk was very small. Xuxub lay a long, long way from the haunt of the most dangerous hostiles left, the Indians of Santa Cruz and their allies near the ancient Maya ruins of Tulum and Coba. Indians who invaded the northeast back in 1872 ventured only as far as Kantunilkin, which they overran and burned. That time they walked twenty-eight days to hit their target and get home again.

It was one of their longest marches ever, directed at people they especially despised, former rebels who had surrendered to the whites. An attack against Xuxub would cost them even more days of marching through difficult terrain for little gain. And they had probably never even heard of Xuxub or where it lay. There were plenty of other places in Yucatan and Campeche to which hostile Indians could turn their murderous attentions. If the Urcelays planned to destroy their rivals that way, it was a long shot at best.

Or was it? Hostile Indians did not actually have to attack and burn the place. It was enough for people to *believe* they might do it. Then potential buyers and investors would be frightened off. Workers would flee the danger of their ill-stared frontier employer. New laborers would refuse to go there unless paid exorbitant wages. And with no laborers, the place would resort just as rapidly to bush as if hostile Indians had laid it to waste. There was more than one way in which Montilla's little road might yet doom Xuxub, unless the American consul could help Robert Stephens to get the Urcelays off his back.[29]

12 October

The day dawned pleasantly cool. Workers were out early again at their chores, some preparing ground for a new planting of sugarcane, others harvesting corn in fields further away. A canoe made its way up the Xuxub River through the predawn mist bringing mail to the plantation, and by eight that morning Robert Stephens and Joseph Byrne were poring over it. The public in Merida had already been treated to several volleys in the press campaign over the "Stephens affair." But Xuxub was far away, and Stephens and Byrne had read only the first couple of articles, written in their favor, all about how a bad government vexed the valiant immigrant Roberto Stephens and exposed him to danger from an Indian invasion. Not much else had happened in the last few weeks to irk Stephens. He complained to the American consul, the consul intervened with the governor, and he believed that would restrain the Urcelays and their agent Montilla. Mary would be sailing back in just three weeks. Next year's harvest should be the biggest ever. No hurricane would strike that year to set them back again. None warned Robert Stephens how closely death then hovered.[a]

The hostile Indians who had been lying nearby the whole night did not stir before dawn as frontier raiders would. The sun had been up two hours or more before the sixty-odd armed men and boys walked across the savanna and into the cane fields of Xuxub. They fired no shots, and like the deep shadow of a passing cloud, Xuxub silently fell under the power of the invaders. In the big house Stephens and Byrne had no time even to jump from their seats. Armed strangers grabbed them, tied their arms behind, and hitched them to a crossbeam overhead. Leaving the captives guarded there, others went out to look for anyone else lingering about. Raiders commenced to ransack the big house, going through the trunks, taking out clothes, money, demijohns of rum, weapons, anything of use or value, and piling them up outside in preparation for the march home.

They worked at a leisurely pace. Xuxub was their target. No racing far off this time to surprise and sack other estates on that stretch of the frontier. They had come just for Xuxub.

After about an hour and a half they took Stephens, Byrne, and others from the big house over to the plaza near the houses of the plantation workers. They tied their prize captives to coconut trees there—Stephens, Byrne, foreman Baeza, sugar master Marvilla, carpenter Najera. Workers were collected there too, many of them also bound.

Two groups of Indians then left. One went to round up the twenty or so laborers in the cornfields. They found most of them. One or two ran away. The other group, led by their most renowned general, headed a short distance to the coast to capture the three families who lived in a tiny hamlet there, including Stephens's fisherman. By the time they reached the place, however, the families had taken to their boats and from just offshore they taunted their Indian enemies.

The Indian general returned ill-humored to Xuxub. It was time to liven things up. He broke out some of Stephens's stockpiled alcohol, served himself, and distributed hearty doses to his men. Soon all showed signs of growing very drunk.

Now it was time for the business that had lured him and his men so far from their homes. The general walked over and through an interpreter spoke to his captive Robert Stephens.

Three

Protection

A S ROBERT STEPHENS TOOK HIS PROTEST TO THE CON-
sul, his partner Ramón Aznar took care to validate his citizenship. So prominent in Merida, Aznar had a little secret not
widely known in capital circles. Like many other children of the elite when
the Indian rebellion broke out back in the 1840s, he had been shipped off
for safekeeping to New York City where he lived for several years until, at
the age of twenty-five, he appeared before the Superior Court of the City
of New York and swore everlasting allegiance to the United States of
America.[1]

Ramón did not become an American citizen because he intended to
settle in the U.S. On the contrary, within months of getting his citizenship
he returned to Yucatan to live there the rest of his life. American citizenship was only a kind of insurance that various members of Yucatan's elite
quietly acquired for themselves. It would protect them, they hoped, from
forced loans or extraordinary taxes levied by revolutionaries and by
regimes fighting insurrection. The insurance proved of little worth for
Ramón Aznar. After failing to avoid one such forced loan, he ended up
paying out like the rest of the businessmen of Yucatan, and he kept his
American citizenship under wraps for use another day.[2]

The day had come. With trouble brewing over Xuxub, Aznar applied
to the American consulate to renew a long-expired passport, and he registered for the first time with the Mexican Ministry of Foreign Relations as
a resident foreigner. Aznar almost received a rude surprise regarding his
passport renewal. Lespinasse opposed acknowledging him, and a handful
of other Yucatecans, as American citizens. At least one had surely obtained his citizenship fraudulently (from the same Southern Court of
New York where Aznar took his oath), and others, including Aznar,
clearly never intended to reside in the United States. Lespinasse's superiors at the embassy in Mexico City agreed, but the State Department in

Washington overruled them, since it wasn't their place to question acts of the New York courts. Aznar's American citizenship was revalidated and his passport renewed.[3] That done, he turned to mobilizing still other support to protect Xuxub from enemies.

Robert Stephens had urged the inexperienced consul to bring his complaint directly to the attention of the United States minister in Mexico City. Eager Lespinasse decided instead to take steps on his own. In early August he protested to the governor of Yucatan that:

> In view of the facts that an application has been made to me by Mr. Robert L. Stephens an american citizen for protection against the abuses which have been committed on his estate "Xuxub" by the authorities of the district in which he resides, such as marching with armed forces through his property thereby damaging his crops, tearing down fences, opening roads on the estate, which may lead to serious results as it may be the means of indicating to the indians the way to his place, using threatening language towards him and committing a number of other arbitrary acts which are ruinous to his interests, I therefore have the honor to request as the representative of the United States at this place that your good services may be used to protect the property owned or in any way interested in by the above named person.

To that breathlessly long sentence Lespinasse added more pointedly, "I respectfully protest against such treatment being visited upon the said American subject."[4]

Americans in Mexico often ran to their consuls to complain about Mexicans, seek protection, or demand money for damages they claimed they had suffered. The habit hardly endeared them among Mexican officials, who came to view every American as a potential claim jobber, seeking any pretext to enlist their powerful government in an unjustifiable raid on the Mexican treasury, or worse. The claims of Americans had served before as convenient pretext for war, as the excuse the United States needed to indulge an appetite for Mexican land. Lespinasse's request to the governor was simple enough: protection for Robert Stephens. International law and bilateral treaties and common decency assured that the man was entitled to protection, just like anyone else. But the governor knew, better than young Lespinasse, the sordid history of "diplomatic protection" as practiced by Americans in Mexico and the viperous pit of dangers that could lurk beneath the surface of such a note.

Governor Ancona had been installed provisionally back in November. That ended two years of war and anarchy in the state provoked by the illegal efforts of a previous governor to extend his term. Things had spun so out of control that the federal government dispatched troops and declared martial law. In the election that followed, murder, intimidation, and fraud provoked dissension and uprisings. Passion and the warring habit, as well as insatiable lust for power and patronage, seem to have driven men mad, until the central government finally imposed Eligio Ancona to restore order in his beleaguered patria.[5]

In general elections the following March Ancona appeared to emerge honestly victorious, the seventh governor of Yucatan in less than five years. He brought some strong credentials to the office. He was trained in law, and was a former alderman of Merida, publisher, sometimes opponent of the French imperial regime, secretary-general of the new republican government of Yucatan, congressman in the republican federal congress, and fortunately absent from Yucatan during many of the recent years of turmoil. He was also a prolific novelist, good enough for writers in Europe and the United States to bother plagiarizing him.[6]

As one of his first official acts back in November, Ancona had appointed Andrés Urcelay to be chief of the Merida district. Now he had to inform Urcelay of the American consul's protest and have him instruct the local authority to investigate the matter. Of course the local authority was Baltazar Montilla. While waiting for a report from them, Governor Ancona also began seeking passage for a judicial commission to go out to Holbox, Isla Mujeres, and Cozumel. It was a routine gesture. From time to time such a commission had to visit distant or isolated parts of the state to check on the conduct of judicial affairs, the condition of facilities, archives, and the like. If necessary, this one could investigate the Stephens matter, too. Unfortunately, the governor soon learned, no government vessel was available to take the commission east, nor would one be until the beginning of September at the earliest.[7]

Meanwhile the Urcelays had been busy using the powers the governor had granted Andrés. Their first order of business was to settle a problem that had nagged them for years with their properties just north of the capital. Ten years earlier the Urcelays had bought a hacienda from an aging figure of Yucatan's elite. The only problem was that some Indians claimed part of those lands and they weren't going to move nor labor for the Urcelays. The previous owner had tried to resolve the problem by paying off all the heirs of the original Indian owners of the disputed parcel. But each generation of children and grandchildren brought new claimants and new court battles over the almost worthless parcel. The Urcelays bought the land and the problems and got a bit further in court, winning some eviction orders, and it didn't hurt them either that years of prior case records disappeared. Still, they couldn't shake a few remaining heirs and their dogged lawyer. When the Urcelays won in lower court, the heirs went to superior court. When the Urcelays won there, heirs appealed to the president, and the Supreme Court granted the heirs the right to try again. Meanwhile nearby a minor skirmish between soldiers and Indians involved in another land dispute (one that had included the Urcelays, but they had since sold their problems to another) kindled fears of a new Indian insurrection and prompted authorities to try to resolve such land disputes more quickly. On and on and on it went, until Andrés Urcelay became district chief. Then the litigious claimants to the disputed parcel gathered at the Urcelays' hacienda, Chumoxil. They dumped their intrepid lawyer of so many years' standing and hired a new one. They declared in writing that they were, in fact, not the owners of the disputed parcel, and never had been, since it had long ago been sold to the previous owner of Chumoxil. They renounced forever any claim to the property and promised ever after to remain silent on the matter. And that was that.[8]

Even as they were resolving their problems north of Merida, the Urcelays had Montilla parade his troops out into no-man's-land and open a trail back to Xuxub. The Urcelays weren't just going to sit around and wait for Montilla's road to work its magic, however.

In August a man arrived at Xuxub looking for work. That was odd enough. People did not just show up at the door of a frontier estate seeking to bind themselves to near-perpetual labor out in the boondocks. But this one had been a worker at Solferino and had been sent by Manuel Urcelay to help Stephens at Xuxub. Mary Stephens later recalled that her husband turned the man away with a note back to Urcelay. Stephens had his own workers and needed none from the Urcelays. The emissary was not so easily gotten rid of, however. He lingered around Xuxub, talking up the Indian menace with other workers and trying to get workers to agree to burn the place down and flee to safety. Stephens became aware of the

plot before it much matured. Five workers did flee one morning, setting
fire to one house before they left. But most of the workers and their families stayed put.[9]

After that, according to Mary Stephens, her husband, "felt so badly he
wished he could fly to Washington where he could get justice for there is
none here for us poor strangers." But "my husband did not want to leve his
Place or his fore years hard labor for he had envested all his Money to inprove it More and More every year."[10] When Mary Stephens started taking ill, she blamed it on the stress of the confrontation with Montilla and
the fear that Indians might come to kill them. Husband and wife talked it
over and decided that Mary would return to West Hoboken with the
child until she was well and the crisis had blown over. In mid-September
Mary Stephens and her husband said their good-byes on the Progreso
pier as she waited to board a steamer for Havana and New York. She
planned to return in five weeks or so. By then her husband and Ramón
Aznar planned to have the Urcelay problem well under control. She and
Robert had weathered difficult times before, after all. Perhaps for a part-
ing moment they reflected on their travails in Cuba, on her husband's imprisonment by rebel forces, on their fear of the Spaniards and Catalan
volunteers, and on their eventual flight from that land in which they had
spent so much of their adult life. Starting over in Yucatan had not been
easy, but it would not be so much longer before they could retire in comfort among friends and family in the States.

Then again, standing on that pier, maybe they just chatted about the
weather.

Whatever they talked about, for the rest of her life Mary remembered
that as "the last day I saw my poor husband alive."[11]

Even as Mary sailed home to the States, Ramón Aznar covertly
launched a press campaign to win relief for Xuxub and punish its enemies.
He influenced the owner and editor of one of Yucatan's major newspapers,
La Revista de Merida, to denounce in print the shameful treatment to
which the American Robert Stephens had been subjected. Mexico, so well
endowed with varied climates and fertile lands, should be the wealthiest
nation on earth, began the first editorial volley on behalf of Stephens and
Aznar. Still far from achieving prosperity, Mexico had not managed to
properly develop its agriculture and fisheries because of the indolent nature of its people, the inadequacy of its laws and institutions, the insecurity of property, and the low prestige enjoyed by diligent, prolonged effort.
If Mexico was ever to prosper, the writer insisted, it needed foreign immi-

gration, especially from the United States, a country that so dramatically prospered from land no finer than Mexico's own. But foreign immigrants seeking a better life would certainly not stay if subject to insecurity and political turmoil. Take Robert Stephens, for example—skilled, honest, hardworking, brave. The newspaper related his story in brief, beginning with his work in Cuba, then the pier at Progreso, then his move to Xuxub, where he put his life at risk on the unsettled frontier to give the nation a productive enterprise. Mexico should protect him, but instead it subjected him to harassment and injuries. The article described Montilla's destructive expedition through Xuxub and darkly noted that the government, although it had been fully informed, had done nothing to stop it or to prevent it from happening again. Only peace and respect for the law, property, and the observance of individual rights would bring immigrants to this land and keep them here. Finally, to impress upon officials the power of the press, the writer noted, "that which happens in the interior of a nation is no secret to others; the press undertakes to carry to all parts the news of even the most insignificant events that occur in any corner, no matter how forgotten it may seem. . . ."[12] Soon afterward the official newspaper of the state government—*La Razón del Pueblo*—denounced the opposition article as an insult to the nation, mocking the black picture one of Mexico's own sons had painted of their mother. The official press would not yet respond further to the calumny and infamy an ungrateful author heaped upon his country.[13]

The next day Governor Ancona did respond in private to the American consul. The governor had asked Andrés Urcelay to investigate the complaint of Robert Stephens. Urcelay instructed Montilla to report. Montilla finally reported back to Urcelay, Urcelay to the governor, and the governor now to the consul. Montilla, it appeared, did no damage to the Xuxub estate. He came onto the property only at the invitation of Stephens, who then surprised Montilla by claiming trespass and threatening to send him tied up to Merida if it happened again. Stephens should have thanked Montilla and his men for the concern shown for the security of the district. Instead, Stephens abused them, which ingratitude, though it momentarily startled Montilla, was not inconsistent with Stephens's known peevish and violent character, and with his bad influence on the inhabitants of the district. The governor could report that a judicial commission traveling east would continue to investigate what was going on between Stephens and the other residents and authorities of that territory.[14]

The opposition *La Revista de Merida* fired a new salvo on 12 October.

Touchy about the charge that the opposition was unpatriotic, the editor now philosophized on the role of the press, under the title "The Means of Defense." He described the free and critical press as a civilizing element in society. No people need fear the self-examination of its faults, conducted with the intention of correcting those faults. The press, he stated, was the only peaceful means of defense the citizenry had against a government that persecuted and jailed hardworking folks. Along with that editorial the paper published a letter received from Ramón Aznar, Stephens's business partner, though he did not identify himself as such. (The press only alluded to a "respectable capitalist in this city" with whom Stephens worked.) Aznar naturally praised the opposition press for its stand on the Stephens affair, and he directed his own sharp barbs at the politicians and bureaucrats then in power, a "privileged class," he wrote, "that lives well off to the same degree that those who work live poor." Aznar heaped praise on Stephens—a man whom all could see had over the last four years proved his honesty and love of work. If the governor did not know Stephens, and if the editor of the official daily did not know him—the official press had referred to Stephens as an "unknown person"—that could only be because the governor had been so long out of the state and upon his return had brought that outsider with him who was made editor of the government newspaper. After that oblique attack upon the two, Aznar went on to report that Stephens had come to this country believing he had the protection of Mexican law (or were those laws just a "dead letter"?). Stephens paid his taxes regularly. He lived and worked in hostile Indian territory (something of an exaggeration, but it would ring true enough to city dwellers) neither expecting nor demanding military protection from the government, impotent to protect him anyway. Stephens certainly did not expect, however, he'd have to count among the threats life and livelihood that government, specifically in the person of Baltazar Montilla, or Miramón Montilla, or Miramón Fernández y Brito, or whatever was the name of the escaped convict made authority on the frontier and acting covertly as an agent for Andrés Urcelay, chief of the Merida district. Aznar alluded to a hidden hand working in still higher circles to protect the persecutors of Stephens and obstruct any investigation of what was happening out east. After all, the commission named to go investigate the matter still had not departed for the east, evidently because it was not in the interest of the government to have matters out there investigated.[15]

In the Great American Republic to the north immigrants are well received, Aznar noted, without revealing that he was himself an American citizen. "Among us," on the other hand, "it only seems that those who govern try to drive away at any cost men like Stephens who bring to us with their honesty and love of work a spark of what could become the immigration on a grand scale of other such colonists." Authorities feared that, Aznar concluded, because they knew that the day would arrive, as it did in Texas, when they would have to go elsewhere to find people to abuse.[16] The next day a second opposition newspaper joined the attack, praising Aznar's contribution to the debate, labeling him a man "respectable, impartial, and beyond all partisan spirit," and taunting the government in verse:

> But in the end the one who suffers
> Is always the poor people
> This people that finds itself
> Converted into a flock of sheep.
> And it is very just that it suffers
> Such great injustices,
> Until it rises up appropriately
> And makes of its executioners an example.[17]

The American consul Lespinasse had been out of town for several days. Upon his return he caught up on the press campaign. It especially irked him to find that all of his correspondence with the governor concerning the Stephens affair had been published in the official press, the better, presumably, to rally the public against the importunity of foreigners. Lespinasse acknowledged in his next missive to the governor that perhaps Stephens had "laid himself open to censure for having interfered with local affairs of his district." The consul continued, "I would however respectfully request that there may be no reason for infringing on the rights to which Mr. R. L. Stephens is entitled as an American citizen."[18]

Two days later the official press responded to Aznar's earlier public attacks, attributing them to discourtesy and passion, rather than to any sense of justice.[19] Sometimes, the editorialist noted, for our intense love of country, when the government does something wrong we respond with bitter, rude words. "We love our country like we love our mother, and the very idea of seeing her injured wounds us, injures us, makes us desperate." Such sentiment, however, could serve as no excuse for Ramón Aznar, he who "though born here, made himself a foreigner of his own free will and who only has the right to feel his patriotism offended when tyranny shall take shelter under the beautiful flag of the stars [and stripes]. Our tricolor banner is no longer his." Aznar should choose his words more carefully, the editorialist cautioned. Aznar should show more respect to a country that is not his but which welcomed him with benevolence. As for the complaints of Stephens and Aznar, they were simply unjustified, as documents published with the editorial would show. Montilla was not threatening the American. On the contrary, his diligence and vigor in the execution of his duties guaranteed that should rebel Indians invade, Montilla and others stood ready to defend Stephens's property with their lives.

In further response to Aznar's broad attack upon the Urcelays and, perhaps, people still higher up in government, a letter supposedly from Baltazar Montilla (but, from the polish, more likely from one of the Urcelays) dated 8 October from Puntachen was delivered to *La Revista de Merida* and published on 17 October. Montilla claimed that during his midsummer expedition to investigate signs of hostile Indian activity he did not touch anything at Xuxub—opened no fences (there weren't any fences to open), frightened no workers. They—Montilla and the valiant volunteers from Kantunilkin—don't forget their public service—conducted themselves in the most orderly manner. Montilla had his own theory for the evident troubles at Xuxub, including the obvious decline in the morale of the workers, who had been happy under Mauricio Palmero, and miserable under the despotism of Mr. Stephens. Montilla indicated that he had already made a full report to the governor and that he himself had requested that a commission be sent out at once to investigate the matter first hand, at the expense of whomever should be judged wrong.[20]

On that warm, rainy October morning when people could read Montilla's attack upon the veracity and character of the American at Xuxub, none in Merida knew that Robert Stephens was already dead, along with many of his workers, their wives, and their children.

12 October

Commander Montilla warned the fisherman to keep his mouth shut, and the fisherman cleared out. Word spread anyway. One of the Xuxub laborers who fled capture in the cornfields ran to Puntachen. He arrived there around nine-thirty in the morning, and the news flew through the tiny waterside village. Indians had overrun the Stephens property.

Still, Montilla did nothing. After all, the report might well be false. Around eleven, though, came word from one whom Montilla could not dismiss. Puntachen's justice of the peace had gone out to Xuxub that very morning. From some safe vantage point he spied the dreadful events and rushed back to alert the others. Why had Morales gone to Xuxub on that morning? The answer to that question soon died with him. Maybe the fisherman had confided in the justice of the peace and urged him to warn Robert Stephens. In any event, Morales made it official. Xuxub had been invaded. Montilla could no longer delay acting. Or, at least, appearing to act.[a]

As word spread of the invasion, men from Holbox who were on the mainland descended upon Montilla. Give them weapons from the small armory, they asked, and they would rush to the relief of Xuxub. But Montilla told them he did not need their help. Some of the frustrated liberators retreated to Holbox Island. Meanwhile, Montilla dispatched a messenger to Solferino, calling upon the Urcelays to send reinforcements. Nineteen or so men, armed by Montilla, took up watchful positions on the outskirts of Puntachen. Some of them also asked Lieutenant Fernández to lead them to fight the invaders at Xuxub. But Montilla firmly rejected the idea. They would wait for men to arrive from Solferino. No one would go that day to save Xuxub.[b]

Four

Between Strength and Weakness

C ONSUL LESPINASSE BLAMED THE INDIANS. AT LEAST
at first. So he didn't mention the Urcelays, Montilla, or all the rest
that Robert Stephens had told him about the vile conspiracy
against Xuxub. Instead he recorded for Governor Ancona that Robert
Stephens had been "unmercifully murdered by a band of savage Indians
who attacked his ranch slaughtering all those who came within their reach
and laying waste all the property around them." Stephens's friend and assistant, Joseph Byrne, witnessed it all and lived to tell, thanks to "the hand
of a merciful providence." From the governor, Lespinasse asked only that
the Indians captured at Xuxub be speedily tried and harshly punished "for
the crimes they have committed in unmercifully sacrificing the lives of innocent and harmless persons whose bloodshed loudly calls for retribution." That the governor could promise Lespinasse.[1]

Things might have gone smoothly had only Byrne perished with the
others. But Byrne survived, and from the moment he returned to Merida
he told his story over and over again. His tale gleaned authority from the
fact that Byrne was no stranger to violence and war. At the beginning of
the American Civil War Byrne enlisted as a private in the 38th New York
Volunteers and later was commissioned as a lieutenant in New York's
101st. He fought at both the first and second battles of Bull Run, at Fair
Oaks, in the Peninsular Campaign, and at Fredericksburg. He knew well
the sights and sounds of carnage.[2]

Byrne told his story to Ramón Aznar, to the American consul, to
those who would prosecute the Indian prisoners. The Indians came down
Montilla's road, Byrne assured one and all. "If this road had not been cut
the invading savages would have to wade through a wide flooded savanna
+ their only route would then be through the fields where the hands were
at work—a Bridge covered with loose plank was between the plantation
house + the fields on that side + there is a moral certainty of our having
been alarmed in time + of being able to make a vigorous + from the na-

ture of the approach to the house a successful defence—We had 4 Winchester Rifles all loaded—a large self cocking revolver + 8 other rifles + muskets—+ could without doubt have driven off the Savages—who do not attack a defended place."[3]

Were that not grounds enough for making Mexico pay, how about the fact that the savages tore up the American flag? Byrne was on a roll: "One or two war vessels sent to the South E. Coast of Yucatan—Bay of Espiritu Santo or other point + a force landed there of 1500 or 2000 men could inflict a prompt and just retaliation for this brutal murder of an American citizen + outrage on our flag."

Two or three days later a letter from Byrne appeared in a new opposition newspaper, *La Union Liberal.* That paper had already announced the death of Robert Stephens and reminded the public how authorities had abused the American. Why was it, the paper now asked, that the commission charged with investigating Stephens's complaint still had not departed? For some time a "hidden hand" had been at work to demoralize or destroy Xuxub. Now Xuxub lay ruined, while the Indian raiders oddly had not touched any other property in the area. "While the whole country deplores this catastrophe, there will be no lack of persons who rejoice in it," the paper suggested without naming any names. Finally, to excite the public with the seriousness of this matter, the paper expressed the desire "that the misfortune which occupies us truly be just a misfortune, and not an attempt that provokes an international conflict and increases our problems, new pretext for the flag of the flaming stars to be in our ports, insulting once again our poor country, hard worked and mocked by its own sons."[4]

With Byrne's letter now in hand, the paper could expose in more intimate detail the tragedy of Xuxub and perfidy of the government. Byrne didn't write that letter, of course— "and when the Respectable Public shall know that it was by this same road that the Indians entered," with correct Spanish subjunctive verb forms for good measure. Aznar wrote it. Pseudo-Byrne informed the Respectable Public that when the acting district chief who would prosecute the captured Indians recorded Byrne's account, the official omitted what Byrne said about Montilla's road. That was why the public would read nothing of Montilla's road in the official newspaper. While tied to a coconut tree on his estate, Stephens asked the Indians by which path they had come. Byrne heard the reply: "By the road newly opened that goes to the well." Byrne's letter spoke for itself, the editor assured the public.[5]

The official press vigorously denounced those accusations. That newspaper, *La Union Liberal*, was not the ordinary organ of any political party. It was the tool of a special enemy of the administration. Those articles about Xuxub exceeded in their maliciousness all the bounds that "national dignity and the noble sentiment of love of one's country" set for those who write for the public. From reading those articles, one would hardly know that it was the savage Indians who killed Stephens, that Mexican citizens died as well, and that local authorities and volunteers heroically and severely punished the criminal Indians by killing them in battle. Robert Stephens established himself at Xuxub in full knowledge of the risks of invasion. The government responded vigorously when the invasion came. That was all one could ask of government. There was no basis here for international complications. Stephens died, Mexicans died, criminals were punished. Was the government to guarantee immortality to every foreigner who passed through the territory? To distort the facts, as the opposition press had done, and so to disturb the friendly relations between Mexico and the Great Republic to the North was inexcusable. In the fever of opposition some newspapers forgot the duties imposed by "universal justice, patriotism, and conscience." That sort of calumny should be forbidden the press, for the honor of the press itself.[6]

Just a day after writing sorrowfully, but cordially, to the governor to seek justice for Robert Stephens, Lespinasse had second thoughts. The savages came down Montilla's road, the path that authorities had cut "with the premeditated intention of affording the Indian easy access to his estate." In his letter to the State Department Lespinasse could not yet provide all details of what had happened, "owing to the rapid succession of events." He begged for instructions.

Lespinasse's immediate superior was the consul general of the United States in Mexico City, Julius Skilton. Skilton was highly educated and experienced, and very much a man of the Gilded Age, too. Consuls general earned a decent salary, but that wasn't enough for Skilton, who found numerous improper ways to line his pockets. Skilton ran the official American cemetery in Mexico City as a personal cash cow, overcharged on passport renewals,[7] and pocketed payments from foreign citizens who needed diplomatic intercession but had no consular representatives in Mexico. Claims by American companies or individuals against the Mexican government provided Skilton his most lucrative opportunities for personal gain, and he embodied the Mexican stereotype of greedy, grasping American claim jobbers who would prey upon the treasury and territory of a weak neighbor. Skilton would take money from Americans eager to have him forcefully bring their claim to the attention of the U.S. minister in Mexico City, who would then unwittingly champion the case with his superiors in Washington and before the Mexican government. Or he would accept payments and contract contingent fees for companies to act as their agent in claims cases. That business alone stood to net Skilton hundreds of thousands of dollars.[8]

When back in August Lespinasse first wrote him about the problems of Robert Stephens, then still alive but molested, the sharp eye of the consul general spied no chance for gain. He just dropped the matter in the lap of the U.S. minister, John Foster, who was then completely ignorant of the scams and schemes of his subordinate and who was happy to conclude that in this matter no action was required. Consul Lespinasse had done all that was necessary and proper, as "in all such cases as this American citizens should seek an adjustment of their local difficulties without a resort to diplomatic intervention."[9]

In his first two years in Mexico John Foster troubled himself with little else than such calls for diplomatic intervention, to the detriment of his grander hopes for improving U.S.-Mexican relations and expanding commerce between the two nations. He had no diplomatic experience before his appointment as Envoy Extraordinary and Minister Plenipotentiary of the United States of America to Reside Near the Government of the United States of Mexico. By his own account he "spoke no foreign language, had never been out of my own country, and had only a text-book knowledge of international law." But he was honest and intelligent, and in the service of America such men were far from common. The Harvard-educated lawyer and Midwestern newspaper editor got the Mexican post for having done such a good job as Republican State Chairman in Indiana during the 1872 campaign. Invited to pick a post as reward for services rendered, Foster chose to be minister to Switzerland, a position where he could do no harm. Instead President Grant gave him Mexico, the most important diplomatic mission in the hemisphere.[10]

The Mexico Foster would find could hardly have been imagined even ten years before. The country's long and devastating war for independence from Spain (won in 1821) had served but as prelude to decades more of equally ruinous civil wars. Should independent Mexico be governed by a monarch of its own or by republican institutions? Should it have a strong central government or a federal system with strongly sovereign states? Must the age-old privileges and power of the Catholic Church and the military be preserved in the new Mexico, or should those privileges yield to the progressive doctrines freedom of religion and equality under the law? Over grand issues such as these, and for motives more base and fleeting, Mexicans time and again turned to destroying one another and plundering the wealth of the nation. Bled weak by interminable strife, the nation fell prey to the demands and designs of foreigners. Even as Mexico won its independence from Spain and recognition from world powers, so too did it acquire internationally accepted rights and responsibilities as a nation. But Mexico was not yet a nation. No stable government exercised authority over all of its far-flung territory and diverse peoples. Mired in civil strife and revolutions Mexico often found itself unable to protect the lives and property of resident foreigners, to administer an orderly and just tariff system, to honor its public debt (much of it owed to foreign bondholders), prevent its territory from serving as refuge for Indians and bandits preying upon the citizens of neighboring lands. It was not long before foreign governments responded to the clamor of aggrieved citizens and decided that Mexico would respect its international obligations only under threat of force. Some reached that conclusion reluctantly. Others did so happily, and they found in the claims and grievances of their citizens pretexts for sating an appetite for Mexico's land and minerals, their greed tempered only by pronouncements about the responsibility of civilized nations toward a people so anarchic and self-destructive. It was a duty, they would claim, to put Mexico out of its misery.

The U.S. took first dibs by contriving a mismatched war in which Mexico lost half its territory. Some Americans lusted for more, but their own civil war consumed the nation's passions and spared Mexico more humiliation from that quarter. After a decade of renewed internal strife in Mexico, France stepped in to impose order, collect debts, and protect the privileges of the Catholic Church then besieged by liberals. France installed a Hapsburg prince as emperor of Mexico, but forty thousand French legionnaires and four years of brutal counterinsurgency couldn't extinguish the nation's republicanism. When the Union triumphed over the Confederacy, and a newly united America sent a forty-thousand-man "army of observation" to the Mexican frontier, France withdrew from Mexico and hapless Emperor Maximilian fell.

Unlike the other bloody episodes in the history of the young Mexican nation, the war against the French appeared to have settled much and republican government firmly established itself in Mexico City. Banditry remained rife. The treasury was broke. Political succession in many Mexican states remained chaotic and often violent. Yet under Benito Juarez, hero of the long struggle against the French, Mexico appeared at last poised to build and extend the foundations of a free, orderly, democratic, and perhaps even prosperous nation.

Juarez appreciated the support he had received from the U.S. during his long struggle against the French. Among the Mexican people more broadly, however, distrust of foreigners had grown stronger than ever, and they did not exempt gringos. Why should they? Many influential Americans had not given up on acquiring all of Mexico. In the place of outright warmongers arose the economic expansionists, men to whom it seemed as obvious as day that American investments and American immigrants must slowly permeate Mexico. As that happened, they reasoned, Mexico would further strengthen its own republican government and discipline itself in the ways of democracy. The two tendencies would draw Mexico and the United States ever closer together economically, politically, culturally, until one day Mexico would freely and joyfully seek admission into the great American union.[11]

Perhaps no Mexican leader was more wary of the Americans than Sebastián Lerdo de Tejada, president when Foster arrived in Mexico. A more tranquil, democratic Mexico would be good for U.S. business, men like Foster thought, and commercial relations between the two nations should rapidly expand. Lerdo had other thoughts on that subject, summed up as, "between strength and weakness, the desert." Lerdo was a true nationalist. As a congressman he was known for his unyielding defense of Mexican sovereignty threatened by foreign treaties and claims. As minister of foreign relations under Juarez he made sure Mexico took no step to renew severed relations with European powers that had supported or recognized the imperial regime of Maximilian. As president Lerdo regarded the United States warily. Mexico would need U.S. capital to rebuild and develop its infrastructure and industry. Lerdo understood that. But he also understood that U.S. capital would eventually threaten Mexican sovereignty as gravely as French soldiers had. President Lerdo would welcome Foster, and all he represented, cautiously.[12]

Before heading on to his post in Mexico, John Foster passed first through Washington to meet and receive instructions from his immediate superior, Secretary of State Hamilton Fish. There Foster had, as he understood in the hindsight of old age, "a foretaste of the duties which occupied much of my time and occasioned me no small embarrassment during my official residence in Mexico. I was waited upon by various American citizens or their attorneys, who sought to enlist my interest in claims against the Government of Mexico, growing out of injuries alleged to have been sustained to their persons or property and for which they maintained that Government was responsible."[13]

Mutual recriminations for harm to people and property had pestered U.S.-Mexican relations for decades and driven more than one diplomat to distraction. One of Foster's distinguished predecessors at the Mexican post, James Gadsen, pointedly complained to his superiors about "the swarm of importunate and complaining sufferers" who gathered around his mission and who appeared to be growing exponentially in number. Most of those Americans, it seemed to him, had only themselves to blame for their woes, and were it not for the ignorance of so many American consuls, most of their claims wouldn't have seen the light of day. Gadsen wanted to stop receiving such complaints and claims altogether.[14] But he couldn't get off that easy. From time to time the two countries would negotiate agreements that, in addition to their main purpose of ending wars or transferring territory, also settled all outstanding claims—as in the 1848 Treaty of Guadalupe Hidalgo and the 1853 treaty that Gadsen negotiated. Yet hardly had the ink dried on those accords before new claims started coming. The most recent housecleaning of old claims was in progress even as Foster arrived in Mexico. John Foster could only pray that he would not be deluged with new claims as he attempted to usher in a new era in relations with Mexico.[15]

In his first meeting with President Lerdo in Mexico City, John Foster conveyed "the earnest desire of the president of the United States that the most peaceful and cordial relations may continue to be maintained between the Republics." American hunger for territorial gain and Mexican anger over the lost territory had both been drowned in the bloody civil strife of each nation, Foster proposed to the Mexican president. Each nation's trials had represented "the contest of modern intelligence and equality against ancient injustice and intolerance, which ages of law and superstition could not render sacred, and which the spirit of Republican justice could not tolerate." The Mexican president had recently proclaimed his country at peace, there being not "a single armed band in hostility to law and authority" anywhere in the Republic. In that case Foster could "entertain the hope that my mission may result in the promotion of more intimate political and social intercourse, an increase of our commercial relations, and the disappearance of whatever of prejudices and suspicions may have existed [between us] in the past." [16]

The cordial relations of which Foster spoke were hard tested during his first years as U.S. minister. Several issues dominated Foster's dealings with his seasoned Mexican counterpart, the foreign minister José María Lafragua. The first and most critical issue was the unruly situation along the U.S.-Mexican border, which threatened to precipitate renewed war between the two nations. From the American perspective the key border issues included the return of Kickapoo Indians who fled into Mexico during the American Civil War, the punishment of Mexican bandits who preyed on Texan towns, permission for American troops to pursue Apache Indians and bandits into Mexico, and the abolishment of the Mexican free trade zone (imports from Europe admitted tariff-free), which Americans considered harmful to merchants on their side of the river. Mexico wanted an end to support from the American side for revolts and revolutionists in Mexico. It wanted Americans to take vigorous action against marauders like the Apaches who preyed upon Mexican settlements in the border region. Mexico insisted that the U.S. should respect its territorial integrity, and that meant no armed American crossings of the common frontier. Those were the big issues Foster hoped to resolve. He was no warmonger or expansionist, nor was his boss back in Washington. But warmongers and expansionists paced in the wings, and a troubled border might give them pretexts and public support they otherwise lacked.

Most of the other issues dominating Foster's dealings with Lafragua concerned the fate of Americans, American property, and American interests in Mexico. Time and again Foster moved to demand better protection for Americans and the punishment of those who harmed them or their property. He tried to get reparations for harm done to American persons or property in Mexico. He tried to stop what he considered unfair or hostile treatment of American commercial interests, particularly of American merchant vessels visiting Mexican ports. Foster often lost those battles with his Mexican counterpart, who knew his international law much better than Foster. When it came, however, to the violent deaths of Americans in Mexico, diplomats could hardly temper their passions, and friendly relations were strained to the breaking point; such was the case of John L. Stephens.

John L. Stephens was a protestant missionary who lived and preached in the small town of Ahualulco in Jalisco, Mexico. On 2 March 1874, a mob shouting, "Long live the priest, death to the Protestants," attacked Stephens's house at two in the morning. They ransacked the dwelling and when they captured Stephens, who had managed briefly to flee out the back, they killed him, splitting his skull into several pieces and mutilating his corpse. They also murdered one of Stephens's Mexican coreligionists, Jesus Islas. David Watkins, a companion of John Stephens's who survived the attack, reported to American diplomats that instead of trying to prevent the assault, local authorities actually had participated in it. Town prison guards egged on the murderous crowd by firing their weapons, and soldiers stationed in the town took part in the assault as well. Watkins laid most of the blame for the killings at the feet of the local Catholic priest. The previous Sunday, the good Father had proclaimed from the pulpit, "the tree which bears evil fruit should be cut down. You may interpret these words as you like." After the assault, church bells pealed in joy, Watkins reported.[17]

When he got Watkins's telegram, Foster beat the well-worn path to Lafragua and insisted that prompt measures be taken to punish the offenders. The Mexican government did move quickly. By the time Foster met with Lafragua two hundred federal troops had occupied Ahualulco and several men had been arrested, including two priests. Further, a judge had gone there with extra clerks to conduct a speedy investigation and trial. Satisfied for the moment, Foster reported as much back to the states, where news of the "fearful outrage" hit papers and caught the attention of Secretary Fish.[18] The Secretary of State promptly let Foster know he expected a speedy trial of the accused and compensation for surviving dependents, if any, of the slain Stephens.[19]

Within a month seven men stood convicted and sentenced to death for the murders of John Stephens and Jesus Islas. Fifteen others still awaited trial, the local priest among them. Meanwhile President Lerdo met with a delegation of Protestant missionaries in the capital and assured them that he'd use all his power to protect them and ensure religious tolerance throughout the nation.[20] Despite the speedy convictions, however, proceedings against the killers bogged down. Six months after the first guilty verdicts none of the condemned had been executed. Meanwhile, in May, two Americans in Mazatlán were taken from the street, robbed, and slain. The American consul in that city reported that six men had been arrested and tried in the murder of one of the Americans, but after a long trial they were set free, although "the proofs were very strong against some of them."[21]

In August, six months after the killing of John Stephens and three months after the Mazatlán murders, Foster lost patience and fired off an angry note to Lafragua. "During the short time that I have been in charge of this Legation," he wrote, "I have been officially informed by the consuls of my Government . . . of the death of thirteen American citizens by violence and outrage, some of them murders of the most horrid character and revolting to our common civilization. . . . I am sorry to state that up to the present date I am not aware that there has been one single punishment inflicted for all this long list of murders and personal outrages."[22]

Foster protested the indifference of local authorities towards the welfare of Americans living in their district, and he demanded that the federal government use its power to punish those who murdered or maltreated Americans. Resolution of the case of John Stephens was especially urgent, it having created such a stir in the United States. Secretary Fish instructed Foster to inform Lafragua, orally and confidentially, "this must necessarily become an international affair unless it shall be satisfactorily disposed of and without unreasonable delay."[23]

What was holding things up? The now six men (no priests among them) condemned to death for the Stephens and Islas murders were undergoing religious preparation for their collective execution. A district judge in Jalisco stayed their sentences and the case went on appeal to the supreme court. Eventually the supreme court rejected that appeal, restored the death sentences, and did what it could to speed up the executions.[24] In response to Foster's repeated complaints about the snail's-pace proceedings against the killers of John Stephens, Lafragua had leaned on the court. After an October meeting in which Foster confidentially warned that the Stephens case could become a serious international affair, Lafragua addressed the supreme court in the name of the president. He drew the court's attention to the case and urged that they "dictate the measures they deem conducive to the quick conclusion of the stay of execution, as are involved in the matter the good relations of Mexico and the United States."[25] The court obliged by instructing the district judge of

Jalisco to terminate quickly the condemned men's stay of execution. It also issued a circular to all lower courts in the nation, urging them that "as soon as you may have knowledge of any crime committed against the rights or persons of American citizens . . . you should proceed to effect the arrest and punishment of those that may be found guilty, with the promptness and energy which the dignity and good name of the Republic demand."[26] Seven weeks later, with no one yet put to death and after another meeting with Foster on the matter, Lafragua again wrote to the supreme court, asking that they "stimulate the proper persons so that as soon as possible is ended such a painful matter. . . ."[27]

Before the supreme court could speed things along in the Stephens affair, there occurred another much publicized attack on an American missionary in Mexico, this time in Acapulco. A mob attacked and killed four members of a Protestant congregation, including one American, though their American minister managed to flee. Foster again urged that the Mexican government take vigorous measures, and he warned of "grave international difficulties" if this case went the way of the Stephens affair. The Americans even sent a man-of-war to the waters off the port to spur federal officials into action.[28]

The Mexicans couldn't or wouldn't act quickly enough to suit Foster, whose frustrations were only partly checked by calm counsel from his American superior. Fish reminded Foster that some martyrs were to be expected in the missioning of new lands. The U.S. should require of the Mexican government only that it do all it could to punish criminals who harm Americans. If it tried and failed, it could hardly be held responsible, just as, Fish could have added, the U.S. did not consider itself responsible to Mexico for the lynching of seven Mexicans in Texas, a claim that he had rejected just the week before.[29]

Two months after the Acapulco attack, and a year after the murder of John Stephens, none of the attackers in Acapulco had been arrested, and the condemned killers of John Stephens still awaited the supreme court's decision on a second appeal they had filed, which the court again rejected.[30] By mid-October 1875, the Americans had the bodies they required. Four Mexicans were put to death in Jalisco for the murders of John L. Stephens and his Mexican coworker, Jesus Islas.[31] Foster acknowledged Lafragua's report of the executions, took the opportunity to thank the Mexican authorities for "the exemplary manner which they have, in this instance, manifested their desire to afford protection to the citizens of the

United States as also to guarantee the freedom of religious worship in the Republic."[32] The Acapulco situation, and the other unsolved cases of murdered Americans, lingered on. For a few days, though, Foster could still hope the time had come for U.S.-Mexican diplomacy to break free of those fetters to tackle more substantive issues of trade and commerce. Until, at least, he received word from Lespinasse concerning the murder of Robert L. Stephens in Yucatan.

Foster had just applauded the vigor with which Mexican authorities protected American citizens in their country. Now he had to read from young Consul Lespinasse that:

> authorities here have played such a contemptible part, neglecting to fulfill their obligations, and I do not hesitate to say have done so with the fixed purpose of incompassing the death of Mr. Stephens upon whom they have always looked with the greatest enmity owing to the great importance his estate was acquiring to the detriment of others belonging to persons holding high positions under the Government, moreover to his great popularity with the working classes whom he always assisted when persecuted or abused by the authorities at Puntachen, however he always positively refused to interfere in political affairs although it is well known he was constantly requested to do so by the inhabitants of his district.

According to Lespinasse, Montilla's little road was but the last, alas successful, device they employed for the ruin of Stephens and Xuxub.

> The authorities have never failed to throw all the impediments they could in his way in order to force him into any rash act for which they could render him responsible but failing in this they determined at any sacrifice to get clear of him and under the pretence of making a road into the Indian country they succeeded in this manner in opening a path on his estate to the Indian territory thus under the cover of friendship obtaining the desired end as it would lay the deceased at the mercy of the savages who would certainly not be long in finding their way to his residence as they had been attacked and would in all probability seek to avenge themselves, and finding a road open which led them to their point of attack the late Mr. Stephens would be the

first one who would have to face their assault therefore the nefarious plot so successfully carried out has just seen its Completion in the death of a true and loyal American citizen whose death certainly cannot remain unpunished.[33]

Indians had killed Stephens, but his Mexican enemies were behind it all. Byrne said that the Indians came down Montilla's road, just as those at Xuxub had feared might happen. Authorities betrayed their guilt by the way they acted after Stephens had been killed. Three Indians had been captured at Xuxub and sent bound to authorities back in Merida. The governor had told Lespinasse he could be present when the captives were interrogated. That party the governor had been planning for weeks to send to Xuxub, to investigate the original complaint of Robert Stephens, was still due to depart, and Lespinasse thought the governor had promised that he could send an observer with them. Now, at the end of October, Lespinasse had to protest bluntly to the governor that he'd learned the prisoners had already been interrogated without him being present. As for the investigative commission, either it still hadn't departed or it had gone without Lespinasse, neither of which seemed acceptable to the consul. Lespinasse pointedly asked the governor that the Indians be questioned again in his presence and that the commission depart at once accompanied by someone who would represent him. Further, "as serious and grave charges have been imputed against the Commander Montilla," the governor should require that he appear in person and "refute with positive and sufficient proof any and all charges in which he is implicated respecting the death of the late American citizen R. L. Stephens." Finally, Lespinasse wrote, "I moreover forcibly protest against the manner in which the authorities whose duty it was to punish the Criminals in a summary manner have endeavored to elude the fulfillment of their duty through unjust and feeble reasons and who will be rendered responsible if the ends of justice are thwarted."[34]

Lespinasse alluded to the handling of three Indians captured at Xuxub. Governor Ancona had instructed the district chief, Andrés Urcelay, to try them under a harsh federal decree, the Law of Highwaymen and Kidnappers, which limited proceedings to fifteen days at most and allowed only one penalty—death. Urcelay, however, noted that since workers from his plantation had captured the Indians, he had a conflict of interest and would have to step aside. The president of the city council of Merida would act as district chief to prosecute the prisoners. That was Urcelay's idea, at least, until a district judge stepped in, ruled the district chief had no jurisdiction, and took charge of the case himself.[35]

At that juncture someone surely explained to Lespinasse how torturously long court proceedings could be, that Yucatan had outlawed capital punishment years before, and that the fact that the prisoners would be tried in court meant they would live. They might even be acquitted or otherwise evade punishment. No one bothered to tell the consul that no captured Maya rebels had actually ever been tried. They were just killed by their captors, farmed out to haciendas, sold into slavery in Cuba, or otherwise made to disappear (not that any rebel Indians had been captured in recent memory).[36] Nor might Lespinasse have realized that the federal law under which the governor wanted them tried was relatively new and had been little applied yet in Yucatan. Given the extraordinary publicity and controversy surrounding the events in which they were involved, the trial of these prisoners was going to be complicated. Anyone could see that.

The governor responded to Lespinasse's angry communication two days later.[37] The interrogation of the prisoners was in the hands of the court in a phase of proceedings not open to the public. (Yet the official newspaper had reported days earlier that the prisoners had been interrogated before the chief of the Merida District, Andrés Urcelay, the governor, the head of federal forces in the state, and "a large crowd."[38]) As for the investigative commission, it would leave the next day. The consul could go with them, but under provisions of the Consular Law of 26 November 1859, he could not send someone in his place. In any event the commission would investigate only the original complaint of Robert Stephens. It would not investigate the circumstances of his death, since that would be done by the court trying the Indians captured there.

Concerning Lespinasse's demand that Montilla come to answer charges, the governor thought it: "truly strange that it be supposed that the valiant Commander Montilla could be involved in the death of Mr. Stephens, he who with no garrison at his command spontaneously rushed to the rancho of Xuxub with a few armed citizens of Puntachen and Solferino." The governor knew well that Montilla did not fly to Xuxub on the very day it was invaded. He waited twenty-four hours to gather men and prepare. That was only prudent. More than one intrepid commander in the past had flung his men headlong against invaders only to find that they faced not scores of the enemy, but hundreds or thousands, with results inevitably tragic. Montilla acted as quickly and boldly as he should. As it was, the governor noted, Montilla and his men managed to save Joseph Byrne and prevent the ranch from suffering even more damage than it did. "If despite this fact that has been public," the governor continued, "if despite this position based in all the facts that have been collected, you still harbor any doubt, the courts of the country will always be available to administer prompt and full justice, and you can go to them with the accusation you see fit to formulate."

As for the accusation that authorities wanted to avoid punishing the captured criminals, by making that claim Lespinasse violated consular law. The governor would forward Lespinasse's last note, and all of the prior notes, to Mexico City and ask that the federal government take appropriate action. The governor wanted Lespinasse gone.

The young consul didn't understand that his job hung by a thread. "As my demands have met with such an unfavorable answer," he testily replied, "I desire to end all discussion on the subject in question," but not before he did "forcibly protest anew that the Government has neglected to fulfill its duty in the past and is not respecting its obligations in the present." To that the governor coolly responded that Lespinasse had once again violated consular law, and he would also forward that most recent note to Mexico City. They had no further communication on that matter and little on any other in the months that Ancona remained in power.[39]

The same day as Lespinasse's last spat with the governor, Ramón Aznar dropped his claim off at the consulate. He'd been working on it since Byrne's return from Xuxub. Aznar had tinkered with Byrne's first account of what happened at Xuxub and turned it into an early draft of his own claim-in-progress. "The undersigned citizen of the United States of America, merchant of this city, owner and possessor of the sugar plantation called 'San Antonio Xuxub,' situated in the Municipality of Puntachen under the immediate jurisdiction of the district of Merida de Yucatan," as Aznar introduced himself, "finds himself compelled to expose to you for the Knowledge of our minister and for the safety of his outraged rights of which he expects and solicits full reparation, the following facts...."[40]

Aznar constructed a history of the whole affair. How he and Stephens had entered into partnership back in 1872. How all was going fabulously well until Stephens had to struggle with the rivalry of the neighboring estate, owned by the Urcelays. Once Andrés Urcelay became Jefe Político of the district, that struggle left "the legal ground of private rival interests." Urcelay appointed Montilla, "a man of very bad antecedents" to be local authority at Puntachen. Montilla was intended more "to serve as able tool in the execution of a malicious plan than to be the agent of a civilized government." Aznar related once again in detail the story of Montilla's road, how Stephens complained and sought official protection, and how that protection was not forthcoming until:

> It happened, Mr. Consul, that your foreboding was fatally fulfilled and on the 12th of October two months after you foretold it the savages marched confidently into the ranch by the path that had been traced for them going in contrary to their usual custom with the greatest silence, they surprised Stephens to whom they gave cruel death, his two interpreters of the Maya language partaking the same fate.
>
> Having taken possession of the plantation and after ransacking all they pleased they stayed there without being molested by anybody twenty-six hours, although Puntachen is but three or four miles distant, at the end of which time Mr. Montilla armed with a force of fifteen men from Puntachen, who had been furnished with arms taken from private citizens and twenty-five armed men that were sent by Urcelay from Solferino . . . attacked the Indians left behind, undoubtedly for their state of drunkenness.

To add outrage to injury, Aznar claimed, after defeating the Indians Montilla permitted his own troops to complete the pillaging of Xuxub. "For all the above related by the exponent, reserving therefor the widow and heirs of Mr. Stephens their rights safe and in full force in regard to his death, protests once, twice, and as many times as is right and permitted, against the military and political authority of Puntachen, against the superior authorities on which it depends, and against whoever is concerned for the damages and losses caused in his plantation."

An award of about eighty thousand dollars gold should make things right, Aznar's claim concluded. Lespinasse dutifully forwarded the claim to his superiors in Mexico City.

Even as Lespinasse waited for guidance either from Washington or the Consul General, Governor Ancona sent his own complaint against Lespinasse to the minister of state and minister of foreign relations. He denounced the consul's insulting and libelous notes. How absurd it was, the governor insisted, to suppose Montilla had encouraged the attack. If he'd done anything to attract or assist the rebel Indians, that would have imperiled all lives and properties in the area, his own included. Besides, rebel Indians don't need any agreement or assistance from locals before they attack the frontier. They are fully capable of doing that on their own. They don't need any roads or paths to travel down, either. In sum, the governor was certain that Aznar and Stephens had deceived their consul and encouraged him to make such absurd accusations against Mexican authorities. Unfortunate that was, but the American consul had gone too far, and the governor trusted that the supreme government would determine what should be done in favor of the decorum of the nation. In Mexico City they acted promptly on the complaint, forwarding it to the Mexican minister in Washington for him to take up directly with the American secretary of state.[41]

The State Department responded to Lespinasse's plea for instructions on 6 November. They had no guidance to offer. Lespinasse had promised to forward more details. The department would await that information before giving the matter any further consideration.[42]

Meanwhile the opposition press in Merida wasn't done with the Stephens affair. La Union Liberal responded to the recent attack on its credibility and patriotism from the state's official newspaper by noting that Joseph Byrne was there, and Joseph Byrne said the Indians came down Montilla's road.[43] "Can it be," mocked the opposition, "that the events at Xuxub were not planned in advance, and that the investigation of this matter is proceeding with impartiality? Or is it that the editor of the official press wishes to deny the witness [Byrne] even the faculty of sight and hearing, because outside of the realm of government no one is permitted to see or to hear?" In any event, that a crime had been committed was obvious. The problem was to discover who were the "true perpetrators." That would be difficult, the editor lamented, as those who should investigate in fact took charge of hiding the truth, those people whose influence in the regions of power had left their mark on everything. The way proceedings were going, the punishment of the guilty would have to await the coming of the Antichrist, unless the United States took greater interest in the matter which could, the paper again insisted, lead to an international conflict.

Of course it was just a coincidence, but the same day *La Union Liberal* again trumpeted a warning of international conflict, former Union general and Massachusetts congressman Benjamin Butler met with the U.S. secretary of state to suggest they make war on Mexico.[44] As Butler explained it, at the end of the Civil War almost a million and a half soldiers mustered out. Many returned to productive lives. Many others however had "furnished the violent and idle element of society, the tramps and thieves at the north and the outlaws at the South." Butler laid it out:

> A war would furnish the best means of using up this population; that the business of the country was stagnant; and that a war would give stimulus to all enterprises; that history shows that in time of war even the peaceful classes were stimulated; that a war with Mexico would be popular at the South, and would put an end to all the questions arising out of the Reconstruction; that the disorderly population would rush into the war and that "a larger part of them would be left in Mexico either under or above ground." He thinks that by sending some coloured troops, the fact of fighting side by side would relieve those who might survive and return home from all prejudice of color against the negro.

For good measure Butler proposed a simultaneous ocean war against Spain, as "the two wars would greatly stimulate all the national industries of the country; give employment to what is now idle population, and would in its effect inure wholly to the benefit of the Republican Party." To this the secretary of state wryly replied, "one war was bad enough, but that two at once were more than I would have expected even him to have suggested."

Hamilton Fish had labored tirelessly for years as secretary of state to fend off the warmongers in Washington and stave off the foreign conflicts (especially with Great Britain and with Spain) in which many powerful Americans envisaged only profit, glory, and aggrandizement. Increasing agitation against Mexico concerned him some. He confided to one colleague, "I have no doubt of the desire of a class of persons in Texas to get up a war with Mexico; the speculating contractors all over the country sympathize in such object, and there is at present a very large class of unemployed who would see adventure and excitement and chances in a war."

Weeks later to another he commented, "our Eastern states have this 'noble army' of contractors, quite as numerous, quite as rapacious, and quite as patriotic as that blessed band of sharks in any part of the world." So long as he stayed in office and had the confidence of President Grant, the United States was not going to go to war over one aggrieved American, nor even over a roster of wronged citizens.[45]

John Foster did lug Aznar's complaint over to the office of Foreign Minister Lafragua, asking as usual "that vigorous measures be taken to punish all who may in any way be found responsible thereafter."[46] Foster also picked up on parts of Lespinasse's communications with the governor of Yucatan that might give offense. He knew Ancona had already filed a complaint against Lespinasse. Foster instructed his consul general to tell Lespinasse not to accuse Mexican officials of wrongdoing "except upon very clear evidence."

In the meantime, still without any instructions from superiors, Lespinasse continued to accuse officials of wrongdoing, especially after he learned of further complications in the trial of the Xuxub prisoners. A district judge had reinterviewed survivor Joseph Byrne, and according to Byrne had done a full and impartial job of it. Just to make sure, Lespinasse asked the judge to provide him with a copy of Byrne's testimony as well as transcripts of the testimony of the three prisoners captured at Xuxub. Within hours Lespinasse learned in response that the court was not handling that case any more. One judge had hastily accepted jurisdiction, it seems. A second judge found, however, that the court was not competent to try the case.[47] Lespinasse did not then know that it was only that very day—the day that Lespinasse had requested court documents—that the court decided not to handle the case and to send the whole troubling matter back to the district chief of Merida.[48] Then, to make matters worse, attorneys named to the defense refused their appointments, because they rejected the legality of the proceedings. Under such circumstances, the attorneys reasoned, the supreme court must decide who had jurisdiction. Until then, no one could proceed with a trial.[49] Of course with each twist and turn in the proceedings, the chances only increased that the prisoners would escape severe punishment. The Law of Highwaymen and Kidnappers was an extraordinary law crafted to deal speedily with urgent, dangerous situations. Though the supreme court had recently rejected an appeal of two convicted highwaymen in San Luis Potosi, who had argued that they were convicted and sentenced after the fifteen-day deadline established by the law in question, the court might respond differently to an appeal based upon much longer delays.[50]

So the consul again saw fit to charge that "state authorities here have endeavored to prevent me from ascertaining the true facts and have answered all my just demands with the fixed purpose of screening their officers from all seeming complicity in the murder of Mr. Stephens...."[51] Late in November young Lespinasse finally received some guidance. Consul General Skilton assured Lespinasse that the U.S. minister had carefully reviewed all the materials the consul had forwarded. They sent Aznar's claim on to Washington, and they would continue to give the matter their careful attention.[52] Meanwhile Lespinasse ought not to so readily accuse "judicial authorities with willful omission of duty and bad faith," as the consular law then in effect in Mexico (a copy of which he enclosed) established "the convenience, if not the necessity of sustaining by complete testimony any charges you have made or may make against the authorities or tribunals of the country."

His superiors wanted evidence. Lespinasse set about getting it for them. He'd prove that the loyal American Robert Stephens had been destroyed by corrupt and envious officials of the government of Mexico.

12 October

He'd led them on a three-week trek to fall upon Xuxub. So far from home they'd risked everything—disease and death on the trail, ambush from Indian enemies, discovery and annihilation by government forces. It had gone well enough so far. Xuxub had fallen to them quickly, the party was about to begin, and the leader of the raiders now wanted the prize for which they had come so far. "Where do you keep your money?" he asked his captive Robert Stephens. For four thousand dollars he would spare Stephens's life and not burn his plantation. That was all it would take.

Awkwardly and puzzled, Stephens told him that he had no money at Xuxub. It was all in the keeping of his partner Ramón Aznar back in Merida. But they could still get what they wanted, Stephens quickly offered. The Indian general only had to allow Stephens to send word to a contact among the Englishmen in Belize. The contact would raise the money and send it in less than a day.

His captors were displeased. They'd come for money. They'd walked a long way just to find there was no cash at Xuxub.

The Indian officers briefly huddled, then called for the Xuxub workers to assemble in front of their fallen master. Each stepped forward one at a time, spoke against Robert

Stephens, then struck him once—with more or less joy, who can say? For good measure, one of the Indian officers struck Stephens, too, knocking him to the ground. They'd soon lead Stephens off to meet his fate.

Five

The Will of God

HE'D BEEN IN MEXICO LESS THAN A YEAR. STILL THE consul thought he knew better than his Washington superiors the character of Mexicans. "Unless a person is on the spot where this event has occurred," he lectured them, "he can but form a very restricted idea of the prejudice which exists against foreigners."[1] His elders claimed they did understand. "The Department is well aware," they told him, "of the jealousy of foreigners in Spanish countries generally, a jealousy which is apt to be sharpened if the stranger shows superior enterprise and thrift to the natives where they may settle."[2] But they couldn't really understand, not like the consul who lived in their midst and himself saw and heard how among Mexicans, envy bred malice, then murder. They didn't realize how the superior morals and values of an ordinary American like Stephens could enrage the near-idle rich of Yucatan and the authorities who served them, authorities whose word was worthless and who evaded their responsibilities toward citizens and foreigners alike. If Lespinasse had any moments of doubt, he had the much-vexed Ramón Aznar to coach him in the devious and predatory ways of that class of men Yucatan seemed to spawn in agonizing numbers—to prod him on toward the certainty that powerful and envious neighbors had decreed Xuxub must die.

Lespinasse let Byrne inform Mary Stephens back in the States. Byrne hadn't known Robert or Mary very long, nor grown familiar with them. He called his boss Colonel; echo of some story Stephens had spun about his days in the Cuban Revolution. Mary to him was Mrs. Stephens, and it fell to him to send her "sad news about Xuxub. On the 12th inst. at 8 o'clock in the morning the estate was invaded by a band of seventy savage Indians. The Colonel and myself were reading letters (just received) at the time: there was no one else in the house at that hour when, without the slightest warning the room was filled with savages and we were securely tied without the slightest chance of making any resistance. They carried off everything of any value and led us over to the ranchos, from whence at 3 p.m. the same day the Colonel was led off to his fate. He was courageous and firm, and had hopes to almost the last moment that they would spare his life." To ease her fear of penury, Byrne assured the new widow that "Mr. Aznar, the consul and many influential people here are confident that the Mexican government is liable in a heavy indemnity to you for the outrage on civilization."[3]

As hard as it was for Byrne to tell Mary from afar, he'd have to do it again soon, in person, since before his letter reached West Hoboken, she'd already sailed to join her husband in Yucatan. The steamer was due at Progreso on 4 November. As it plied the Atlantic south, she knew nothing about her husband's fate. All of Yucatan knew. Her eldest daughter back in West Hoboken knew, for she had received Byrne's letter. Their friends already knew. Washington knew. Only in the mind of Mrs. Stephens did her husband still breathe with life.[4]

Three days before she landed, the judicial commission the governor had tried (or not tried) for months to dispatch set sail for the east, still charged with investigating Stephens's first complaint against local authorities. The Superior Court of Yucatan had appointed a criminal judge to make the trip along with a secretary, José Río. After waiting weeks for a customs vessel that would never carry them, they hired a private boat, the *Conchita*, owned by Nicolás Urcelay, and left without Lespinasse.[5]

They took seven days to make the beach at Puntachen, counting a stopover for supplies at Urcelay's old haunt, Dzilam Puerto. At five o'clock in the morning, two days later, they boarded canoes to ascend the Xuxub River. A few workers who survived the killing went along. Montilla sent Lieutenant Fernández with twenty armed men to escort them all. The party proceeded east along the south shore of Conil Lagoon before turning into the Xuxub River. While they paddled south, the beauty of the winding mangrove-draped stream impressed José Río. At around eight that morning, the Stephens' house at Xuxub came into view. As canoes drew up, masterless dogs ceased their plaintive howling. Then all fell deathly silent.

Montilla's men went first. They jumped from the boats onto logs bridging the water and filed cautiously to the Stephens' house. The judge and his secretary followed. They found the house empty. Papers and correspondence lay strewn about. All the furniture and utensils had been smashed.

The commissioners backtracked, crossed the bridge, and paced over to the main plaza of the farm. There, scattered around, lay kitchenware and empty rum jugs. It looked like people had partied. Ropes still hung from some of the coconut trees edging the forlorn plaza. A bit further on, the sugarhouse and the machinery and supplies it sheltered for the processing of cane juice appeared untouched. But the houses of the workers were open, abandoned, and in disarray. Lying here and there on the ground were gourds and sombreros, and twenty well-rotted corpses.

Robert Stephens was not among them. They'd fished his body from the river weeks ago. They had already collected the remains of his chief overseer and foreman, too. The chief herdsman for the estate had survived. Cut with machetes he'd fallen in the river, but was able to swim away. The remains of thirty-odd men, women, and children who had lived and worked at Xuxub fouled the savanna a few miles away. The commission did not go check on them.

The corpses at their feet were the remains of savage Indians. Barbarians. Enemies of civilization and of the white race. Rebel Maya from Santa Cruz. They could not name any of them, except one—the one upon whose opened skull still clung some clumps of graying hair, who still wore a brightly colored belt and gold earrings distinctive of his rank. He was, had been, the most feared man on the peninsula of Yucatan: Bernardino Cen, since the early 1860s a commander of the army of the rebel Maya of Santa Cruz.[6] The judge ordered the men remove Cen's head. They'd box and ship it to the governor as proof that their savage nemesis was dead, that civilization had won a great victory at Xuxub.[7] As for Stephens's complaint against Comandante Montilla, the judge neither saw nor heard anything to support it.

Maya General Bernardino Cen had walked a long road to die at little Xuxub. He had ignored the will of God, his followers later said, grappling to explain how the great general could fall in battle. God did not command that he attack Xuxub. As long as General Cen followed the will of God, patron and protector of His rebel Maya children, he was invincible in battle against the whites. So they believed. But Cen came to measure himself against God. So he was bound to perish in such an insignificant place so far from home.

Americans like Robert and Mary Stephens, Byrne, or the consul Lespinasse knew nothing of men like Bernardino Cen. They would have called him a savage Indian, conjuring images from the American west of feather-headdressed horseback-riding "redskins" roaming the plains in search of buffalo or stray wagon trains; from time to time, federal troops would sally from stockades to punish Indian marauders, return renegades to their reservations, or otherwise secure for white people the opportunity to fence the range, farm, or mine where they wanted. Just months after a New York daily announced the atrocities at Xuxub, newspapers nationwide bewailed the loss of General Custer and all his men in the far Black Hills of the Dakotas. Those were the kinds of Indians Robert Stephens had in mind when he told Commander Montilla that it was best to leave them alone in their places out there beyond the frontier. Ancona, Aznar, the Urcelays, and their underlings harbored very different images of the Indian. They and every other white man in Yucatan had rubbed shoulders with Indians almost all their lives, on the street and in the marketplace—not as equals, but as intimates nonetheless. They knew the Indians as ubiquitous, servile, often childlike subordinates who did all the work of Yucatan and happily accepted little food or pay, so simple were their needs. The independent, armed, and proud Indians of the forest led by men like Cen were of the same stock, and yet they'd made themselves people of a different kind, almost as unknown to the whites of Yucatan as were the Sioux to denizens of New York.

Maya Indians like Bernardino Cen were descendants of the builders of the ancient pyramids and temples at Tulum, Chichen Itza, Uxmal, Coba. Spaniards conquered the Maya in the 1500s, but for centuries thereafter they let Indians largely govern themselves so long as they abandoned their religion, paid tribute and tax to the Spanish state and church, and labored when called by any white men with the right. Though Mayas constituted the overwhelming majority of the population, once the Spanish colony rooted itself on the peninsula, Indians seldom really challenged it. Instead, they adapted to it, tolerated it, resisted it in minor or elusive ways. By the turn of the nineteenth century, that was getting harder to do. The Spanish crown developed an insatiable appetite for money from the colonies to fund its European wars. When the colony had to pay more, Indians got squeezed. Independence from Spain brought a confusion of new philosophies and necessities into play on the Yucatan Peninsula—tribute and taxes were abolished, only to be instituted again; Indians were finally recognized as full citizens, only to lose those rights again; Indian lands were taken for new commercial ventures and to dislodge labor for use on the new sugar and henequen plantations. The rulers of the free and sovereign state of Yucatan repeatedly called upon Indians to fight their battles against political rivals or against the central government of Mexico. In 1846, still three-quarters of the half million or so inhabitants of the Yucatan Peninsula were Maya Indians. Finally they'd had enough of affronts to their rights and dignity, threats to their lands and livelihood, and the broken promises and lying ways of their white neighbors living mostly in the cities and towns. Called to arms to fight one more battle for the whites, many of those Maya decided to fight for themselves instead. Early rebel leaders hoped to reform society. They demanded an end to discrimination. Whites and Indians would continue living alongside each other, but would be equal under the law, even as they were equal in the eyes of God. But early rebel leaders and white officials of Yucatan could not long control the passions the conflict unleashed. Prolonged violence shattered the fabric of Yucatecan society, and up welled a horrible torrent of fear and animosity between whites and Indians. What commenced as a reaction to social and political wrongs flared into a war of races.[8]

Bernardino Cen was not yet a leader when his people rose in rebellion in 1847, laid waste to most of the peninsula, and bottled up the whites and their Indian allies in small areas around the cities of Merida and Campeche. Before the last of the whites boarded ships for other lands, the Indian rebellion faltered. White forces regrouped and slowly began to push the rebel Indians back east, southeast, and south. By the end of another year large numbers of rebels had been killed and large numbers returned to submission. Up to a hundred thousand Indians, however, receded into uninhabited forests along the Caribbean coast and south towards British Honduras and Guatemala.[9] There white forces took a frightful toll on the Indians, with hunger and cholera exacting their quota, too. The rebels might well have been exterminated in just a few more months of campaigning, had God not come to save them, his favored children.

The Maya had always been a pious people in their way. Made Christians by conquest, they had long ago adapted the foreign creed to their own concerns and ways of thinking. They worried little about the salvation of their souls or the nature of the afterlife. They paid at best grudging obedience to a white-imposed church hierarchy (which taxed them heavily against their will). But they prayed fervently, and sacrificed, and celebrated the divine, and by so doing sought worldly well-being as members of a whole community of similarly devout family, neighbors, friends, and rivals. Through repeated collective acts of prayer and offerings, they demonstrated respect and acknowledged their debts to True God, his son, the Holy Spirit, the Virgin Mary, the local patron saint, and all the other lords and guardians of heaven and earth, field and forest, humans and wildlife. By doing that they tried to ensure that rain would fall, that disease would stay away, that misfortune would not befall the woodland hunter, that crops would be bountiful and livestock fertile and well, that snakes would not infest their villages, and on and on, all practical concerns and fears of subsistence farmers and hunters.

Honoring gods meant not only praying in churches clouded with incense, men on the right, women on the left, seniors in front, juniors towards the back, all facing, on their knees, altars laden with crosses and saints and bedecked with offerings of sacred breads and gruels. That happened often enough, and many days of every year were spent either in preparation for such events or in the acts themselves. However, every other moment of every other day provided occasion for honoring gods in seemingly ordinary acts of correct speaking, proper acting, and the avoidance of improprieties. Everyday blessings bestowed by gods were named as such. Rain wasn't just "rain," it was *u santo ha,* "the holy water." Corn wasn't just "corn," it was *gracia,* "grace." You avoided carelessly offending lords and sprits. You didn't refer to the dead like you would the living, but instead respected their new status and spoke of them as "the spirit so-and-so," as though the life so named were not extinguished, but simply changed to another form. You couldn't just go out and cut down a swath of forest to burn a field in which to plant corn. You asked permission of the guardians of the forest, to whom the farmer called out and offered gourds of gruel and prayer. Once the field was in corn, from time to time you prayed and sacrificed (together with your colleagues in farming) to the *chacs,* the gods who brought clouds and rain. These were not ceremonies to *make* rain, but rather collective acts in which men acknowledged their enduring debt to higher beings who made life, and living, possible. When the harvest was in, gods were first offered their due before humans dared take their share. In myriad other ways people showed respect to unseen forces and took from them—whether forest for farming, or wildlife for food—only in proper measure and with payment of prayer, incense, and special foods.[10]

When the war turned bad for the rebel Maya, whites tried coaxing them to submit by invoking their famed piety. In one such futile effort in 1848, the bishop of Yucatan addressed his rebellious "children of our Lord

Jesus Christ." The bishop complained that his heart was full of pain, as though he'd been mortally wounded, by the murders that had already been committed by Indian insurgents, especially the killing of clergymen. Surely, however, these killings were but divine justice for the sins of all who failed to attend mass and learn their Christian duties. And, of course, Indians had been led astray by the "exaggerated ideas" of the epoch—ideas like liberty, citizenship, suffrage, and the like. The bishop announced that he was sending a delegation of priests to meet with the rebel Maya, listen to their complaints, and seek solutions to the conflict. The rebels were not to provoke God by treating the messengers of peace with ill will.[11]

Don't talk to us of God, the rebels answered in letters back to the bishop and the priests. "We do know that He descended from his holy heaven to redeem the whole world," they acknowledged, and then went on:

> But one thing I say to you and the venerable holy priests: why didn't you remember or protest when the governor started to kill us? Why didn't you show yourselves or raise yourselves up in our favor when the whites killed us? Why didn't you, when one Father Herrera abused the poor Indians? . . . And now you remember, now you know there is a True God? When they were killing us, didn't you know there was a True God? The name of True God we were extolling, but you didn't believe in that name, and even in the dark of night you were killing us in your pillories. All over this world where you were killing us, why didn't you remember, why didn't you consider True God . . . ? If we are killing you now, you first showed us the way. If the houses and haciendas of the whites are burning, it is because you first burned [our] town of Tepich, and all of the ranches of the poor Indians.[12]

Rebel Indians, made arrogant by victory, scoffed at the hypocritical piety of whites and demanded, instead, that whites give up their fight. Among themselves, meanwhile, a more genuine recognition of the power of God permeated even the most mundane of rebel communications. "The enemy who are here," one Indian commander urgently wrote to his rebel superior, "plan to establish themselves in Kancabchen, sir, and for that I ask of God, our Lord, and of your excellency that you help me. Father, by the hand and the holy crown of God, our Lord, the enemy has paid no attention to me because I have so few troops here." A few days later he had to write again, even more urgently, "respectfully saluting the Holy Sacrament on the altar," and asking that "in the name of God" his

colleagues send him twenty-five pounds of gunpowder and the correspon-
ding shot, as he was engaged in such intense combat with the enemy. The
following summer, one of the top rebel commanders had to chastise his
subordinate officers for allowing rebel soldiers to harm Indian civilians,
loot homes, and fight among themselves. "I ask," he wrote, "that you tell
each one of your captains to advise their soldiers not to fight among themselves, for they are violating the sacred law. Don't let anyone go about cre-
ating disorders, and if an enemy ventures among you, seize them in the
name of Saint Isabel, Saint Rose, the Holy Trinity, Holy Mary . . . angels,
cherubim, protestants, martyrs, confessors, the revered celestials, the glory
of heaven, the protecting spirits of the communities, and the birth of the
church in holy Jerusalem. Win the peace of God, our Lord. . . . Do not
harm our companions. Is that what you want? That's not what we want,
that is not love."[13]

That near-rapturous commander didn't survive the next few months
of fighting, nor did many of his colleagues in those most desperate hours
of the Indian rebellion. Those who lived on must have started losing faith
in their cause and their God, until, at a water hole deep in the forest where
Maya men, women, and children paused in flight from government patrols, God began audibly to speak to them. He'd keep speaking with them,
later writing to them, for years to come. The time had arrived, he explained to rebel Maya, "for me to show you a sign upon the land of all my
engendered people in the world . . . that they might know it, all my children . . . Because it was I who caused you to be created, because it was I
who redeemed you, because it was I who spilled my precious blood on
your behalf when I created you."

For reasons lost to history, God the Son who came to the Maya
evoked the entire Trinity and called himself "John of the Cross, Three
Persons." He called on Indians, his "beloved Ye Christians in the world," for
he decreed that soon would come "the hour and the year for the uprising
of my Indian children against the whites." This Son of God understood
the suffering of the Indians in the forest. He too had suffered once, he reminded them, when he was sacrificed on their behalf. So, too, did he suffer now at the plight of his Indian children. "At all hours I am falling, I am
being cut, I am being nailed, thorns are piercing me, sticks are puncturing
me, while I pass through to visit in Yucatan, while I am redeeming you, my
beloved people."

"Whoever is not believing in my commandments," he warned, "will have drunk a draught of suffering without end." However, "whoever will obey my commandments will also win the fullness of my Grace, they will also win my love, I will also shade them beneath my right hand, I will also give them my final Grace, that their souls might attain Final resurrection." But they should not think of death, he added, since "even though they are going to hear the roar of the firing of the Enemy's guns over them, nothing is going to cast harm upon them.... Because know ye, ye Christian villagers, that it is I who accompany you, that at all hours it is I who go in the vanguard before you, in front of the Enemies, to the end that there not befall you not even a bit of harm, o ye my Indian children."[14] If they obeyed him, God the Son could assure the rebel Maya, "My Father has already told me, you my children, that the Whites will never win, the enemies. Truly, the people of the Cross will win. This is the reason, my beloved people in the world, that I am not abandoning you to the Enemies. I am placing myself on your side."

Inspired by divine assurances that they would win that war, beleaguered Indians regrouped around that water hole and built a village, later a town. The crosses, the sign that God had sent them, were first housed in a small oratory, later in a large stout masonry church, which they called the "Jaguar House." From the surviving rebels emerged a new military and religious leadership to guide the Maya in fulfilling divine will and defeating the Enemies, the whites, who, however powerful they appeared, could never win this war. On more than one occasion in those early months and years, government forces arrived at the new rebel capital, which Mayas called Noh Cah Santa Cruz Balam Nah, Great Town of the Holy Cross Jaguar House. The enemy burned the town and carried off the crosses that embodied the rebels' divine patron. Each time Mayas rebuilt their sacred town larger than before, and despite the loss of crucifixes, God continued to dwell among them and speak to them, as the rebel Maya of Santa Cruz grew ever stronger.

By the mid-1850s most Indians in the west of the peninsula had made a separate peace with whites, while rebel Indians in the northeast (those who would later settle at Kantunilkin) were hard-pressed by government patrols. The rebels of Santa Cruz, however, not only had survived, but were ready to resume offensive war against Yucatan. Among the men leading them at the time there was still no Bernardino Cen. He did not command the rebel Maya who sacked the town of Tekax in 1857, killing six hundred of its hapless inhabitants. He did not lead the successful 1858 capture of the fortress of Bacalar, the southernmost town of the peninsula and gateway to the colony of British Honduras, from which rebel Mayas purchased their weapons and gunpowder. Those were not his men who, in 1861, surprised the town of Tunkas, deep inside of Yucatan, and without a shot captured 250 of its men, women, and children, marching them all off to execution or captivity in Santa Cruz. A list of the principal leaders at Santa Cruz drawn up in 1862 included men named Santos, Puc, Zapata, Poot, two Novelos, a Canché, but no Cen.[15] Yet Cen was there, for sure, somewhere in the obscure ranks of rebel warriors who, in parties of several hundred to a thousand or more, had raided the Yucatan frontier a score of times over the previous decade and smashed a massive government force sent to conquer them in 1860. None then knew the name of Cen. Soon they would. They would learn to fear him above all others, until years later, at Xuxub, they took his head for a trophy.

Some disaffected officers at Santa Cruz attempted to overthrow their superiors in the summer of 1862. They were defeated and slain. The tumult provided openings near the top for a man like Cen, evidently then moving up the ranks.[16] In October of that year a large body of rebels pounced on farms around the frontier town of Pisté, near the ancient Maya ruins of Chichen Itza. They took some prisoners, but otherwise busied themselves rustling cattle to offer in sacrifice to God at Santa Cruz. Laborers and travelers who fell into their hands and later managed to escape named as leaders of the invaders the by then well-known Dionisio Zapata, Leandro Santos, Crescencio Poot, and for the first time, Bernardino Cen, who, like the others, was titled Comandante.[17]

The men of a rebel Maya company, kinsmen and neighbors of a single village, elected their most junior officers. When vacancies occurred higher up the chain of command, officers were bumped up a rung, and a new junior was elected. That system of staffing their command with men whom they knew and could trust seemed to work well for Maya. But they had problems getting rid of unwanted officers and leaders, and resolving rival claims to the uppermost positions in rebel ranks. If leaders out of favor or bitter rivals to those in command didn't die in battle or of disease, someone just had to go kill them. That's how Cen got his shot at the top. For years, a man named Venancio Puc headed the church at Santa Cruz and interpreted God's words. Puc's God had an insatiable appetite for human lives, and captives taken on frontier raids, whether whites or Indians, were slaughtered by the dozen. After one such massacre of innocents, Puc explained to horrified British observers, "the Spaniards always treated their prisoners that way. The Indians merely followed a lesson which had been taught them."[18] Puc claimed God wanted things that way, but in at least one written message to his Maya children the deity condemned such killing of captives. "How can ye just brutally kill your fellow creatures," he demanded of his Maya warriors, "while they embrace each other, clasp each other's hands over their hearts, in order to call on my Father's name? They ought not to be killed, because it is a most grievous sin for a Christian to be killed while kneeling and mentioning my Father's name. They ought not to be killed . . . whether they are whites, whether they are blacks, whether they are Indians, whether they are mulattos, whatever may happen, they are our fellow creatures."[19]

Gradually rebel Maya turned from slaughtering their prisoners to allowing them to live in captivity. That grated on Puc, and late in 1863 he let it be known that God wanted them to kill all of their white prisoners, then fall upon frontier settlements and kill still more, "for it was decreed by God that not a single white person should be left alive."[20] That was too much for other rebel leaders to stomach. Besides, some had grown fond of their captives and prized the services white prisoners could provide. So one night, led by a famed war general named Zapata, they murdered Puc and his assistants and confidentially let the British know that they might finally make peace with the whites of Yucatan. In the meantime they would not kill captives or raid the frontier so long as Yucatan left them in peace.[21]

But they'd been killing so long that it was hard for some to stop. After only a month in power, Zapata slew his principal coconspirator.[22] Two or three weeks later, 250 Maya raiders attacked Yucatan, ordered to do so by Bernardino Cen.[23] Another two weeks later, followers of the defunct Puc murdered Zapata and all the white male prisoners he had protected. Some white women and children were spared.[24]

Bernardino Cen and the other two new leaders of Santa Cruz, Crescencio Poot and Bonifacio Novelo, tried partly to excuse their own roles in the bloody succession. Though the assassins of Zapata came from a ranch owned by Cen, he and the others claimed they knew nothing of the plot, and they ordered the execution of several of the killers.[25] The gesture didn't help much. Zapata's followers blamed Cen for the murder, and the English viewed Cen and his colleagues as "distinguished by cruelty and

thirst for human blood." Meanwhile the new leaders of Santa Cruz rebuffed overtures from Yucatan, with whom, they declared, they would
never make peace.[26]

As the new top generals of Santa Cruz (their colleague, Novelo,
headed the church) Bernardino Cen and Crescencio Poot wasted no time
stoking the fires of war. In November each led sections of the rebel Maya
army against the frontier. They destroyed nineteen settlements and farms
north and northwest of the town of Peto, killing fifty people and taking a
handful of prisoners. Six months later they crushed a white army slowly
advancing upon the rebel capital, the last such attempt to conquer the
rebels until the beginning of the twentieth century. The following year
they besieged the forward-most government outpost at Tihosuco. After
the six-week siege Cen's white enemies had to acknowledge he was "emi-
nently suited for the career of arms." Though Tihosuco did not then fall,
government troops abandoned the outpost a few months later, their officers having concluded it could not withstand another siege.[27] The following year Cen and Poot turned their attention to the peaceful Indians of
Campeche, rebels who had signed a separate treaty with the whites. With
troops, arms, and ammunition, Cen and Poot backed a faction of those
peaceful rebels who chose to obey God's most recent commandment that
they return to war against the whites. Civil war among Indians erupted,
and then war between reborn rebels and the government of Campeche.
Cen, now head of the army of Santa Cruz, and his colleagues found their
own forces augmented by several thousand more soldiers and a southern
route into Yucatan opened for future invasions. Whites rightly calculated
that in the four years since Cen's ascension to power, the war had shifted
against them. They feared that the impunity with which rebels attacked
Yucatan might inspire peaceful Indians to rise up again; they feared that
without federal assistance the frontier would bleed until it collapsed; and
they feared most of all that Cen and his people might one day besiege the
very capital of Yucatan.[28]

In those first four years after the overthrow of Zapata and the death of
any chance for peace, rebel Maya from Santa Cruz attacked the frontier or
combated invading soldiers just seven times.[29] But they radically upset the
prior equilibrium of the war, as the governor of Yucatan reported to his
state legislature. Yucatan could not think of undertaking any offensive
against Santa Cruz without major help from the federal government and
without cooperation from the state of Campeche, whose relations with

Yucatan had long been stormy, at best. An offensive against the rebel capital would require at least four thousand white troops, one thousand loyal Indian allies, and money and supplies sufficient to keep such a large force in the field. Until such resources were available, the frontier would continue to suffer punishing blows from hostile Indians, with what ultimate consequence, no one could say.[30]

Rebel Maya waged war at a leisurely pace. During the decade of Cen's reign at Santa Cruz, they raided the frontier on average twice a year, spending a total of forty days in the field, sometimes more, sometimes less.[31] The nature of the rebel army set the rhythm of war. On a rotating basis men and boys from villages all around Santa Cruz devoted two months a year to military duties, whether in campaign against the frontier of Yucatan or guarding the rebel capital and the vital outpost at Bacalar near the border with British Honduras. When not soldiering, they supported themselves and their families raising corn, beans, and squash, tending livestock, weaving hammocks to sell, gathering honey and salt, hunting deer, peccary, or other game. They engaged in the many other traditional pursuits of forest dwellers.

Those pursuits came first. War came second. Occasional raids against the frontier provided them with adventure, some booty they could sell, and the satisfaction of doing their part to fulfill God's commandments. Raids also sated a lust for revenge. The settlements that rebel Maya attacked year after year were the same villages in which they had lived before the war began. Whites had allowed repentant rebels to settle there again, while those who remained faithful to the rebellion punished their peaceful kin over and over again.[32] Since frontier raiders ran little risk of getting killed, at least after they stopped assaulting strongly defended towns and focused instead on scouring the frontier of all its smaller settlements and farms, war against Yucatan remained popular in rebel villages. Too much fighting, demanding too much time away from home or grave risk of injury or death, would have provoked opposition.[33]

The first raid that Generals Cen and Poot led as new leaders of Santa Cruz went like many to come. With cornfields in harvest and time on their hands three hundred or so men of Santa Cruz armed themselves and filed out during the third week of November 1864. They aimed for an isolated hacienda southwest of the frontier town of Peto. Heading out on a raid they did not force their march. They made eighteen miles or so a day, something they could do in six hours of walking at the brisk pace Mayas of those forests favor. That left time to make camp, find water, gather fruits, or hunt game to supplement the otherwise Spartan provisions of hard tortillas. Raiders often chose the night or early morning hours to fall upon their first target. Then they'd move rapidly to strike any other targets when they reached them, day or night.

The raiding party led by Cen and Poot destroyed two small farms and then, on 28 November, overran Hacienda Kakalná. They killed twelve people and wounded as many more. Next they split their forces in two. One section continued rapidly north to attack Hacienda Thuul, on the main road between Peto and the town of Tekax. The other section headed toward the village of Tzucacab, also on the Peto-Tekax road, destroying two more small establishments along the way. At Thuul raiders killed a half-dozen people and seized sixteen mules and some prisoners, like Wenceslao Trujillo. They caught him out in a savanna, loaded him with their provisions, and forced him to follow.

The raiders tarried only a few minutes in Thuul before moving on to

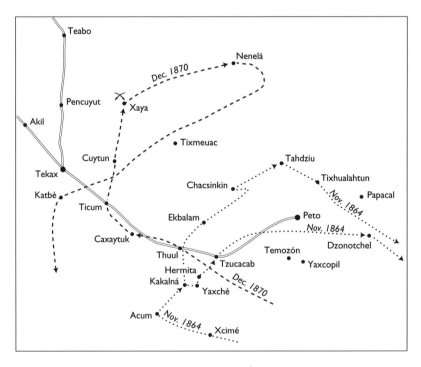

Two Frontier Raids

their next target. Meanwhile the section that attacked Tzucacab had a harder time of it. They opened fire at three in the afternoon but broke off the assault when the defenders of Tzucacab put up stiff resistance.

In the town of Tekax people heard the gunfire, but few troops were on hand to respond. A score of soldiers marched to the village of Tixmeuac in case the invaders continued on a northerly path into Yucatan. Another small detachment left Tekax and marched down the Peto road. By the time they reached Hacienda Thuul, the Indian enemy had departed. They could only bury the dead and collect scattered laborers. When gunfire erupted at Tzucacab, government forces at Thuul hurried on to help out there. Again they arrived too late. The raiders had moved on. Out of rations already, government troops pursued no further.

Meanwhile Generals Cen and Poot continued their broad circuit around Peto. They would not attack Peto itself. That mistake raiders last made in 1858, suffering many killed and wounded in their brief forays into that permanently garrisoned frontier town. This time they circled the town, falling upon one hacienda or settlement after another, leaving a wasteland in their wake. The group that destroyed Thuul marched rapidly on to demolish the small settlement of Ekbalam, and then continued northeast toward Chacsinkin. Expecting perhaps that Chacsinkin was prepared for them, the raiders bypassed it, doubled back, and penetrated the village from the east.

Those raiders, led by Crescencio Poot, spent the night in the village. They wouldn't usually do that. Wary of being attacked by government troops, rebel Maya seldom remained long in a village or hacienda they had raided. Instead, they'd withdraw some miles, set out sentinels and ambushes, and camp for the night in the bush. Maybe Poot knew there were few troops guarding that frontier. Maybe he was covered by the section led by Cen, still out there somewhere. Whatever led them to spend the night in Chacsinkin, the raiders did not sleep late. Around four in the morning they executed some of their prisoners and pulled out.

Government forces, meanwhile, were beguiled by a report that the main body of invaders, led by a General Santos, had headed far west to fall upon the town of Ticul. It was a phantom column led by a ghost; Santos had been dead almost a year. In fact the raiders were moving east. At eight in the morning of 30 November, Cen's section opened fire on the guards of Dzonotchel. The few armed residents of that village fought valiantly to save their homes. After four hours of intermittent skirmishing, however, they exhausted their ammunition and withdrew into the bush. Meanwhile Poot's men attacked the village of Tahdziu, pausing briefly beforehand to execute another of their white prisoners, the hapless Trujillo from Hacienda Thuul who had outlived his usefulness. Ten men fell upon Trujillo at Poot's command, but he survived his mutilation, played dead until nightfall, and made his way to safety.

After their attacks on Tahdziu and Dzonotchel the Santa Cruz raiders vanished, returning at their accustomed pace to their capital with livestock, prisoners, and booty in tow. They had destroyed all or part of nineteen haciendas, farms, ranches, and settlements. They'd killed at least fifty-eight (many of them peaceful Indians), wounded about thirty more, and captured an unknown number of civilians, while losing only a handful of their own.[34] The chief of the district reported to superiors in Merida that nothing was left but the town of Peto. Without prompt and effective measures before long the town itself would fall. That news prompted Serapio Baqueiro, one of the most astute observers of the war (and its future chronicler), to pronounce that the conflict had entered a new and especially dangerous phase, more perilous than at any time since the opening year of the endless struggle. He reckoned there were four thousand rebel Maya, better armed and more seasoned in battle than ever before. He should have noted, too, that they were led by exceptionally capable commanders whose hostility was unremitting and against whom the frontier was ill prepared to stand.[35]

Sometimes rebel Maya from Santa Cruz swept broad swaths of the frontier clean of people and the works of man. Sometimes they focused on fewer, more specific targets. Before daybreak on 16 January 1870, for example, about two hundred raiders from Santa Cruz attacked a thriving sugar plantation eight miles south of Tekax. They took the place easily. The estate machinist, who had just installed a new sugar mill, escaped. So did the managers and most of the workers. The rebels caught and executed a few workers, burned key installations, and herded off eighty to one hundred head of cattle. Guided by servile laborers who had fled to rebel Maya in Campeche, the invaders raced on to hit four neighboring farms. At each they smashed all the tools and utensils they could find. At one they paused long enough to torch the cane fields, then withdrew a short distance and set up an ambush. A small government force came upon them there, bringing with them the machinist whom they found lost in the bush. The Maya raiders fired first. Soldiers returned fire, and two detachments charged the Indians with fixed bayonets. At that moment another detachment of government troops arrived and opened fire. The charging troops thought they'd been surrounded by the enemy. They broke rank and chaos ensued, allowing the rebel Maya to inflict a humiliating, though not particularly bloody, defeat upon the Yucatecan forces before returning in triumph to Santa Cruz. Near the site of the skirmish someone later found the mutilated body of the hapless mechanic.[36]

Not every clash went so well for the men of Santa Cruz, and raiding parties usually moved quickly to avoid battles with regular soldiers. Maya rebels were just as well armed as their enemy counterparts. They had more experience in the use of their weapons. They usually outnumbered the government forces they encountered in villages or on the trail. Still, the outcome of fighting depended as well upon chance turns of event—as when the firing of their own rear guard spooked Yucatecan troops—and twists of human emotion, courage, doubt, and imagination.

At least that's how we might explain the strange fortunes of war. But the Maya did not believe in chance or in the randomness of human events. They understood that behind the inexplicable worked an all-powerful and all-knowing God, and ultimately the fate of battle rested in His hands. As long as they followed His commands, they could not fail in war. As pious as they were, though, Maya men could turn cocky, or greedy, or reckless, just like anyone else. Sometimes they wanted to prove themselves, even measure themselves against God. The son of God once warned them of that very failing: "Thus then my most beloved Christian villagers, anyone whom I propose or make Chief will have to fulfill my holy Commandments and his life will be lengthened and his life will be eternal with God, and anyone who will not obey, his life will end soon and his soul will go where the fire is never put out for all eternity. Because nobody should come out with his own and follow his own will, neither my white children nor my Indian children, but the will of my true Lord and my true Lady and also I."[37]

That's what Mayas say Bernardino Cen did; he followed his own will when he went to destroy Xuxub. That's how his people explain his fall there. Defeat was impossible as long as God protected him. But Cen measured himself against God at Xuxub. Others had foolishly tried that before. At a place called Xaya they paid dearly for their error.

Crescencio Poot had taken four or five hundred men from Santa Cruz and a contingent of fighters loaned from Tulum to raid the frontier south and west of Peto again. He told them they would hit Hacienda Thuul, just like back in 1864. Poot's men protested. "Why must you lead us to an old settlement that doesn't have anything?" Poot explained to his men that such was the will of God as revealed through the servants of the oracle at Tulum. Poot's men didn't buy that. They said their commanders were just afraid to get into real action. Challenged like that, Poot had to relent, and as he explained to his offended religious superiors, they all went on "looking for death."[38]

As ordered, Poot's raiders hit Hacienda Thuul early on 17 December 1870. Then instead of turning back, they kept on moving up Royal Road, which connected the town of Peto, behind them, with the more strongly garrisoned town of Tekax, a day's walk or so ahead. They destroyed two farms on either side of the way as well as the village of Ticum, on the road itself. There they spent the night. They pulled out at five the next morning, turned off the road, and headed north to the village of Cuytun. After wasting that place they continued rapidly northward, occupying the village of Xaya, as Poot later recorded, "at the holy hour of twelve day-time on a holy Sunday." Two hours later officers ordered their men to move out. Again the men balked, however. They wanted to rest longer. Officers insisted they pull out, stay together, and follow a single trail, rather than breaking in sections to scour the countryside. That way they could better protect themselves from counterattack. But the men would not budge. They defied Poot and the other commanders, boasting "Why do we have to go out and sleep in the bush, when we are in a village? If they [government forces] have arms, well we have them, too."

A detachment of soldiers from Tekax was already hot in pursuit of the raiders. They had missed them by only an hour in Cuytun, and reached Xaya at three in the afternoon. Poot's raiders were still lounging about the place. Firing commenced immediately and lasted two hours. Opposing forces battled house-by-house, street-by-street, hand-to-hand, until finally the Maya raiders fled with unaccustomed losses. The governor of Yucatan learned that fifteen enemy bodies were found in Xaya, including that of a Maya officer. Blood trails suggested many more wounded had been carried off. Crescencio Poot later admitted he had lost 16 dead and 19 wounded, and he claimed that his men had slain 179 white soldiers; at least that was how many bodies they counted on the ground in Xaya. On both counts Poot deceived. Only a handful of white soldiers died at Xaya, while Poot suffered losses much heavier than he said.[39] Maya rebels were reminded of a lesson they'd learned before—do your damage, keep moving, and avoid battle with the soldiers of Yucatan. Their failure to do so at Xaya cost them dearly. It was a mistake they'd not make again until they took Xuxub.

Year in and year out they raided the frontier almost with impunity, burning farms and ranches, haciendas and villages, killing inhabitants or making them prisoners, hauling off to their homes whatever they could or cared to carry (or could make their prisoners lug), destroying anything they had to leave behind. The men and boys who went on those raids were otherwise peaceable, orderly folk. They had families to care for, fields to tend, obligations to fulfill to neighbors and gods. They practiced the piety they espoused and lived by strict moral codes. Each time they went out raiding they may have believed it necessary to keep at bay the whites who had amply proved their murderous hatred of Indians. Each time they went out raiding they knew they fulfilled a part of True God's plan for his children and the world. Most of all, each time they flung themselves against the frontier of Yucatan, they did so in fulfillment of the orders of superiors and the shared expectations of family and friends.

From time to time their superiors still voiced grand hopes like those that had inspired an earlier generation of Indian rebels. They would yet conquer the entire peninsula, "land that had always belonged to their ancestors," as Bonifacio Novelo once explained to a British visitor.[40] After a force led by Crescencio Poot dealt government troops a crushing blow deep inside Yucatan, the rebel general boasted that soon Merida would burn and all the state would be theirs.[41] Still others, on appropriate occasions, declared that ancient prophecies would be fulfilled: whites would disappear from the earth; war to the death between the races would enter its final stage; the white man would turn his face to the west (i.e., go back from whence he came).[42] But despite the boasts of commanders and the call of prophets, after each assault the men of Santa Cruz turned their faces east and took the trail home.

The war they now waged had no grand objective. The conflict had an origin, but no purpose. War had become an end in itself, at least for the leaders who kept it going.

Many of those who went on raids, year in, year out, had never actually harmed anyone—shot them or slashed them with machetes. That kind of war they could work into their lives, it seems, without the habitual violence degrading their spirit or sickening themselves, their families, and communities. Not Bernardino Cen, though. On him the years of warring, intrigues, and alcohol took a heavy toll and warped his humanity.

Naturally whites feared Cen, calling him the "most intransigent and violent of the enemies of civilization." But Cen's own people came to fear him, too. Even his equal, General Poot, feared the man for his periodic displays of drunken, murderous abandon against any who angered him.[43] Two men who labored for Cen on his farm once asked to leave his service. Cen butchered them. A white defector to the rebels fell out of grace by courting an Indian widow. It was likely Cen who had him executed in the streets of Santa Cruz.[44] When Cen returned from a trip to British Honduras, he learned that his favorite daughter had died. In drunken anguish, as "vent for his grief," Cen ordered the destruction of a small settlement in English territory. (A subordinate officer had the order countermanded.)[45] Finally, Cen horrified his colleagues by murdering two of his own sons in a drunken rage. That was the last straw, it seems. The Queen of Tulum, wife of each of the last several heads of the church at that important Maya center, removed Cen from command of the rebel army and put General Poot in his place. Cen wasn't left idle for long.[46]

On 30 January 1871, one thousand Yucatecan soldiers and three hundred Indian allies surprised the coastal rebel canton of Tulum, captured a son and assistant of the rebel queen there, and burned the village to the ground. The next day they destroyed another rebel canton, Muyil, and the following day, yet another village, Chun Pom. The Yucatecan force then quickly retreated to the safety of the eastern city of Valladolid. That daring raid heralded a new but short-lived strategy. Yucatan would abandon the costly, wasteful, demoralizing, and in any event inadequately successful static defense of the frontier, and instead make war against the rebel Indians like those Indians made war against them. They'd launch lightning raids into enemy territory, burn Maya villages and farms, but avoid the enemy's main forces. They would slowly (and at little cost to themselves) bleed the enemy into submission. Had they relentlessly pursued that new kind of war, they might have forced the rebel Maya to make peace with Yucatan. As it was, the raid was repeated only one more time— by the Urcelays and Indian allies from Kantunilkin against San Antonio Muyil.

After the destruction of Tulum, one person who escaped captivity in Santa Cruz returned to Yucatan and reported that the rebel Maya would retaliate with a raid against the easternmost settlement of Yucatan,

Chemax, from which whites had launched their attack against Tulum. The escapee claimed General Cen would personally lead the raid, since General Poot had recently done so poorly at Xaya, and because Cen was "the bloodiest of them all, which circumstances make him feared even among his own." Cen reportedly boasted that he was best suited to make a good harvest of squashes, "or heads, attempting perhaps with this phrase to inspire spirit and faith among his subordinates."[47] Such reports of impending rebel attacks were notoriously unreliable. This one was dead accurate. Rebel Maya burned Chemax in June 1871.

It may have been the attack on Tulum that turned rebel Maya attention to the northeast. There had been little rebel activity east and north of Valladolid since resistance there was suppressed in the 1850s and a peace treaty was signed, allowing former rebels to settle at Kantunilkin. While General Poot continued focusing on the central frontier, the leaders of Tulum, Chun Pom, and San Antonio Muyil sent raiders into the northeast. Cen evidently led the Chemax raid, and subsequent events suggested that Cen, too, cast an eye toward that new field of action.[48]

Rebel religious leaders at Tulum ordered a raid against the peaceful Indian community of Kantunilkin in July 1872. Forces from San Antonio Muyil, lead by Juan de la Cruz Pomol, carried out the successful assault. In reprisal, the Urcelays assembled a force of their own workers and Indians from Kantunilkin. In August 1872 they destroyed San Antonio Muyil and killed Pomol. Mayas there quickly chose a new general, Juan de la Cruz Pat. But neither they nor their brethren in Santa Cruz retaliated promptly for that invasion—not against the northeast, anyway. But that long-neglected corner of the peninsula—where Solferino, Xuxub, and other new sugar estates began to flourish—fell again into the rebel Maya ken.

In January Santa Cruz launched a massive raid against the central frontier, destroying seventeen settlements and farms, as well as the small town of Kaua. They annihilated a small force of the Fifth Battalion of the National Guard that had rushed precipitously to challenge them in Kaua (30 men against, it was later estimated, 1,000 invaders), and they seized 160 captives, only 30 of whom ever reappeared in Yucatan.[49] The rest of that year the rebel Maya of Santa Cruz remained relatively quiet. Santa Cruz allies in Campeche launched two raids against the frontier, one in February, another in October. General Poot instructed his allies there to prepare for a massive joint operation against Yucatan and/or Campeche, but not until the following year did Santa Cruz make any major move in

that direction. An accidental fire at Santa Cruz in May 1873 may have delayed rebel plans for an offensive, and a raid that Poot led against the frontier in August 1874 may have been the long-expected campaign. Still, as
late as December of that year, escapees from Santa Cruz were still reporting that a major joint offensive was in the works. Santa Cruz would attack
and destroy Peto and Valladolid, the last two standing towns on the Yucatecan frontier, while allies in Campeche launched diversionary attacks
against southern Yucatan. Meanwhile, Bernardino Cen planned to strike
again far into the northeast of the peninsula.[50]

They had big plans, campaigns to crown themselves with glory, to
shower themselves with cattle, horses, loot, and captives. And nobody
could stop them. That's what they believed. But was that really the will of
God? Or did they seek only to satisfy their lust for war and bolster their
hold on power? They don't seem to have stopped to ponder that vital
question. They should have. Before long they'd realize it hadn't been the
will of God at all. For their hubris, God abandoned them to their fate.
After Xuxub, they looked back and reckoned their fall had begun around
Christmastime.

In that Christmas season of 1874, Alphonse Lespinasse was just en-
tering upon his duties as American consul in Merida, and had not yet
heard of Robert Stephens. Eligio Ancona, governor for a month, hadn't
yet appointed Andrés Urcelay district chief and thus given him powers
that he could unleash against Xuxub. Stephens, meanwhile, looked bliss-
fully ahead to record harvests the next year, ignorant that events on another frontier were stirring up a tempest more dangerous than any he'd yet
weathered.

12 October

They'd come all that way for money and found none at Xuxub. A little killing might make the trip worthwhile. The day was already long when General Pat gave the order to untie Stephens from the tree and for two Maya soldiers to bring him along. They would not need their guns, only machetes. Two fugitive laborers joined the party as well, and they walked Stephens over toward the big house across the river. The squad stopped on the plank bridge spanning the narrow stream and decided right there to kill Robert Stephens while his old laborer Cosme Cob spit bloody insults at the dying master. Then they dumped Stephens's lifeless body in the water, and turned to fetch Joseph Byrne.

Byrne was lucky that day. While Pat and his men dealt with Robert Stephens, Byrne recalled how much the savages liked music. A Merida merchant once told him that. So when Byrne saw one of his captors with a violin looted from the house, he signaled he wanted to play. Apparently Byrne could carry a tune, as the fiddling pleased General Cen. When General Pat and his men returned for Byrne, Cen told them to leave Byrne alone; Byrne belonged to him now.[a] Pat and his men took the rest of the management of Xuxub, one by one, to the plank bridge and their deaths.

The invaders spent that night at Xuxub, confident that no one would disturb them. Some went out to gather firewood so that the captive women could prepare dinner for all. Cen dined in the big house, where he had Byrne join him for a meal and a smoke. Then they fetched some women. While Byrne fiddled away, his captors danced. Alcohol flowed freely.

Later they secured Byrne again to the coconut tree and stood guards over him and the bound laborers scattered around the plaza. None of the captives could sleep that night for the popping of fireworks, the shouts of drunken men, and the screams of women being raped.

General Pat and his men rose early the next morning, hungover or not. They gathered up all the prisoners except Byrne, loaded them with plunder, and started down the long trail home. General Cen still lay in his hammock. Fifteen or so of his men stayed behind, including the general's loyal secretary and a servant boy, José. Some of Cen's men, like their leader, had not yet shaken off the debauch of the night before. Others were up. They put Byrne in the big house in which the general slept and tended to their cut of the plunder—four head of cattle, two horses, a few things from the houses.

Six

Hubris

NDIANS FROM SANTA CRUZ WOULD ARRIVE AROUND
Christmas, looking to sell hammocks, pigs, and plunder from their
frontier raids, and to buy things they needed back home—salt, cloth,
gunpowder, flints and shot, liquor. They might visit Corozal any other
month, too. But you could bank on them showing up at Yuletide.

Residents of that northernmost town of British Honduras awaited
them with mixed feelings. The hundred or so merchants of Corozal
prayed for a prosperous Christmas. Sales of alcohol and supplies to newly
contracted loggers or plantation laborers represented a great part of their
entire annual income. Whatever they could sell to visiting Maya rebels
was frosting on the cake. Yet as the strength of the rebel Maya grew under
Generals Cen and Poot, so too deepened the wariness of their English
neighbors. Year after year officials griped to one another about the "excessive arrogance" of the Indian visitors, of their "insolence of language and
conduct" as they strutted, armed and in military array, down the streets of
Corozal. Claiming already to have conquered the Yucatecans, Mexicans,
French, and Austrians (they'd fought some during Maximilian's reign),
rebel Maya failed to appreciate the great power of Her Britannic Majesty.
Though generally well behaved during their visits, they clearly thought
they could do or say almost anything they wanted.[1] So back in December
1867 they snatched some seventy people from the British side, deserters
from the rebel ranks or people with unpaid bills back in Santa Cruz.
Bernardino Cen threatened to round up more at Christmas in 1869.
Bloodied at the battle of Xaya in December 1870, rebel Maya did not appear in force at Corozal. But they were back in large numbers for Christmas of 1872, just weeks before a massive raid against eastern Yucatan.

Corozal was a ramshackle bayside town with several hundred houses
lining straight, often muddy streets. The settlement and its environs were
home to the largest share of the population of one of England's smallest,
poorest, least significant colonies.[2] The heyday of mahogany cutting, the

reason there was a colony there at all, had passed. The colony's capital, the town of Belize City, still served as point of entry for British imports to Central America (legal or smuggled) and for that region's exports to Europe. But other ports were cutting in on the trade that Belize City once dominated. If the colony had any future, many then supposed, that future was taking shape in the colony's northern district. When the Indians rebelled in Yucatan, thousands of people fled into British territory and settled around Corozal. Years of warfare added to their numbers there. The refugees—almost two-thirds of the population around Corozal was born in Yucatan—brought know-how and labor for building a sugar industry in the north of the British colony. Englishmen, mostly, owned the land and supplied the capital. By the early 1870s, nine sugar plantations with modern machinery surrounded Corozal, while numerous smaller operations using more primitive techniques dotted the flat landscape between the Río Hondo and the sea.[3]

The prosperity of Corozal depended on good relations with the powerful rebel Maya to the north. Under the leadership of Cen, Poot, and Novelo, those relations were usually pretty good. Their impetuous and blood-lusting predecessor, Venancio Puc, would threaten the English on a whim. His successors wouldn't. They valued the relationship, soberly understood how much they needed the English (or at least merchants under English protection), and sought to keep things orderly and calm on their common frontier. They became so good at it that officials in British Honduras toyed with the notion of recognizing the rebel Maya as the de facto government of over half the Yucatan Peninsula (with all the economic and diplomatic prerogatives such recognition would bring).

Some Englishmen dreamed even of a closer union, and relations with the Maya were never better than when John Carmichael Jr., a captain in the British Honduran militia and son of the most important and influential landowner around Corozal, traveled to Santa Cruz early in the reign of Cen, Poot, and Novelo.

Upon arrival in the rebel capital, according to Carmichael's report, "Crescencio Poot, the third principal chief, accompanied by a guard of honour of 200 men and a band of music of 30 performers came to meet me; by [them] I was conducted into the town through triumphal arches."

In the suburbs of the town of about seven thousand people, Carmichael noted, the numerous houses were of typical rural pole and thatch construction, each surrounded by fruit trees and each lot surrounded by low stone walls. Closer to the center of town, structures were built of stone. The grandest of all was the massive church that dominated one side of the plaza and the construction of which, he remarked, "reflects the greatest credit on the masonic skills of the Indians."

On his way toward the center, Carmichael was greeted at "each cross street [by] soldiers who presented arms." He continued: ". . . on arriving in the plaza or principal square I found about 1000 men under arms who saluted as I passed. I was taken to one of the best houses at the corner of the plaza built of stone with a raised verandah, which I found comfortably furnished as well as refreshment provided."[4]

Around the central plaza of Santa Cruz Carmichael found a school "where children are taught the early rudiments of Spanish and [written] Maya," a prison, barracks, the council house, and the palace of the "Patrón," or head of the church, Bonifacio Novelo. The next morning Carmichael enjoyed an audience with the man. Upon arriving at Novelo's house,

> I was shewn into the reception room at one end of which was an altar with a cross profusely ornamented with gold and jewels. Presently the curtain dividing the room from an inner one was drawn aside and the Patron [i.e., Novelo] appeared. Without noticing me he prostrated himself before the cross, and after five minutes devotion rose and welcomed me. He is a man of about 60 years of age, immensely stout, and is of a lighter shade of colour than the generality of the Indians. His expression or countenance is decidedly pleasing. He was dressed in a many coloured blouse made of cloth of Indian manufacture, white loose cotton drawers, trimmed from the knee downward with rich lace, sandals of embroidered leather, and a scarf also of Indian manufacture round his waist, while round his neck was hung a massive gold chain with a cross attached.

Novelo immediately acknowledged the bravery of the young Englishman in coming to that place. They had a bad reputation, he knew, because of their war with the Yucatecans. "Whatever our conduct may be towards them," he quickly added, "I can assure you that our feelings are nothing but those of friendship towards the English." According to Carmichael Novelo then "vehemently denounced the cruelties and treacheries that have been perpetrated on the Indians by the Yucatecans and frankly confessed to a retaliation on their parts towards them, and stated that the war they

were now carrying on was to recover their lands which had always belonged to their ancestors."

As curious as Carmichael was about his rebel hosts, they were just as
curious about the British: "[Novelo] asked many questions respecting Her
Majesty the Queen, her relations with Her subjects, the English code of
laws and mode of punishment with an intelligence which, considering his
complete isolation, astonished me; whilst the firm yet impartial manner in
which he administered justice, his kindness and benevolence to the lower
class of Indians, and the many good traits his character displayed convince
me that he is peculiarly adapted to govern these Indians and a very different character from what is represented by the Yucatecans."

Carmichael next met with General Cen, who, like Novelo, prostrated
himself before his altar cross for a good long while before acknowledging
the presence of the Englishman. In Cen, Carmichael found "a pure Indian,
short, somewhat stout, with a frank, open countenance and an eye indica-
tive of courage and resolution." Cen described for Carmichael the size and
organization of their army, and he claimed that his subordinates performed their bellicose duties willingly, even cheerfully. In contrast, according to Carmichael, Cen "spoke with the greatest contempt of the courage
of the Yucatecan troops."

Before leaving the rebel capital the young Carmichael attended a
meeting of the principal officers of Santa Cruz where a welcome question
was put to him: If the rebels could secure a peace agreement with Yucatan
acknowledging their permanent separation from Mexico, "would England
be willing to take over this territory and make it part of British Honduras,
they, the Santa Cruz Indians, laying down their arms, and becoming
British subjects in every respect?"

Carmichael, like perhaps a few others back home, was ecstatic at the
notion. "It is not for me to attempt to point out to Your Excellency the in-
calculable benefits that would accrue to our colony by this new accession
to her territory," Carmichael offered in his report to the lieutenant governor, before going on to point out just what those benefits would be: "Fresh
capital and that of no inconsiderable amount [Novelo had told Carmichael
their church coffers held over $200,000 in coin, not to mention jewels, gold
ornaments, and more], an addition of some 15,000 laborers, a fresh impetus to trade, and above all, a state of security conducive to immigration,
which would cause the colony to become one of the most flourishing and
prosperous of Her Majesty's settlements in the West Indies."

That was all just a pipe dream. A few past officials in British Honduras had toyed with such ideas. The current chief executive of the colony dismissed it out of hand, along with the notion of having any other kind of formal treaty or agreement with Indians. At most they'd try informally to nurture good relations, let the Indians buy what they needed in Corozal, insist that the Indians maintain order on their side of the common frontier, and hope for the best. As long as the English allowed them to buy and sell in Corozal, the Maya of Santa Cruz tempered any aggressive impulses against the colony's white Englishmen and Indian and Hispanic refugees. Rebel Maya leaders reassured their doubting English friends, writing things like "there is not one evil in our hearts against you," and "may our Father the True God never permit that there should ever be any dislike between you and us, but peace and love one to the other," and "we will never act treacherously with your Excellency as the Spaniards do, but we ask the Lord God and the most Holy Virgin Mary, who is in Her Glory, that there be one love between us."[5]

But how long could love last? Englishmen asked themselves that from time to time. They got along decently with the likes of Crescencio Poot. Cen could be dangerously hotheaded, but his colleagues were keen to the value of the English, and they kept the general in line. Still, a change in the leadership at Santa Cruz might yet unleash chaos and put the colony at risk.[6] Dark imaginings of what could happen cost some English a good night's sleep. By day, though, the people of Corozal sold gunpowder and shot, salt, cloth, and whatever else Mayas asked for. They employed rebel Indians from time to time on their sugar farms. They paid them for permission to cut mahogany or logwood in rebel territory. While privately calling them insolent, bloodthirsty savages, again and again English officials sent polite and friendly missives to the leadership in Santa Cruz. And upon each anniversary of the birth of the Infant Jesus, they showed their Indian neighbors a good time in Corozal.[7]

Each year the magistrate in Corozal reported to his superior how well the Christmas selling season went. He would inform the lieutenant governor, too, about the rebel Maya visitors—how they conducted themselves, what they bought, what news they brought of affairs on the other side of the frontier, whether or not they still seemed friendly toward the British colony and English interests. For several Christmases past, the magistrate had penned little unpleasant about Corozal's Maya guests. In his expected Christmas dispatch to Belize City in 1874, however, the magistrate had something entirely new to report, "a circumstance of unusual character." Two days before Christmas a boat arrived from the rebel Maya outpost at Bacalar. It carried eight Indian soldiers, their commander Vitoriano Vitorín, and a thirty-four-year-old white woman named Josefa.[8]

Josefa Romero de Rodríguez was a captive of the rebel Maya of Santa Cruz. Raiders seized her, her daughter, sister, and hundreds of her neighbors by strolling unopposed into the town of Tunkas on 7 September 1861. On the trail home to Santa Cruz they killed many of the captives—those who could not move fast enough or refused to go any further. A week after reaching the rebel capital, they executed all of the white male captives. (Most of them, anyway. A couple offered up Maya surnames and could pass for Indian.) They spared the white and Indian women and their children, rebaptized them in the church of Santa Cruz, and distributed them among the households of Maya officers.[9]

The service of captives was an important perk of leadership in Santa Cruz. All of the top officers there had farms on which servile laborers toiled. Most of those workers were Indians captured in frontier raids. Some were the children of captives who had died. Some were defectors to the rebel side, people who fled bondage on the haciendas and plantations of Yucatan. A hundred and fifty or so were Chinese—hapless men who after immigrating from Asia to labor on British plantations decided they didn't like the work and food offered by their English masters. They thought the Maya would treat them better and many crossed over to them, only to discover too late that servitude awaited them there, as well.[10]

Bernardino Cen had two farms on which captives and Chinese toiled. His colleague, Crescencio Poot, had two or three. Officers lower in the hierarchy had only one. Cen set his people to raising corn and tending cattle. Poot used captives on one of his farms to cultivate sugarcane, which they crushed in wooden mills they had fashioned.[11] They made sugar and distilled rum on equipment plundered from farms in Yucatan or acquired in some other fashion from English territory. All that corn, beef, sugar, and rum didn't just go to feed officers' families, or to liven up fiestas. The officers' servile laborers produced goods that could be sold for money. In that society of corn farmers there would always be some looking to buy grain. As for rum, most men would drink it, but none could make it, except for the officers who controlled the stills. Rum fetched a good price in Santa Cruz. Officers also sold liquor to their allies in Campeche and their colleagues near the coast, and sometimes even across the border in the English colony.[12]

In a rebel society where every free man labored for himself and his family, none of that would have been possible without the captive workers, slaves in all but name. At first, captives who were not killed were sent to labor on public works in the capital—leveling its hilly plaza, building the high walls of the church where the rebels spoke with God, weeding streets, and the like. Over time captives spent ever fewer days in such public labor, only to be sent more quickly into the private service of officers like Cen and Poot.[13]

The captors of Josefa Romero didn't send her to toil in the fields. She was special. Her husband, absent from Tunkas that fateful September morning, was a well-known Yucatecan military officer and player in political revolutions. On the day of Josefa's capture, her twenty-eight-year-old husband Manuel, like most of the men of Tunkas, was away or in the fields. When he learned of the disaster, he led men in hot pursuit of the fleeing Indians. But the raiders moved too fast. In the days that followed, searchers found only the bodies of forty-seven villagers along the cold trail back to Santa Cruz.[14] In the ensuing years, Manuel built himself a reputation as an avid Indian fighter, and he did not quickly abandon hope of freeing his wife and the other Tunkas captives. More than once, it seems, the government declined to aid him in that challenge, so eventually Manuel decided that before he could make war on Indians, he'd have to make war on the government of Yucatan.[15] In March of 1863 Colonel Manuel Rodríguez, then head of the garrison at the town of Izamal, and Felipe Navarrete, military chief of the eastern line based at Valladolid, declared themselves in rebellion against the governor of Yucatan. They pledged that if they triumphed in their cause, conquering the rebel Maya would be their first order of business. Thanks mostly to Rodríguez's persistence and daring, by September, the revolution triumphed. Navarrete installed himself as governor, while Rodríguez returned to Izamal to take charge of the central line and prepare for war against Santa Cruz.[16]

By the middle of 1864, Navarrete and Rodríguez prepared to launch their promised invasion of Santa Cruz. Military units from the eastern, central, and southern defensive lines converged upon the government outpost at Tihosuco. They waited there for the governor who would personally lead the invasion against the rebel capital recently rocked by the coups that killed Venancio Puc, Dionisio Zapata, and Leandro Santos, and brought Novelo, Poot, and Cen to power. Early in July Navarrete's army seized Kampolkolche, an abandoned ranch close to Santa Cruz from which government forces had repeatedly attacked the rebel capital more than a decade earlier. They got no further. Even as rebel Maya gathered to counter a thrust toward their capital, Navarrete discovered that his food stocks were rotten. Other critical supplies were just as bad. At least that was Navarrete's excuse for calling off the final push to Santa Cruz. He ordered his troops to retreat to the safety of Yucatan.

Manuel Rodríguez obeyed, but instead of leading his men back to the barracks he marched them off across northern Yucatan. Rumors flew that he had again raised rebellion against the government. He claimed he was merely rounding up deserters. The governor chastised him for having annoyed in transit so many landowners and for having thus deviated from the ideals of the revolution they had made together, "which was to provide guarantees to our working society and open for it a new era, if not of prosperity, at least of peace and order. . . ." Rodríguez was not punished for his excesses, but never again did he have the chance to bring war to Santa Cruz. He finally broke with his revolutionist colleague Navarrete and tried to organize armed resistance to the expected arrival of French and Austrian troops in Yucatan, coming to impose Maximilian's empire on the peninsula. But Rodríguez failed and had to lay low for a while to avoid arrest.[17]

Manuel Rodríguez married Josefa when she was only sixteen. They had at most five years together before she and their only child, Eulalia, were marched to captivity in Santa Cruz. From time to time, he received news of his wife: in 1864, that she still lived; sometime later, that she was the woman of a rebel Maya leader. Early on Rodríguez wanted to fight to free his wife. Later on he stopped trying, not least because she'd become the woman of another man, and one of the barbarians, at that. With wife and child five years gone, Manuel found himself another woman, nineteen-year-old Jacinta Gómez, and conceived another daughter, this one, too, christened Eulalia.[18]

The world would have forgotten Josefa Romero. She'd been gone thirteen years. After their first year in captivity, about forty-six of the Tunkas captives still lived. Shortly before the assassination of General Zapata in 1864, a list of captives who survived the bloody mania of Venancio Puc included only eleven of the women of Tunkas, along with twenty-five of their children.[19] It had been a long time since anyone had heard of Tunkas captives still alive around Santa Cruz, when Josefa's husband suddenly died and left a plump estate consisting of five haciendas, a large house in Merida, and five smaller houses in other towns of Yucatan.[20] The estate was clear of debt and valued at sixty-one thousand pesos. One claimant to it all lived there in Yucatan. For the time being, however, a court would consider only the daughter of Josefa and Manuel as legitimate heir.[21] The court wondered too whether some of the property in question had belonged in fact to Josefa, not Manuel. But no one knew for sure if Josefa and her daughter Eulalia were still alive. Somebody would have to find out. Noting that the very existence of these two women was "problematic," a judge appointed a representative for each while seeking information about their fate.

Josefa and her sister, Encarnación, were still alive, though Josefa's daughter Eulalia had died in captivity years before at the age of eleven.[22] Early in their captivity they'd been sent to the household of Dionisio Zapata, then the most renowned of rebel Maya generals.[23] After Zapata's assassination in 1864 they remained in that household serving his widow, for a while, at least.[24] Sometime during Josefa's years of captivity "one of the most prominent chiefs of Santa Cruz" took her to be his wife, and by him she bore a child. Public sensibility prohibited the press of Yucatan from ever naming Josefa's other, Indian "husband." Crescencio Poot took one of the Tunkas prisoners as his wife, but not Josefa. Poot's son married another, but not Josefa. No "prominent chief" of Santa Cruz showed more interest in Josefa's journey to British Honduras than did Bernardino Cen.[25]

Within a month the court received word. People who had recently fled captivity in Santa Cruz confirmed that Josefa lived, but added she was "enjoying some consideration among those Indians," an oblique reference to her concubinage to a high Maya officer. Delicate arrangements were made to get her out, and as her canoe approached Corozal, only one man knew she was coming. Henry Trumbach, a merchant and sugar planter around Corozal, had never met Josefa. But he was expecting her. When she came, he'd buy her freedom.[26]

Precious few people ever returned from captivity among the rebel Maya. Once distributed among the officers, they either labored for their masters the rest of their lives, were killed for insubordination, were given away to others, or, in some cases, were freed upon the master's death—not

to go home again, but to live on in rebel territory.[27] Precious few ever managed to escape back to Yucatan. To trek back through the forest took the
few who made it anywhere from two weeks to three months, and some
caught trying were killed. One's likelihood of escape dropped sharply with
each passing year in captivity, and lone women like Josefa were but a small
minority of those who ever tried.[28]

Some captives had family or friends who tried to ransom them, but
ransoming captives from the rebel Maya was a complex and dangerous affair, as the friends of Josefa would soon learn. A Maya officer could not
just ransom or release any of the captives assigned to him or his household. All the top Maya officers and God himself had to concur. Decades
after his liberation from captivity, José Maria Rosado described how it had
worked for him.

Rosado was eight years old when taken prisoner to Santa Cruz after
the fall of Bacalar back in 1858. Maya victors put his mother and all the
adults to death, and most of the children, too. Before killing the children,
though, Maya officers selected a few to keep. Rosado made the cut because
he could read. He joined the household of General Santos and served as
instructor to the general's children. About nine months into captivity
General Santos cautiously informed the boy that his father in Belize was
trying to ransom him. The general claimed at first to be shocked by the
proposition. If it came to light it would mean death for the boy and any
emissary the father sent. After several entreaties from the boy's father,
General Santos broached the subject privately with the head of the church
at Santa Cruz. The general's wife conferred with the wives of the other
Maya generals, trying to get them to intercede with their husbands on so
delicate and dangerous a topic. Finally everything was arranged—almost.
General Santos coached the boy concerning his final test. He told the boy
that he'd be taken into the church where God would question him. The
boy must respond saying he did *not* want to be ransomed. He must say he
lived happily in captivity and did not want to return to his father in Belize.

According to Rosado, the general coached him well. In the dark interior of the church of Santa Cruz, after a long sermon about the war
against the whites, the loud, whistling voice of God finally addressed the
boy.

"You young white face prisoner listen to me! Our beloved General
Don Leandro Santos in whose custody you are has pleaded for your

freedom, asking us to allow you to return to your father who is in the English territory of Belize. Now tell me with all truth: Do you wish to go? Or do you wish to remain?" My reply through the general who was holding my hand was as he had instructed me:"I wish to remain with you; I do not wish to go, as I am well treated by General Don Leandro Santos."Then the Cross said in a very loud angry voice:"You have not told the truth, I know the sentiments of your heart, that you are anxious to go to your father. You will be allowed to go to your father, but now you will be punished for telling a lie and trying to deceive me."

Rosado was lashed for his troubles, leaving his back blistered and raw. Back in the house of the general the whole family kneeled before an image of the Infant Jesus and prayed, thanking Him for having spared the life of the boy. Soon after, Rosado joined his father in English territory.[29]

Little wonder so few captives were ever ransomed. As for Josefa, she was no captive child. She was the concubine of one of the principal leaders of Santa Cruz. Her ransoming would be an even more delicate affair.

In Corozal the commander of Josefa's Indian escort met with Henry Trumbach to receive the money he was holding. Immediately a problem arose. Trumbach thought the two thousand dollars he held was for the ransom of Josefa. Comandante Vitorín thought it was just her inheritance. He had been ordered to bring Josefa to the English side, pick up her inheritance, and return with her and the money to the Maya side of the river. Vitorín carried a letter from Santa Cruz that seemed to confirm Trumbach. Santa Cruz had approved Josefa's ransom and freedom. But that was not what Comandante Vitorín had been told, and since he could not read the letter, he would not relinquish the woman.

Trumbach immediately sought help from the magistrate in Corozal, Edwin Adolphus. Would not Adolphus talk to the woman and find out what she wanted? Adolphus obliged. Josefa was being held in the house of a sister of the most prominent trader from there to Santa Cruz, a man well known and trusted by the Santa Cruz leaders, José Andrade. Adolphus went there with Trumbach and an interpreter of the Maya language, the only language Josefa then spoke.[30] The Indian guard presented Josefa, who seemed to Adolphus to be"in a state of abject terror." Adolphus asked the Indian guards to leave the room. Comandante Vitorín"demurred for some time, but at length retired looking much annoyed."

Free now to speak openly, Adolphus tried to fathom Josefa's wishes. "I then inquired of Doña Josefa if she were a prisoner—she replied that she had been so for many years at Santa Cruz. I thereupon asked her if she wished to stay on British Territory, or to return to Santa Cruz. The unhappy creature, who appeared almost afraid to speak, answered that she would like to remain, but could not, as her sister, who had been her fellow prisoner for so many years and to whom she was greatly attached, would surely be killed if she did, and therefore she was compelled to return to Santa Cruz."

Adolphus asked Josefa if she wanted Trumbach to raise money in the colony sufficient for her ransom. Captive so long to the will of others, however, she could not answer for herself. She said Andrade would answer any such question, presumably because in Corozal he spoke most directly for the rebel Maya leadership. Adolphus asked Josefa several times whether she wanted to stay in British territory. He finally gave up after receiving the same equivocal answer over and over again, concluding that Josefa was "evidently labouring under very great fear and is quite unable to express her own wishes."

Comandante Vitorín and his men planned to leave that very night for the Indian side of the border. They'd take their captive back with them. Later that day Trumbach tried again to get the magistrate to stop them. This time he bore what he claimed was Josefa's handkerchief, given as a sign that she wanted to stay. Adolphus could not act upon so vague a gesture, however. Josefa had to tell him directly.

The way Adolphus explained it, he later happened to be visiting someone in an apartment adjoining a store where the Indians who had brought Josefa were just then making purchases (a silly story Adolphus surely made up once he realized he had precipitated a crisis). All of a sudden Josefa slipped through the door. Her departure for captivity imminent, she now "earnestly implored me to rescue her from her keepers." Adolphus agreed, but dared not take her away just then. Josefa returned to her captors. Adolphus prepared to act.

Adolphus sent Trumbach to wait on board the *Alert* in Corozal harbor. Trumbach still had not given the Indian comandante the two thousand dollars for which he had come. That was all that delayed Vitorín's departure for Indian territory with Josefa in tow. Best then to keep Trumbach out of sight until Josefa was in English hands. Once they brought Josefa to him, Trumbach would depart with her immediately for the safety

of the sea and Belize City, hours away. Adolphus notified the commanding officer of the Second West Indies Regiment in Corozal to have troops
ready in case the Indians put up a fight. "The unfortunate lady was
brought here by but five Indians, [but] there are always many more about
the place." For good measure British troops at another frontier town, Orange Walk, armed themselves and awaited a call to action.

Then came a glitch in the plan. The owner of the *Alert* refused to
transport any freed captive. The magistrate could not force him, so Adolphus had to change the plan. Josefa would be seized and brought to the
local courthouse. There police and soldiers of the Second West Indies
Regiment would protect her until she could be spirited out of town.

Night had already fallen when four policemen abruptly grabbed Josefa
and took her to the courthouse. That part proved easy. Her puzzled guard
did not resist. An hour before midnight police removed her from the
courthouse, escorted her to the wharf, and delivered her to Trumbach.
Somehow he had come up with a dory in which they'd try to reach Belize
City, stormy weather notwithstanding. The two set immediately out to
sea, feeling their way through the dark to safe harbors and to the few years
of freedom Josefa's tubercular body and tormented mind had left.[31] She'd
never see her captive sister again.

Nothing else unusual happened that night in Corozal, but early the
following morning Comandante Vitorín appeared at the door to Adolphus's home. He "begged" for a letter attesting to the fact that he had not
willingly surrendered Josefa. The magistrate complied. The note to Crescencio Poot, Bernardino Cen, "and the other Commandants" explained
that Josefa Romero de Rodríguez became free as soon as she stepped onto
British soil. She requested to go to Belize City and was taken there. Henry
Trumbach left two thousand dollars with Adolphus for the ransom of
Josefa (which sum Comandante Vitorín said he was not authorized to accept), and the magistrate would gladly deliver the money to whomever the
leaders in Santa Cruz sent for it.

With the exculpatory letter in hand Comandante Vitorín could return to Bacalar. Before going he let Adolphus know that General Cen was
already there, awaiting the return of Josefa and the money. If the letter did-
n't satisfy Cen, the general might act immediately. After conveying that
news to the lieutenant governor in Belize City, Adolphus thoughtfully
added, "Cen, I think it right to observe, has the reputation of being the
most impetuous and unrelenting of all the Indian Chiefs."[32]

News that Cen was in Bacalar alarmed English authorities and sparked some second-guessing. In a letter that day to the colonial secretary in Belize City, the captain commanding men of the Second West Indies Regiment in Orange Walk regretted that when they seized Josefa they hadn't detained her Indian guards, too, so that they couldn't so speedily alert their colleagues on the other side of the border. After all, the Indians had come into British territory for an unlawful purpose—i.e., holding a woman prisoner and ransoming her. But the damage was done. The captain sent reinforcements to Corozal expecting Cen might attack, and he instructed his subordinate officer there to man the stockades and take other necessary precautions.

Back in Belize City there was hand-wringing, too. They could still return Josefa to the Indians. The attorney general advised the lieutenant governor that what Adolphus had done was perhaps not "strictly legal (technically speaking)." On the other hand, the magistrate had in effect protected Josefa from assault and battery "which in law every illegal imprisonment is." It was just as well, he reflected, that Adolphus had not tried to arrest the Indian guards. Josefa might have been injured in the fracas, and other Indians thereabouts might have tried to rescue the guards and recapture Josefa, exposing her again to injury. The most proper course would have been for municipal authorities in Corozal to have obtained a writ of habeas corpus from the court in Belize City, and to have served that writ on Comandante Vitorín. In any event, while it may not have been illegal for the Indians to hold Josefa captive in their own territory, it was clearly illegal for them to hold her prisoner on English territory, and since they were preparing to remove her again from English territory, there was no time to get a writ from Belize City. In sum, it seemed to the attorney general, "The occurrence is exceedingly awkward, as it may induce hostile action by the uncivilized Indians of Bacalar; and yet it would not, I think comport with the honor of the Crown to surrender the poor woman into their hands."

Troop reinforcements were ordered up to Corozal from Belize City. But the lieutenant governor countermanded that order. He gave no reason. He probably didn't want to commit the few troops available for defense of the colony to protect a single point of the exposed northern frontier.

The English breathed a bit easier on 2 January, when the trader Andrade returned from Bacalar where he had gone with Comandante Vitorín. It turned out Cen hadn't arrived there yet from Santa Cruz. So Vi-torín continued on to the rebel capital with Adolphus's letter in hand. The English would get a response in ten days or so. Unless, Andrade added, General Cen decided to act sooner with the two hundred troops then on garrison at Bacalar plus the two hundred who always accompanied him as his personal guard.

Reports from rebel territory soon confirmed that Cen opposed letting Josefa go. In fact her loss enraged him, but he blamed his own, not the English. Meanwhile he tried unsuccessfully to claim the money paid for Josefa, sending messengers to Adolphus. Adolphus had been around long enough to suspect that missives not signed by all the top leaders at Santa Cruz might be hoaxes or unauthorized, so he held on to the ransom.

Back in Santa Cruz General Cen vented his anger by slugging Cres-cencio Poot. To resolve the matter a meeting of all the important rebel of-ficers was called. When the Belizean trader Andrade, a major arms dealer and close confidant of General Poot, arrived in the rebel capital, he joined the heated meeting in progress. The enraged General Cen moved impul-sively to kill him. Cen's colleagues intervened and threatened that if he made another move toward Andrade, they would kill him on the spot. Joint leadership at Santa Cruz died with those words.[33]

The other chiefs agreed to accept Josefa's ransom and use it to buy more weapons and ammunition. In his struggle with Cen, Poot had the key backing of a new comandante, Alonso Chablé, who had been pro-moted after his superior, Alvino Aké, commander of the vital outpost at Bacalar, was murdered by his own men in late 1873.[34] Still, from now on Poot alone stood above the rest, and when he wrote to Adolphus for the ransom of Josefa, the letter bore only his name. Of Cen no more was heard for a while.

Back in Yucatan word arrived of the split between the generals Cen and Poot. Captives who had escaped from one of Cen's farms confirmed the news, which was received in Merida with joy and trepidation. With the rebel leadership so gravely divided, the end of the long struggle might finally be at hand. Two years earlier, after rebel Maya had extinguished so many settlements around Kaua and the state had again descended into political anarchy, the elite in Merida had campaigned in earnest to get the federal government to impose martial law in Yucatan and send troops and money sufficient to conquer Santa Cruz. A lengthy open letter to the president of Mexico, signed by dozens of the leading merchants and industrialists of Yucatan, declared it the sacred duty of the federal government to win once and for all this "savage war which damages humanity, offends civilization, humiliates the national dignity, complicates our relations with foreign powers, and which will later or sooner end the social and political existence of an important state of the Republic."

Ramón Aznar headed the long list of signatories. A few weeks later, Yucatecan deputies to the federal congress, Andrés Urcelay among them, requested that the Ministry of War report on what it would take to conquer the rebel Maya. The Ministry obliged, but Yucatan wouldn't like the answer. Yucatan would have ended that war long ago, the war minister concluded, had it not indulged itself time and again in political revolts, squandering in those struggles resources the federal government had provided for fighting Indians. Now it would be much harder to subdue the rebels. It would require at least six thousand troops operating in the field for at least a year. Mexico could not spare any federal troops for Yucatan, nor could the Mexican budget, then only adequate to meet normal administrative expenses, fund such a massive campaign. Now was simply not the time to go fighting rebel Indians on the Yucatan Peninsula, concluded the minister's report. Yucatan was on its own.[35]

So people naturally rejoiced in 1875 when it seemed that the rebel Maya might turn to fighting themselves, rather than Yucatan. Even as it conveyed the good news to its public, the official newspaper of Yucatan had also to warn its readers that the final moments of the war would surely be cruel, without quarter, terrible. Of the outcome none should harbor doubt. "Before the light, the shadows must disappear, even as before the civilizing impulses of the times, barbarity must die." The future looked so bright. Once those thousands of rebels, withdrawn from the authority of government, soldiers without cause or wage, returned to civilized life and lent their labor to industry and the arts, and once their uncultivated lands were crisscrossed with the furrows of the plow, then Yucatan would recover its former, famous power. Before that, however, "the last tremor of that sick lion will be terrible," the press again warned, "but the day is already approaching when it must happen, shaking even the very forests."[36]

The frontier held its breath. In March news flew. Rebel Indians had invaded the eastern line. They attacked one small settlement, Chacsikin, then divided up and headed off simultaneously to overrun the eastern

towns of Tizimin and Valladolid. Gunfire echoing in the countryside signaled their movement. When word reached Tizimin in the middle of one
night, townspeople and federal troops hurriedly manned strategic heights
and barricades along country roads. As dawn broke experienced Indian
fighters announced that the hour of greatest peril had arrived. Still, all remained oddly quiet. The defenders stayed anxiously at their posts all
through that day and the next night too. Only with the dawn could people discern the truth. Reports of Indian attacks were false. Anxious
denizens of the frontier, unnerved as well by an epidemic of smallpox, had
conjured up executioners.[37] Still, everyone knew that something had to
happen. Somewhere. Soon.

The tremor struck on 12 April. Not on the frontier, though, but in the
rebel Maya capital itself, where men loyal to Cen and those loyal to Poot
and Chablé slew each other in the streets. Cen's side got the worst of it,
and the intrepid general finally took to a trail and fled for his life with the
hundred or so men and boys who remained at his side.[38]

In the past Maya leaders who had to run headed south, trying to reach
sanctuary in English territory before their colleagues caught them. None
ever succeeded. After the battle in Santa Cruz hundreds of people flowed
out of rebel territory to the safety of British Honduras.[39] Cen was not
among them. He struck out in a different direction, not yet resigned to
abandon rebel territory or his leadership of the rebel Maya. He went east
toward the sea and the coastal village of Tulum, whose rise as an oracular
center Cen had once favored, and whose soldiers might yet protect and
support him from any men Poot sent in pursuit.[40]

Poot didn't send his army after Cen, for a while, at least. As Cen's
small group of followers shrank further from desertions, his situation
grew more perilous. Poot might yet attack. Or Cen's Tulum hosts might
weary of him and decide to do away with their controversial guest. After a
couple of months in Tulum, the fallen general left with the thirty-odd men
left him to test the hospitality of a Maya garrison still further from Santa
Cruz—the village of San Antonio Muyil, near the ancient Maya ruins of
Coba.

Almost hidden as it was in the forest far from Santa Cruz, San Antonio Muyil had remained independent until the early 1870s, when it was
brought into the fold. Its links still remained closer to Tulum than Santa
Cruz. Muyil's first major contribution to the war against Yucatan was its

1872 raid against Kantunilkin. In retaliation the force led by Nicolás Urcelay located and burned the place, but Muyil was rebuilt and garrisoned again.

Cen went to Muyil to bide his time—for what purpose, or for how long, he likely didn't know. When he arrived, the leader of Muyil, Juan de la Cruz Pat, was considering a suggestion to undertake another raid into the northeast. There was a rich sugar estate up there that would be easy pickings and yield rich plunder: Xuxub.

General Pat had, so far, resisted the temptation. Cen's arrival changed everything. He was game for attacking Xuxub. Cen boasted that he was accustomed to winning all his battles, and that he could take Xuxub with only thirty men from Muyil, in addition to the thirty he had brought with him. Cen forgot what most of his followers knew. He won battles because God willed it. He won because he bent himself to the will of God. But God had not sent him to attack Xuxub. Cen would go on his own, without God along to watch over the general and his loyal men. Cen chose Xuxub because of Josefa, because of the money, because he had nowhere else to go but into battle again. In any event, it was Cen, not God, who decreed Xuxub must die.

If Cen was going to Xuxub, General Pat could not refuse—not if he wanted to retain the respect of his own men, not if he wanted continue in command at Muyil. Pat relented. He and Cen, with thirty men each, would destroy Xuxub, take its workers captive, and carry off whatever was worth grabbing. Still, Pat may have thought that this raiding party, as General Poot had once said of his willful subordinates, just went out looking for death.[41]

Cen, Pat, and their combined forces departed San Antonio Muyil the last week of September. They traversed the forest in a direct line to the Caribbean coast, then followed the coastline northward to well-known Point Maroma. Somewhere between present-day Playa del Carmen and Puerto Morelos, they turned northwest, inland, through the Mulchí pass, and began crossing the immense savannas and forests of the northeast corner of the peninsula of Yucatan. The trek then became difficult. They crossed long stretches where fresh water was hard to find. They slogged for hours through the mud and water of the flooded landscape. Without men from that region showing the way, they might well have wandered for days or weeks on end without finding their target. Worse still, they might have stumbled upon Kantunilkin, whose peaceful Indians would have welcomed the chance to slaughter them. With the help of their guides, however, they avoided Kantunilkin and after three weeks on the march, reached the Río Turbio, very near Xuxub.[42]

It was the morning of 11 October. They could have attacked that day. Instead, they rested. They had come a long way, no one knew that they were there, no one would oppose them, so they believed. Xuxub could wait until the morrow.[43]

13 October

Reinforcements from Solferino arrived about four that morning, almost two days since the fisherman first spotted signs of trouble. Only twenty-five men came, two armed only with machetes. That was all the Urcelays would spare, though they sent for help as well from Kantunilkin. With the nineteen or so on station in Puntachen, forty-four men stood ready to liberate Xuxub. Still, it seemed to Montilla, they should wait, perhaps rest a while longer. It was eight-thirty when they finally set out in boats to ascend the Xuxub River. Short of their objective they disembarked and continued on foot toward the cane fields.

At ten the sun was high, but Cen had not yet stirred. Why should he? The great general had nowhere left to go. A single shot broke the morning quiet. Then another. Indians rushed into the big house, grabbed their firearms, loaded, and poured out again. More shots sounded; this time the Indians were firing on figures advancing through the fields. A bugle blared. The shrill music of impending battle penetrated the fog of Cen's slumber and struck a chord deep in him. He swung out of his hammock, grabbed his machete, and stumbled out of the house, into eternity.

Montilla later claimed the battle at Xuxub lasted an hour and a half, and that when the Indians ran out of ammunition they hurled themselves upon Montilla's force to fight hand-to-hand with machetes. A wild exaggeration. When the short fight was over, Cen and most of his men had been killed.

Montilla's party captured two. Two others escaped, one leaving a trail of blood along the path into the savanna. Montilla's force suffered only two men lightly wounded and the loss of brave Justice of the Peace Morales, tragically killed in the encounter.

Montilla's men freed Byrne, still tied up in the big house, but otherwise unharmed. From him they learned that many of the raiders, with prisoners and booty, had left Xuxub hours earlier. Montilla, however, had neither the inclination nor ammunition to chase after them. Instead, they quickly prepared to leave Xuxub for Puntachen. Some of Montilla's men took charge of the cattle and horses Cen's men had set aside and led them back to Puntachen. Others, upon Montilla's orders, loaded boats with casks of alcohol, sugar, and other things the Indians had not ruined. It was all to be delivered to Manuel Urcelay's house in Puntachen. As for the bodies of Robert Stephens and his slain colleagues, Montilla would have left them floating in the river. Byrne was so insistent, however, that finally they fished them out. Then it was time to go.

Seven

Unnatural Cruelty

C ONSUL LESPINASSE DIDN'T TALK WITH JOSEFA, though she lived, in seclusion, not very far from his office. He knew all he needed to about envy, greed, and official duplicity. Josefa could have taught him about the depths of cruelty to which men can descend, about how egos can soar beyond all restraint, and about men who commune with a bellicose God. Caught up in the furor of the moment, Lespinasse just blindly accused Indians about whom he'd never tried to learn much. He couldn't fathom their motives, except to call them savages. Within days he returned to more familiar terrain. Envious, powerful men were to blame for the destruction of Xuxub. The Indians were just their tool. Ramón Aznar kept that story going. The grieving wife would embrace it, too.

Mary learned the terrible news when she landed at Progreso. Aznar gave the distraught woman shelter, and Lespinasse met with her to console and advise. Maybe it was his suggestion, maybe Aznar's. In any event, Mary composed herself enough to write to President Grant in the "hope to Almighty God and in the name of the United States of America you will do something for me."

Mary explained to the distant president how her husband was hired to build the pier at Progreso. While working there he became friends with many people, including the Urcelays who asked him to install steam machinery for making sugar. He did a good job but they paid him only half of his promised fee. In any event, while out there, her husband visited the Xuxub estate, which was up for sale. He returned to Merida, convinced Ramón Aznar to buy it, and "from that time he improved and cultivated it more and more every year."

> There we lived comfortably and my dear husband worked very hard to make some money with which we might go home to the States and live happyly. All was very pleasant indeed, until last May one of the

brothers Urcelay was elected Governor of the district of Merida and, of course, that gave him an opportunity to show his jealousy towards my husband. It was then he began to disturb us in every way. Last August his brother sent a servant to our place to work for Mr. Stephens; Mr. Stephens thought this was very strange and therefore wrote to him telling him that he did not want his servant for he had his own. My husband found out he had been sent to burn down our place. But the poor servant had not the heart to do it and confessed it. Mr. Stephens wrote concerning it to Merida, but as one of the Urcelays was the Governor of the district, there was nothing done.

"I am here all alone," Mary Stephens paused to tell the president. "I write to you as a daughter would to a father and I hope that your kind heart will listen to me." She went on to tell all about Montilla's strange mission through the lands of Xuxub and about her husband's angry reaction. "Mr. Stephens thought they would not come back the same way, but in twelve days they returned. My husband asked him why he did not ask him his permission and told him he had done wrong in cutting a road through his land and that some day the Indians might come that way; that there were other roads outside his land by which he could have gone, but that he did it to molest him. Montilla ordered his men if Mr. Stephens spoke another word to fire at him and said he had never seen the color of an American's blood and hoped soon to see it."

The continuing tensions with the neighbors so upset Mrs. Stephens, she told the president, that she began taking ill and decided to return to New York to recuperate. Of course, by the time she returned, her husband was dead. The Indians came just as they had feared. They came because of Montilla's road. They seized Robert Stephens, and "they cut my dear husband down and stabbed him to the heart and threw him into the river and all who spoke in Mr. Stephens' favor they did the same to," Mary Stephens had learned from the trusted aide Byrne. Montilla and his men in Puntachen did nothing to help Mr. Stephens, even though they knew that hostile Indians had invaded Xuxub. Montilla and his men went there only after most of the Indians had gone. One of Montilla's men found Robert Stephens's account book, Mary claimed. Montilla seized it "and tore off the account my husband had against the Urcelay brothers so it could not be paid." She went on, "Everything we had was lost or stolen. This is the kind of Government there is here. Nothing but they were jealous of Mr.

Stephens because he knew his business better than they did and improved his place more and more every year. Mr. President, this is the truth and nothing but the truth and I can prove it all. Please Sir, do something for me and my poor child."[1]

Days later the *New York Herald* trumpeted Stephens's murder. A bold title crying "Wholesale Butcheries by the Indians" caught the attention of a public weaned on continuing reports of Indian troubles out west. Reading on, however, the public learned that Mexican authorities were to blame. "The insecurity to life and property in the State of Yucatan is frightful to witness," the New York public was informed, though the writer likely held vivid in mind conditions elsewhere in Mexico, not really the Yucatan:

> Large and well armed bands of enemies to the government of Lerdo de Tejada are marauding over the country and killing and destroying whomsoever and whatsoever comes in their way. The burnings, assassinations, and robberies committed by these enemies of the public peace are attributed to "the barbarous Indians"; but it is a well-known fact that the poor Indians, if left to themselves, have neither the power nor inclination to commit such gigantic crimes as those that are now about to be recorded. It is the political demagogues and partisan leaders of Yucatan, who have first excited the worst passions in the bosoms of the unhappy, uncivilized Indians, and then placed arms in their hands wherewith they might devastate the country and inundate it with blood.

Americans have no right to intervene in that sad state of affairs, the *Herald* advised, so long as "the inhabitants of the country limited themselves to cutting their own throats." However, "when the lives and property of American citizens are ruthlessly sacrificed to the fury of the rabble, then indeed it seems that the administration ought to take such active measures as would prevent the recurrence of such deplorable deeds as those here spoken of."

The New York daily went on to repeat what Montilla himself reported about the Indian attack on Xuxub, and it published the letter of "Englishman" Joseph Byrne to Mary Stephens—the letter Byrne sent not knowing that Mary had already embarked for Yucatan, and which "was received in this city by an orphan daughter of Stephens." The article closed with the last line of Byrne's letter—"there is no doubt but that the Mexican government will be made to pay dearly for its carelessness."[2]

Byrne had no doubt that Mexico should pay, but the State Department did. When the Stephens' eldest daughter, Catherine, received Byrne's sad letter about Xuxub, she appealed directly to the secretary of state, Hamilton Fish. "You may judge, Sir, of the consequence of so terrible a blow for us all his wife and children. Besides the loss of a good husband and father we remain now deprived of his support and in want of means to live on, lest our government would as ever be just and kind enough to claim from that of Mexico some indemnitation [sic] for us."[3]

Secretary Fish could send only condolences, not encouragement. You couldn't hold Mexico responsible unless authorities were complicit in the death of Robert Stephens—unless they'd killed Stephens themselves or ordered others to do so.[4] To his people in Mexico City, Fish added, "it is presumed those gentlemen [Aznar and Stephens] well weighed the possibility of attack from that direction before they embarked in the enterprise which has been so unfortunately defeated. It is not unlikely that persons of mark and influence in that quarter may have been envious of their previous prosperity, and would not grieve at their failure, but we must be slow to believe that any person in authority under the Mexican Government would by act or omission contribute to the success of the attack of the savages. This, to be credible, must be supported by proof."[5]

The White House relayed Mary's letter to the president over to the State Department. The response from the assistant secretary of state, John Cadwalader, again offered condolences but no encouragement. He echoed the belief expressed by Fish "That some of the Mexicans in that quarter to whom you refer may have borne malice towards Mr. Stephens and were envious of his superior skill and success is probable, not only from precedents in that country, but in others formerly under the dominion of Spain."[6] All the more unfortunate it was then, "that in casting his lot in that strange land, impelled as he no doubt was by a spirit of generous enterprise, Mr. Stephens may not have taken that peculiarity of the people there into due consideration, or perhaps other risks to which such an undertaking was inevitably exposed not the least of these was the danger of hostility from Savages." It was, however, a well-established principle of international law that governments need not insure foreigners against all risks, any more than they could insure their own citizens against all misfortune. Unless it could be demonstrated, as Mary Stephens alleged, that Mexican authorities had incited the attack, then nothing could be done.

Meanwhile the Mexican government aimed to have Consul

Lespinasse held accountable for the wild charges he'd been leveling against officials in Yucatan. Late in December a new Mexican minister to Washington, Vicente Mariscal, went to the State Department to discuss the Lespinasse affair. The governor of Yucatan had prepared a long, detailed bill of particulars against the brash consul, and he made no secret he wanted Lespinasse withdrawn. With an appropriate measure of coy discreteness Minister Mariscal broached the topic with the assistant secretary of state. His government would not publicly demand the withdrawal of the consul. It did not want trouble with the United States over the little affair. However, Lespinasse had repeatedly offended the governor of Yucatan and accused officials of involvement in the murder of Robert Stephens. They had to do something about that. Minister Mariscal suggested Washington might recall Lespinasse not because Mexico insisted, but because the consul had conducted himself in a manner of which the State Department disapproved. Assistant Secretary Cadwalader could not promise that. He did promise to conduct a thorough review of the matter, after which the Mexican minister and the secretary of state would meet to discuss it.[7]

U.S. officials told Lespinasse to get proof before accusing his Mexican hosts of being liars and criminals. Although he had already cried foul several times, if he came up with some proof soon, he might yet save his skin and make everyone see the plain truth.

Apart from Joseph Byrne, who'd already told his story several times, and the three Indians captured at Xuxub, who'd never be made available for questioning by Americans, only the surviving workers of Robert Stephens could give eyewitness testimony. Some of them would have seen the damage done by Montilla's men back in June. They would have been there when Montilla threatened Robert Stephens. Someone must have seen from which way the Indians invaded when they surprised Xuxub in October. The Indians came down Montilla's road, the road that Montilla had cut for just that very purpose. Loyal workers of the late Robert Stephens would surely swear to that.

Ramón Aznar had already asked the federal district court in Yucatan to take depositions from Xuxub laborers. The court declined. They could take such testimony only if it pertained to a trial, such as the trial of the three men captured at Xuxub. But that court was not trying those criminals. The court could not take testimony relevant to a claim against Mexico, except in the unusual circumstance that witnesses were very old or might disappear and testimony had to be recorded before they died or vanished. Aznar appealed the decision to the federal circuit court, arguing that, in fact, there was some urgency to taking testimony from his workers. His workers were then in Merida, but once they left Merida it might be hard to find them again. The circuit court rejected the appeal, wryly noting that these were, after all, Aznar's servants and he could be expected always to have access to them.[8]

Aznar didn't ask the state superior court. He didn't trust it. That court had before it the original allegations made by Stephens. It took the court months to act on the matter. When they finally received the report from the commission that had gone out to Xuxub, the superior court handily dismissed the complaints of the dead American as sheer fabrications. The Xuxub workers to whom commission members spoke (in the presence of Montilla's men) didn't corroborate Stephens's version of events. Two declared that when the Indians attacked, they came across the savanna, not down any road Montilla had supposedly opened. Everyone knew, the court observed, that Indians did not need roads to travel down. In sum, the court concluded, "all these data collected with due impartiality, far from proving the existence of the alleged offenses . . . on the contrary reveal that Mr. Stephens, lacking due respect towards the Consul of his nation, disfigured the facts in an alarming and exaggerated manner." Case closed.[9]

Early in December Consul Lespinasse learned that Andrés Urcelay had reseated himself as district chief, ceased all proceedings against the Xuxub prisoners, and referred the matter to the Supreme Court of Mexico. For Lespinasse, this was more evidence of the "wanton neglect displayed by the authorities" in the whole Xuxub affair.[10] If no judicial authority would take depositions from Aznar's workers, then Lespinasse himself would do it, even if it took him weeks, with Aznar bringing the witnesses in twos or threes into the Spartan consulate office.

Twenty-nine-year-old Aquilino Bautista went first. He'd labored at Xuxub two and a half years, and could solemnly swear:

> from the time of my arrival at the farm it has been increasing ever more in value and products. That I was an eye witness to the return of Comandante Montilla and the force that had gone at his orders for an incursion against the Indians [back in June]. That I was at work opening rows in the field at about eight-thirty or nine o'clock in the

morning on the twelfth of October when I was made prisoner and
then taken to the plaza of the farm and tied there where were Mr.
Stephens, Mr. Byrne, and the other workers of the farm. That I saw
when one of the Chiefs named Juan de la Cruz Pat took Mr.
Stephens towards the house. That said Chief gave the order that two
men go with him, ordering that they not take firearms, rather just
machetes. That on the morning of the thirteenth I left the farm with
all the other workers and families escorted by twenty-five or thirty of
the invaders. That when we were in a part of the bush called San Pastor, about two leagues from Xuxub, at about ten or eleven in the
morning, there arrived two of the invaders who had remained at the
farm, one after the other saying that a misfortune had occurred. That
I did not see nor knew of any troops that had been sent to protect
these places since the return of Montilla's incursion which I witnessed up until the twelfth of October when I was made prisoner.[11]

Bautista had more to say. Lespinasse did not ask or did not write it
down. When the Indians invaded, they came across the savanna, not down
Montilla's road.[12]

Another field hand, Ceferino Guevara, went next. Twenty-eight years
old, he'd worked at Xuxub almost two years.[13] Like Bautista he acknowledged that Xuxub had been increasing in value year after year, "especially
in the area of sugar cane." He said he "saw the path opened by Montilla and
his people at the end of May towards the enemy territory." He knew of, he
said:

the animosity that Don Manuel Urcelay, brother of the District
Chief Don Andrés and both owners of the farm Solferino, [had]
against Don Roberto L. Stephens. That I know of the two incursions
made by Montilla to the enemy territory, and that the force that accompanied him was composed of laborers of [Solferino] and peaceful Indians of Kantunil. That the path that was opened was not only
of no use, but on the contrary it exposed the farm to an invasion of
the barbarians. That I was made prisoner around nine o'clock on the
morning of the twelfth of October when with the other laborers of
the farm I was occupied in opening rows in fields in order to plant
more than two hundred mecates of cane. That like the others they
took me and tied me up in the plaza. That I saw them take Don

Roberto L. Stephens around two in the afternoon of that same day and I never knew anything more of him. That on the morning of the thirteenth I was taken with the other prisoners, but in the rearguard. That about two leagues from the farm the invaders received word from three fleeing men who arrived saying that they had been defeated. That from the time of the incursion made by Montilla at the end of May until the farm was lost on the twelfth of October I did not see nor had any word that any force had been assigned to protect the farm and neighboring settlements against the attacks of Indians.

Francisco Hernández went next, fortunate man that he was. After two days out on the trail, while being led into captivity, he managed to escape. Though unfamiliar with the territory, he wandered back and was found by peaceful Indians about a league from Kantunilkin. They turned him over to the Urcelays at Solferino. He spent a month or so there, before presenting himself to authorities in Tizimin, by his own account then eager to rejoin his master, Ramón Aznar.[14] Hernández told the American consul he was:

forty years old, married, from the city of Oaxaca in the state of Oaxaca. I had hardly arrived a week before at Xuxub along with the majordomo Baeza leading a replacement of horses for the service of the farm and I found myself planting two hundred mecates of cane with the rest of the workers on the morning of the twelfth of October of 1875 around nine in the morning when I was made prisoner and led to the plaza of the farm and my hands were tied. There was Mr. Supervisor, Mr. Roberto L. Stephens, Mr. J. Byrne, the majordomo Baeza, the sugar master Marvilla, the carpenter Najera, and the rest of the workers who had been made prisoners. Around two in the afternoon of that same day I saw Mr. R. L. Stephens taken away by a force of four men, among them the prisoner Cahum, the order, having heard the order that it was not necessary to take firearms, rather, machetes, which indicated they were going to kill him, as I learned later. On the morning of the thirteenth I was led along with all the prisoners except Mr. Byrne by part of the invading force and when we were still three leagues from the farm those who guarded us learned from two of those left behind, saying that their companions had been defeated, for which reason he saw thirteen of his companions killed. The invaders believed that they had been attacked by the peaceful Indians of Kantunil, since for their stay of twenty-six hours in the farm and the extreme confidence they displayed, drinking, dancing, lighting off fireworks, they did not appear to fear in the least anything from Puntachen where Montilla commands even though it is not more than five miles distant from the farm. Upon learning of the attack [upon their companions back at Xuxub] they complained they had been deceived with the promises that had been made to them, they seized Cosme Cob who appears to have been a former worker on the farm and who was the one who guided them there. A few days before the event the child Ramón Guerra, son of the carpenter Fernando Guerra, informed me that the Indians were coming, because they had gone to find them.

Lespinasse took one more deposition that day from a Xuxub laborer, Pascual Koyoc. Koyoc had little to add to what the others said. He had been ill in his hammock the morning of the invasion and did not see how the Indians had come before they made him prisoner, too.

In weeks to come Lespinasse took more depositions, but none more from Xuxub workers.[15] They had little helpful to say. None would say the Indians came down Montilla's road, and some had stories to tell that no friend of Robert Stephens wanted to hear. How could the carpenter's boy know that the Indians would soon arrive? The boy said "they" had gone to find the Indians. Who had gone to find them?

What if the Indians had not come down Montilla's road? Byrne after all was the only witness who made that claim. That part about Stephens having asked one of the Indians by which path they had come, and the Indian having answered, "by the new path that goes to the well," that was a bit of silliness that Byrne never repeated. Byrne only supposed the Indians came down Montilla's road. Had the Indians crossed the savanna and come into the fields where laborers were working, then "with a moral certainty" someone would have raised the alarm. But no one did. Was that because the laborers did not see the Indians coming? Or had they spied them, led by one of their own, and welcomed them as angels of their vengeance?

The workers didn't have to tell Lespinasse. The captive Indians had already declared that a fugitive worker from Xuxub led them to their target.

Cosme Cob fled from his obligation to toil for Robert Stephens. He had
set that brush fire that had served as pretext for Montilla's infamous forays. Cob wandered all the way to San Antonio Muyil, where for several
months he tried to convince General Pat to raid his former estate.

It was a hard sell for the fugitive. Xuxub was far away, and who had
ever heard of it? The last time they attacked up there, lured by a fugitive laborer, they hit Kantunilkin. That raid invited the devastating retaliatory
strike led by an Urcelay. Little wonder the new leader of Muyil balked at
returning to that frontier.

Then along came General Cen, eager for a fight and hungry for cash.
To keep his followers, recruit more men, and challenge Poot's lone rule
back at Santa Cruz, Cen needed guns, powder, and food. To get those, he
needed cash. Cosme Cob said to all who would listen that there was
plenty of money at Xuxub, and no one would or could stop them from
taking it.[16] That was all Cen needed to hear. And if the fabled general was
game, the general of little Muyil could hardly stay behind. When they finally set out for Xuxub, they left guided by Cosme Cob and one of the
Dzaptun workers who had showed invaders the way to Kantunilkin three
years earlier, Encarnación Cahum.[17]

Whether they escaped to a city and lost themselves, or ran to the forest Indians and took their chances there, fugitives like Cob and Chum fled
the debts that bound them to a master. A liberal Mexican Constitution
declared that no one could be forced to work for another. Labor codes on
the Yucatan Peninsula followed suit, but ingeniously added that someone
could be forced to work if it *was* in accordance with his will. If, that is, he
had agreed to be forced. As far as the law was concerned, virtually all of the
full- and part-time laborers on the estates of Yucatan had voluntarily entered into contracts, oral or written, to serve their masters, if necessary
under duress, because they'd taken money.[18] Once he'd taken money and
agreed to work, a laborer could not leave his employer's service with debt
outstanding and tasks incomplete. Indebted workers could not even
briefly venture off the hacienda or plantation without written permission
of the master.

In return for their loyalty in bondage, workers could expect to receive
modest pay or the right to farm some idle land, food rations, access to
water and firewood, and shelter and protection. Indebted laborers were
shielded from onerous, sometimes dangerous military service against rebel
Indians or manning frontier posts. In times of drought- or locust-induced

famines, such workers might fare better than their relatives in the ever-dwindling free villages of Yucatan. Whatever the advantages or disadvantages of putting oneself in debt on a hacienda, as time went on and estates expanded across the countryside of Yucatan, the landless found they had little other choice.

Some workers came cheap. For as little as 25 or 50 pesos, Ramón Aznar could bind in service part-time workers for his cattle hacienda Chablé. They were the so-called *luneros*, or "Monday men," who'd agreed to labor only a day or two each week for their master. Sugar estates like Xuxub or Solferino, however, required full-time laborers, bound by debt to toil every day for small pay and a ration of corn, and they didn't always come so cheap.[19] Manuel Urcelay paid 170 pesos to acquire Guadalupe Cardos (paying, that is, Cardos's debt to his previous employer). So it especially irked Urcelay when only a month later Cardos fled Solferino and, Urcelay later discovered, went to work for Robert Stephens at Xuxub.[20] Cardos was a bit pricey. Most men on those eastern estates owed much less than he, but it didn't really matter. A debt of 15 pesos could bind a man to servitude under one master or another as firmly as 150. Aged Estanislao Tzek knew that all too well. He worked on Andrés Urcelay's estate Papacal, north of Merida. When Urcelay bought the property, Tzek owed 17 pesos. So he had to stay on to work for Urcelay. He had no choice. Years later, Tzek still owed 17 pesos. Old, infirm, without the use of one arm, and hardly able to complete his chores, he still couldn't leave Urcelay's service, unless he came up with the 17 pesos.[21] When Vicente Yam, a laborer on Andrés Urcelay's Chumoxil estate, turned twenty-one, he longed to start working for himself, to support himself and his family, having labored two years already for Urcelay. Yam only owed 15 pesos—money that Urcelay gave him to get married. Yam hoped that since he had contracted with Urcelay as a minor, that contract no longer bound him in his maturity. A court figured differently. Imagine the chaos that would ensue all across Yucatan, a judge noted, if children could repudiate their contracts upon reaching adulthood. Yam must toil on for Urcelay.[22]

The indebted laborers of Xuxub would have had similar stories to tell, had anyone paused to listen. Nominally free, but bound by chains of debt, a laborer was subject not only to his master's will, but to his whip, also. Masters enjoyed the right to "correctionally punish" the minor faults of workers.[23] Those faults could include failure to complete assigned tasks on time, disruptive drunkenness, lack of respect shown the owner or others in charge, leaving the estate without permission, fighting, theft of small sums, and admitting guests from outside to his home without permission from superiors. Acceptable forms of corrective punishment included whipping in moderation (a half-dozen to a dozen blows), the kind of corporal punishment a father might use to correct his misbehaving son.[24] Only public officials could administer punishments more severe. That was the law, and that was the consensus among the elite of Yucatan.

But some estate owners lived beyond the pale. Everyone knew that. Even the green consul Lespinasse would have heard of Kancabchen, a hacienda near the capital on which the master-as-father had sadistically tortured his workers while mother justice looked idly on.

Hacienda Kancabchen lay within easy walking distance of Merida. Its owner, Manuel Solís, had bought the run-down cattle hacienda, stocked it with indebted laborers, driven them hard, and rapidly transformed it into a prosperous henequen plantation. There the thirty-six-year-old Solís lived with his mistress and young daughter, lording over his little realm not only as an ambitious or greedy master, but as a bold and violent man whom none in Yucatan dared cross.[25]

The horrors of Kancabchen should have come to light in October 1868, when Felipe Dzul escaped the plantation and complained to a Merida judge that Solís had given him two hundred lashes, hung him from a tree, and thrown him in a cell. All that, just for having asked for an account of his debt, as prescribed by law, so that he could go find another employer. And Dzul wasn't the only one so mistreated by Solís. According to Dzul none of the workers there received any pay from Solis, who forced even the children to labor for him. All they got was a ration of corn each day. The judge listened to Dzul's tale, let him recuperate in a city hospital for a few days, then returned him to his master. Solís welcomed the fugitive home with twenty more lashes, hung him from a tree again, and threw him in the cell. For good measure he confined Dzul's wife and one-year-old child in a walled pen behind the big house. While his family was imprisoned, Dzul would not flee again.

Dzul failed to free himself, but he managed to start something rolling that, months later, Solís could not easily stop. In early May most of the workers of Kancabchen assembled in the pre-dawn darkness and started walking to the capital. The sun was up when they arrived at the palace in Merida, and the governor immediately sent the tattered and gaunt petitioners to tell their stories to a criminal judge.

Thirty-year-old Saturnino Pinto talked first. He had been whipped and jailed three times. Once he spent five days in a cell without getting anything to eat, and another time his wife was whipped and jailed, too. Pinto had contracted to work for Solís as a supervisor for thirty loads of corn a year. Solís simply ignored the contract, however, and put him to work running the henequen rasping machine, having to strip the fiber from an exhausting four thousand henequen leaves a day in return for a meager corn ration, not enough to feed himself and his family. When Pinto and the others left Kancabchen for the city, Felipe Dzul and his wife were still in confinement. The woman had been in the pen for six months already. In all that time she and her husband could not communicate with one another. Another worker, Mauricio Chan, was also in jail, along with two old men.

Judge Juan Buendía suspended proceedings and went immediately with a city official out to Kancabchen. There he found the cell Pinto had described. He addressed several men milling outside of it. Yes, they said, they were prisoners. They were put out to work during the day. That evening they'd be locked up again. Going behind the big house, the judge found the pen Pinto described. Two women were within, one of them Dzul's wife. The outraged judge had seen and heard enough for the time being. He ordered all prisoners freed and issued a warrant for the arrest of Manuel Solís on charges of coercion and cruelty. When judges resumed taking testimony, police seized Solís and jailed him in Merida.

The workers told chilling stories of the monotony of cruelty at Kancabchen. All complained Solís didn't pay them for their work and that their corn rations were so meager that they and their families were slowly starving. They complained of unrelenting labor by day—6:00 a.m. to 6:00 p.m., seven days a week—followed by the obligation to guard and patrol the hacienda at night. Single men had to work all day every day and patrol all night every night. Married men fared slightly better—they only had to patrol three nights in a row before having the next six off. All, of course, for no pay. All children had to labor from 6:00 a.m. to 1:00 p.m. No pay, no food for them. Then each night the children had to assemble at the principal house and dance for Solís. If they did not dance well he would hit them. If they irked him, he would lock them up.

Workers complained most, however, about the whippings, the incessant flailing away at human flesh. Justo Cocom got one hundred lashes. Manuel Solís delivered the first few, then tired. His supervisor Pinto took

over, whipping others even as he himself had sometimes to bear such punishment. Solís joined in again for the final few blows. After that they hung
Cocom from a tree for three hours, before taking him down and jailing
him for two months. Cocom's wife got thirty blows with the lash. Her
children got the lash because they could not dance well enough to amuse
the master. Gerónimo Balché fell asleep on guard and got the lash for it
three times. Solís did not want anyone leaving his little kingdom. Ever.
When Francisco Mezquita sent his daughter to study in the city, Solís ordered him to bring her back. The father refused. For that he got the lash
and jail for five days, until he finally relented and called his daughter home
from freedom in the city. The boy of Felipe Chim fared better, if not the
father himself. He went off to work for someone else and escaped the per-
petual ire of his father's master. For that Felipe Chim earned fifty lashes
and hanging all day from a tree. On another occasion Chim got six lashes
since illness kept him from helping others to erect a dwelling that day.
Like all sick laborers, he was docked for treatment and fined as well. So
grew the debt that bound him to Solís. Ill José Canuto Cocom couldn't
finish his work—twelve lashes. Sick again, twenty-five blows, jail for a day,
and no corn ration.

María Antonia Pech dared criticize Solís's order that her niece's hair
be cut—six lashes. Estéban Gamboa never knew why he was whipped.
Manuel Cauich got drunk and got a hundred lashes, hanging for three
hours, and jail for a month. Cauich got drunk again and earned two hundred lashes, hanging, and jail for two months. That time all the workers
had to join in whipping him. One of Cauich's colleagues, Marcelino Kú,
did not strike him hard enough to suit Solís. Solís whipped Kú, giving
him twenty-five lashes. Juan Catzim would get twenty-five lashes from
time to time for failure to complete his daily assignments. Domingo Canché got fifty lashes once, fewer on other occasions, who knows why? Eduardo Carrillo argued with the wagon master. For that they whipped him
fifty times and bound him naked to the railing of a corral. He stood there
all day long in the hot sun and all night in the chill. The next morning they
threw him in jail for eight days. José Gil Castillo had been whipped several
times, once getting twenty-five lashes for poor workmanship, another
time only six and jail for a day because someone had escaped.

If someone escaped, those left behind must pay. If a male worker fled
the estate, Solís took the children from his wife, put them to work by day,
and confined them in the big house by night. When José Facundo Chim

went with another worker to pick up rope in Merida, the other worker
fled. For that Solís had Chim bound hand and foot and lashed a hundred
times. For good measure, Chim inherited the fugitive's debt and the cost
too of the rope they were supposed to get. If a prisoner escaped, the guard
would have to pay. Juan de Palma Cen got fifty lashes for having "let" a man
flee the cell. Then he had to go try and get the man back, following the
fugitive for twenty-eight days all the way to Puntachen. He never did find
the fellow, but he caught the fugitive's wife and children and brought them
back to Kancabchen. Soon thereafter the children managed to escape and
never were found again. For the flight of Felipe Dzul back in October, the
jailer got fifty lashes and was locked up for two days.

Because he was partially disabled, Juan Pablo Huxim did not have to
work as many days a week as most of the others (even the so-called *luneros*,
who had signed up for part-time labor, were coerced and threatened into
laboring for Solís seven days a week). But he was still subject to the lash,
on ten occasions, for not completing his work on time. Victoriano Cen got
twelve lashes once, then twelve more, just why he could not say. Eduardo
Carrillo, Casiano Gamboa, Anselmo Uicab, Domingo Canché, Luciana
Tek, Juan Caamal, all were whipped repeatedly. Poor Pedro Chalé got the
lash because, desperate with hunger, he left the hacienda to beg in the
streets of Merida. Inocente Cocom got the lash, too. He died, it was said,
from complications of his injuries. No one remembered or cared to tell
just what his guilt had been.

It took judges four days to record all the horrors of Kancabchen. The
outraged Judge Buendía who had jailed Solís had just been sitting in for
another. When that other judge returned he continued the inquiry, maybe
with less outrage than the first.

When called upon to respond, the still-jailed Solís denied it all, all the
lies told by his rebellious workers. He never gave workers at Kancabchen
more than six or a dozen lashes for their correction. Two people received
much more severe punishment, but that was for infractions of military
law. As an officer in the republican army besieging the imperialists in
Merida, Solís duly ordered that punishment. Kancabchen had no jail.
Judge Buendía had not actually seen anyone locked up, had he? Some
workers, like Dzul and Cauich, had to be kept under watch, of course, because they kept fleeing their obligations. As for Dzul's wife, she was confined in that pen only because she was addicted to alcohol and made such
a scandal whenever she got drunk. Solís denied forcing the children to

work and mistreating them at their nocturnal dances. It was his custom simply to invite the children to come pray and dance at his house, and out of the goodness of his heart he often gave them clothing. Yes, Solís had coerced Mezquita to retrieve a daughter from Merida. Why, if he hadn't insisted, all the other workers would send their children away, too. The guard service of which all had complained was greatly exaggerated. Only five men stood guard each night, and then only to protect the main house. As for the arsenal of military weapons and munitions found at Kancabchen, military officials had asked him to store those at his estate. Lies, lies, lies, all the accusations against his good name and honor.

The following month judges heard from witnesses for the defense. They were all men from the area who were friends of Solís, who frequently did business with him or who occasionally did skilled jobs on his estate (a machinist, a mason, a blacksmith), or who frequently had to pass through Kancabchen on the way to and from their own properties. Virtually all could swear that Solís treated his workers well, paid them on time and at a rate higher than customary for that region, gave workers any extra money they needed, allowed them all the time they needed to rest, and so on and so forth. Kancabchen was, were these witnesses to be believed, a workers' paradise in the countryside of Yucatan. When asked about "corrective punishments," however, the witnesses balked. Did Solís ever use cruelty or coercion to punish laborers or their families? One witness said he did not know. Another had not witnessed punishments so he could not say. Still another did not know. Eusebio Quijano did not know what Solís used to do, but he was sure Manuel didn't do that anymore. Three Alcocer brothers did not know. José Cámara didn't know. Misters Rosas, Mijangos, Méndez, Díaz, none of them could say.

In August, Solís's attorney, Juan Antonio Esquivel, one of the finest in the state (the same fellow who had delivered Felipe Dzul back to Solís after Dzul's flight to the judge in Merida), formally refuted the charges against his client, by that point out on bail. "The intense light of the truth has shown with all its splendor and it has completely tumbled the edifice," he said, of the case against his honorable client. He picked at this or that weak point in evidence, but his main argument was simply that Solís's accusers must be lying, for how could Solís single-handedly have tyrannized so many men without them striking him down?

With a concluding flourish, Solís, in words penned for him by the attorney, belittled the workers:

Coercion! I am charged with coercion! Yes, just one man has coerced more than forty! This fact would be appropriate to the times of fable, it would be the height of heroism and might! As long as we don't accept as true the fables attributed to the Twelve Peers of France, to the famous Amadís of Gaul, to Don Belianis of Greece, and to others whom the old books of chivalry tell us about, it lacks common sense to believe that I have been able to coerce and defeat more than forty men, gathered together and living in the same settlement where this took place. The immortal pen of Cervantes with prodigious success conjured from the fertile fields of verisimilitude the conquerors of monsters, the beheaders of giants, and those valiant men who by themselves defeated numerous armies, leaving us a testament of their nature in the creation of the famous Hidalgo de la Mancha. These kinds of stories are only heard near the cradle, where governesses entertain themselves in capturing the attention of children, wounding with frightening stories their weak and easily frightened imaginations. I dwell no more on this point, for to do so would be to offend the enlightenment and good judgment of this court.

A month later the judge delivered his verdict. It was true, he concluded, that all of those who accused Solís sought to leave Solís's service. Therefore they had an interest in having Solís convicted. They were not impartial witnesses—on the contrary, they quite clearly did not like Solís. Testimony from partial witnesses alone, from people who have animosity against a person, was not sufficient for a finding of guilt. The charge of cruelty, the judge found, had been ill chosen, since under the law cruelty was punishable only when exercised by a superior against someone under his authority. But the complainants were free workers, not the children of Solís. Felipe Dzul's wife obviously could have left her detention pen anytime she wanted to. As for the other charges of illegal imprisonment, those charges had not been made in a timely fashion.

Finally, the judge noted troubling inconsistencies in the testimony of Solís's accusers. Witnesses agreed that after his beating Felipe Dzul was suspended from a sapodilla tree, and Justo Cocom dangled from the custard apple. Felipe Chim was suspended from the orange tree, and Pedro Chalé from the breadnut. Manuel Cauich was strapped to the poplar the first time, but the second time, some said he was tied to the custard apple, others said it was a coconut. One witness thought Cocom hung from the orange, like Chim, not from the custard apple, like Cauich. Such inconsistencies, the judge said, made all the testimony suspect.

The judge acquitted Manuel Solís of all charges, and delivered the wretched men and women of Kancabchen back into his service. Adding insult to injury, a higher court upheld that verdict in January, reasoning that the testimony of the witnesses was actually too *consistent* to be credible.

Shortly after the dark secrets of Kancabchen spilled out, an article appeared in a Veracruz newspaper. It denounced the sad lot of Yucatan's agricultural laborers and likened them to the slaves of Cuba's sugar plantations. The article made the elite of Yucatan uneasy. They did not welcome scrutiny of their labor practices or of their age-old techniques for stimulating the Indian, indolent by nature, as everyone knew. It especially galled some that someone from Yucatan, living in central Mexico, one Mr. Sosa, son of a hacienda owner, had seconded the denunciation of slavery in Yucatan.

In response to the attack from afar, a distinguished writer undertook to refute, point by point, the charge that there was slavery in Yucatan, much less radical, Cuban-style slavery.[26] According to Apolinar Garcia y Garcia, Yucatan's agricultural laborers, or servants as they were called, enjoyed as Mexican citizens all their constitutional rights. None of them did any work for which they were not paid. In Yucatan any laborer who suffered mistreatment could complain to authorities, and justice would be done. None of that could be said of Cuban slaves. Unlike the Cuban slave, the laborer in Yucatan lived in his own house, far from that of his master, surrounded by his wife and children. He ate what he wanted, got drunk after hours if that pleased him, sang, danced, and laughed at the top of his lungs, entertained friends in his home, or took his family to fiestas on neighboring estates, all without encountering the least opposition from his master—as long, of course, as he finished his daily chores. In Yucatan a worker was master of his own family. If he wanted to, he could go to work for someone else, taking his family, his animals, and his property with him—so long, of course, as someone would assume his debt and he had completed all the work he had started. None of that could be said of Cuban slaves.

That critic of Yucatan's labor regime made much of the fact that masters publish advertisements in newspapers offering rewards for the return of fugitive laborers. What was so peculiar about that? asked Garcia y Garcia. Runaways abandoned contractual obligations that any honest man should fulfill. Besides, the very fact that laborers fled revealed they were free, for if they were not free, then how could they have fled?

According to Garcia y Garcia by treating their laborers well the hacienda owners of Yucatan simply served their own economic interests. Work to be done abounded. Labor was scarce. By keeping labor content, owners kept hands working on their estates and not on someone else's. As for the debt that bound laborers, many of whom were Maya, maybe people in central Mexico did not realize that the Indians of Yucatan liked debt. They preferred to be indebted rather than pay what they owed to their masters. Otherwise they could simply sell some of their many domestic animals to liquidate their debt. Yucatan was not Cuba, and its rural workers were not slaves.

Garcia y Garcia believed some of the nonsense that he wrote. That is what Yucatan's elite had been telling themselves for years. They kept telling themselves that on into the twentieth century, until the Mexican Revolution came and freed the slaves of Yucatan. But what about Kancabchen? Garcia y Garcia knew about Kancabchen. Everyone knew about Kancabchen. Men like Garcia y Garcia simply chose to ignore the injustice. They had higher principles to protect, like the sanctity of contracts, the right to maintain order with "corrective punishments," the right to get wealthy off the backs of Indians. They would not jeopardize such principles by punishing one of their own, Manuel Solís. They had the chance. They chose to look the other way.

The brave workers of Kancabchen did not give up. Francisco Mezquita, whom Solís had forced to fetch a daughter back from Merida, filed another complaint against his master. Again a judge ordered the arrest of Solís. He evaded capture for a while, and by the time they found him, he was ill, so the court let him remain free. Meanwhile a judge dismissed the case, since obviously Solís was no longer coercing Mezquita. Justo Cocom and others again accused Solís of mistreatment and nonpayment of wages, only to watch their complaint demoted from criminal to civil branches of the judiciary and then fade from view altogether. Once again, Justo Cocom and others sued to be allowed to leave the service of Manuel Solís, but a judge ruled against them and returned them to Kancabchen.

Eventually, the workers of Kancabchen lost all hope that the law would rescue them from the blind cruelty of their master. There were honest judges like Buendía who would listen to their complaints and arrest even so wealthy and prominent a man as Solís. But Manuel Solís had the money and lawyers to beat any case and then return to beating his workers. The debt of the workers of Kancabchen was so large as to make it unlikely any other landowner would redeem them, even if other landowners did not fear Solís, which they did.[27]

For the workers of Kancabchen, only death offered freedom from the tyranny and cruelty of Manuel Solís. They must either kill themselves or kill him.

Almost four years to the date of their mass exodus to see the governor of Yucatan, Justo and José Canuto Cocom and Juan Catzim freed themselves, their wives and children, and all the workers of Kancabchen. On a solitary stretch of a lonely road through the estate, as Solís turned his back on them for a moment, they brained him with the blunt ends of their axes. When he fell to the ground, one buried his axe in Solís's neck. Then they did something truly strange. They ran off eagerly to confess to the nearest authority that they had just murdered their master.[28]

Word flew to Merida that the Indians of Kancabchen had risen up in rebellion. Before troops were mobilized, however, authorities revised their characterization of the incident. What happened there was no assault upon public order, only a crime against one man, something for the criminal courts to handle, not the military.[29]

The workers of Kancabchen—three who struck the mortal blows and many others accused of conspiring—waited months in jail before their case came up. Political revolt in Yucatan again threw the machinery of state into turmoil. Not until March of the following year could the public prosecutor present the case against the men. He knew the case very well. He was Solís's former defense attorney.

The prosecutor pointed out that the accused workers of Kancabchen had confessed to an atrocious crime. There was no doubt about what they had done. There could be no excuse for it either. In deciding the fate of these men, the court must not dwell upon the alleged misbehavior of the deceased. Judges listened to all complaints workers had raised against their master and found them wanting. No court had ever convicted Manuel Solís of anything. No fault of Solís justified his murder. Such atrocious acts, the prosecutor warned, were becoming all too common in Yucatan. For once the offenders must receive severe punishment, lest others follow their example.

The accused had able and vigorous defenders who finally got their say in July of 1874. Representing the Cocom brothers and Juan Catzim, Attorney Ricardo Río told the judge that "because of harsh treatment and constant cruelty" his clients were "under force and against their natural instincts led to murder their master." In their ignorance they "had considered this act a just and natural defense, as the only means to free themselves from that tyrannical power." Courts heard their many complaints against Solís and found them wanting, because Solís had at his side one of the ablest attorneys in all of Yucatan, the same man who now as public prosecutor strove to convict these men and so justify his vigorous defense of their brutal master. As for the judge trying these men, had not he, when he was chief of the Merida District, more than once issued warrants for the capture and return of workers who managed briefly to escape from the hell of Kancabchen?

More eloquent and emphatic still was Attorney Perfecto Solís. His clients were the nine accused of conspiring with the killers, of knowing two hours in advance about the plan to murder Solís, yet doing nothing to stop it. Attorney Solís spoke in defense of all the accused when he noted that the crime occurred not under the dark of night, but in the full light of day (perhaps like that bright light that had once shown on the truth and found Solís innocent?). The killers presented themselves immediately to authorities and confessed what they had done. These unfortunates had been "reduced by the whip and the stick to that most sad of human conditions, slavery." Manuel Solís's account books plainly showed how little he paid his workers, how their debt grew and grew, until no other employer would take them and they could never in their lives redeem themselves. The workers of Kancabchen lived in miserable huts. They and their families went about almost naked, starved, and doubled over from excessive toil. When some managed to escape and present themselves before the governor, all saw how Solís deployed his agents, his friendships, his intrigues, and his money to force the return of those now labeled "criminals," just because for a moment they had "shrugged off the immense beam" that oppressed them. Even Solís's neighbors feared him—he had forced one to sell him his property, he stole land from another, he had invaded the property of still another, cutting roads wherever he wanted. All of his neighbors, men of rank and wealth, had to tolerate Solís with patience, since between letting oneself get robbed and killing to stop it, morality dictated the former. All political bands of Yucatan sought to have Solís on their side or tried mightily not to make of him an enemy. "All the landowners fear him; the public administration with all of its elements of force and power refuses to enter into conflict with him. What could his poor servants do?" the attorney asked.

Solís himself, the attorney argued, by his repeated acts of cruelty, brought about his own sad end. Judges had decided that the charge of cruelty against Solís was not justified. "Who in our society does not know," the attorney shouted with his pen, "how those servants were treated?" The unfortunate Manuel Solís "descended prematurely to the tomb," the attorney concluded, "and the Supreme Being, inexorable and just Judge, has already decided who were the victims and who was the executioner."

It was one of the most compelling murder cases Yucatan had ever seen, and maybe it was true that all Yucatan knew who were the victims and who, the executioner. The assassins of Manuel Solís freed themselves and their families from the unending tyranny of Kancabchen. Perhaps they easily accepted having to spend the next years of their lives in prison. In August of 1874 all the accused were judged guilty and given maximum penalties. The three who struck the blows received thirteen and a half years in prison, to be served in the fortress of San Juan de Ulua off the coast of Veracruz. Those accused of having been accomplices received over six years to be served in Merida.

Everyone knew how Manuel Solís treated his workers. Only Attorney Perfecto Solís speculated publicly on *why* he was so cruel. Money was the purpose of that madness. Henequen offspring had to be planted and henequen fields weeded. Someone had to cut the leaves and extract their valuable fibers. It was loathsome toil. The more of it Solís beat out of his workers, and the less he paid them, the richer he got.

Perhaps Attorney Solís was right about the cruelty of Manuel. Maybe there was nothing more to it than that. Certainly as the years passed, as the cultivation of henequen expanded, and as the wealth of the state's elite came to depend more and more upon that export staple, so too did the lot of Yucatan's laborers descend deeper and deeper into slavery. Laborers didn't have it so bad on Solís's other estates where cattle, rather than henequen, was king. Of the nineteen workers on Solís's Tanyá estate, four were not indebted to him at all, yet they worked on for him. Another owed less than two pesos. On average, laborers there owed half what their unfortunate counterparts at Kancabchen owed. Yet they labored on for the notorious Solís and never complained about him.[30]

Henequen plantations were different. Half the value of Solís's estate was standing henequen, not land, buildings, money on hand, or money owed him. To tend his 540 acres of henequen and keep his steam-powered rasping plant humming, he should have had seventy able-bodied men. He had only forty, including the aged and infirm. That's why he needed the children, too, as young as six or seven. That's why he gave out so much work to do and beat those who fell short.[31]

Most henequen planters had the same problem, and it just got worse once all of them purchased labor-saving machinery to rasp henequen fiber. To pay for the expensive equipment, they needed to run it at capacity. That meant harvesting more henequen leaves. That meant planting and weeding more acres, all by hand, just like before. They never had enough hands to do all of the work. Most planters didn't go to the extremes of a Manuel Solís and try to terrorize their workers into greater effort. They feared it would drive their workers to rebellion. They feared, perhaps, the law. Some may have feared for their immortal souls.[32]

Not Manuel Solís. He feared no man or god. Solís was so cruel because he could be. He could get away with it. Other members of Yucatan's elite feared him. The authorities feared him. He had been a leading figure in more than one revolt in Yucatan, and he had stockpiled weapons and munitions sufficient to start another. Few other landowners had such force or such a reputation at their disposal. Rightly could Solís boast to his workers that if they complained to authorities, he would kill them. He didn't care.

Privately people must have speculated on other reasons for the unnatural cruelty of Manuel Solís. They all knew how he treated his workers, and they all knew what had happened to his wife and daughter. Not the mistress and new daughter he kept at hacienda Kancabchen, but those he lost when Indians raided Tunkas in 1861. Manuel Rodríguez Solís—some called him Manuel Rodríguez, others (as he preferred) Manuel Solís—never freed his wife Josefa and daughter Eulalia from captivity in Santa Cruz. Eventually rumors circulated Josefa served another man, one of the principal leaders of the Indians of that place. For a man like Solís, such disgrace was indelible. It must have soothed him some to flail at the bare backs of men and women with names like Cocom, Cauich, Balché, Pech, Uicab, Dzul, Chalé, and, of course, Cen.

13 October

Bloodied but alive, two of Cen's men escaped from Xuxub and kept on running until they caught up with the party led by General Pat. Escorting Xuxub workers and their families loaded with booty, and unconcerned about being followed, Pat's group had made less than ten miles in the previous three hours. The runners babbled out that they had been defeated. General Cen was dead, most of the others, too. Men gathered around to grasp the startling news. They quickly concluded that it must have been the turncoats of Kantunilkin. From the whites at Puntachen, they seemed to believe, they had nothing to fear. It must have been the Indians of Kantunilkin who had attacked. The men of Santa Cruz had walked into a trap, and it was Cosme Cob who had led them there. Pat's men took hold of Cob. Of him no more was heard.

They had now to move quickly. Captives loaded with booty would slow them down, and Maya raiders were not accustomed to relinquishing live captives along the trail. Whether on order or in blind rage, Pat's men set upon their prisoners, hacking left and right with their machetes, trying to kill all of them, sparing no man, woman, or child, though in the confusion some managed to flee, wounded but alive. When the slaughter was over, thirty corpses lay partly submerged in the flooded savanna. General Pat too lay dead, shot in the chest, whether by accident or in mutiny none would ever know.[a]

Eight

Suitable Measures

IN HIS FIRST PUBLIC TELLING OF WHAT HAPPENED AT
Xuxub, Byrne described how the workers had assembled before
Stephens, then stepped up one by one, declared their grievances, and
hit him. The workers only did as they were told, and they only struck
Stephens lightly. You could see on their faces how it pained them. They all
loved Robert Stephens, Byrne claimed. Irritated by the workers' display of
affection for their master, one of the rebel chiefs struck Stephens hard, full
in the chest, knocking him over. Then General Pat, two of his soldiers, and
the two fugitive guides, Cosme Cob and Encarnación Cahum, led Robert
Stephens away.[1]

Byrne stopped telling that story. He realized some might conclude
that Stephens had a problem with his workers. Comandante Montilla had
suggested as much weeks earlier in the Merida press. According to Montilla, when Aznar and Stephens took over Xuxub from Palmero, they replaced a gentle and thoughtful regime with their own harsh despotism.
That's why the workers of Xuxub were demoralized, not because of anything that Montilla had done. It troubled Montilla to see the decrepit state
of worker housing at Xuxub. No wonder people fled Xuxub.[2]

Aznar was more careful than Byrne to avoid branding Stephens a despot. The public still had fresh in mind the notorious case of Manuel Rodríguez Solís. Byrne's only so-called proof that the Indians came down
Montilla's road was that no worker spied the invaders and raised the
alarm, as of course they would have, to defend themselves, their beloved
master, and their prosperous common enterprise. In his first report to
Aznar about what happened at Xuxub, Byrne mentioned that a Merida
judge had already interviewed him and that "those of my answers which
suited the purpose of these gentlemen were written down." In a second
version of the letter, changed at Aznar's wise direction, Byrne noted, "the
answers I made which suited their purpose (but not all) were taking [*sic*]
down. They seemed to lay more stress on the harsh treatment of his ser-

vants by Mr. Stephens than on the criminality of the savages."[3]

That was what today we would call "inoculating" the story. Anything more that came out about harsh treatment or "corrective punishments" they'd just dismiss as lies spread by hostile agents like Montilla and the Urcelays.

Not all the workers loved their master. Cosme Cob ran away. Why, none cared to ask. Fernando Guerra and five other Xuxub workers had revolted against Stephens earlier in the year and tried to kill him. At the time an editorialist sympathetic to Aznar and Stephens claimed a "special enemy" of the two inspired Guerra and his colleagues, and that the incident was just one of many such attempts against Stephens at Xuxub. No one asked in hindsight if Stephens was his own "special enemy," paving a road to the tomb as Manuel Solís had done.[4]

If Xuxub prospered as rapidly as Aznar said—the better to get a large settlement on the claim—just how did Stephens do it? Did he drive his workers too hard? Did he skimp on the corn rations? Cheat on their pay? Did he treat his workers like Cuban slaves (years of experience would have taught him how)?

Under Palmero's "gentle and thoughtful" regime Xuxub had not prospered. A guide for sugar planters published by the state government in 1872 stressed why such weak regimes must fail. The supervisor of a sugar estate should be affable, but he must be just and firm, too, and never submit "his dispositions to the opinion of any of his subordinates by consulting with them, because considering as a sign of ignorance any little deference, and thinking themselves superior in knowledge, they will be given chance to abuse, to do bad work, to refuse that blind obedience and submission which are essential for proper management." The handbook continued, "Goodwill or tolerance towards them [the workers], for fear of displeasing them, harms the owner much, for it is known that on establishments whose administrators or supervisors opt for tolerance, fearing discontent, production drops."[5]

For a sugar estate to prosper, a firm hand was required. Xuxub prospered under Robert Stephens. He did not motivate workers with kind, encouraging words. He could not even talk to most of them, since he didn't speak Maya. The lash did his talking, as it did on almost every other estate in Yucatan.

Was Stephens "excessive" with the lash, like the late Manuel Solís? Many who could have said had already perished at Xuxub. The survivors could have told some tales, but no one asked them before they went back to labor in Aznar's service. Only Stephens's friend and aide, Joseph Byrne, let slip that there may have been harsh treatment at Xuxub; that workers might have helped destroy their master.

The invaders had to have come down Montilla's road, Byrne insisted. Workers had gone that morning to open new rows in the cane fields. If the Indians came across the savanna, workers would have spotted them and shouted or run to warn others. They'd had a dress rehearsal of that just the previous May, when laborers panicked at the approach of armed Indians and ran to alert their master. (It turned out they were part of Montilla's group returning from the well.)

Byrne was wrong. The invaders did not fly unseen down Montilla's road. They strolled across the savanna and through the cane fields, and none who saw them raised the alarm.[6] The workers had been expecting them. The Guerra boy said so. That fateful morning while in the big house reading mail, Stephens and Byrne heard nothing, until the soft fall of a bare foot on tile floor stirred them to turn around. By then it was too late.

None of Stephens's workers was charged with conspiracy. None stood trial for his death. Only Cosme Cob was implicated directly in the killing of Stephens, but Cob vanished. That left Encarnación Cahum to bear the burden for them all. He had never labored for Stephens, but he was a fugitive worker who embodied the enduring menace from the forest and a danger lurking close by on any hacienda or plantation in Yucatan.

When Comandante Montilla liberated Xuxub on the morning of 13 October his men captured two of the invaders, José Chan and Perfecto Chimal. The next day an intoxicated Encarnación Cahum was brought into Puntachen. Who found him, where he was found, and how he got liquored up while wandering in the bush were never explained. Montilla's men just sent Chan, Chimal, and Cahum by boat to Merida to pay blood owed for the death of Robert Stephens.

Governor Ancona sealed the fate of the prisoners when he decided to apply the Law of Highwaymen and Kidnappers, crafted to suppress an epidemic of assaults by armed gangs on travelers and settlements elsewhere in Mexico. That law suspended key constitutional guarantees. The accused lost any rights to know who accused them, and of what. They lost the rights to make statements in their defense, to challenge testimony, and to have legal counsel.[7]

Under that law Comandante Montilla could legally have executed Chan and Chimal right after their capture *in flagrante* at Xuxub. They were lucky Montilla was a tool of the Urcelays. He could not kill his prisoners without the Urcelays' say-so. Besides, having living, dangerous barbarians and a notorious fugitive worker like Cahum to parade in Merida might help deflect attention from Montilla and his patrons. The only thing was, when Montilla decided not to execute his prisoners, they inadvertently recovered some rights. Since he'd not killed them in the field, they'd get a kind of trial after all and could have attorneys, too.[8]

Back in Merida the prisoners were interrogated and incarcerated in the city jail. Andrés Urcelay stepped down as chief of the Merida District since he had an apparent conflict of interest in the case—his brother's workers were among those who had captured the prisoners. The head of the Merida city council, Juan de Dios Espinosa, took over as acting district chief and prepared speedily to try the prisoners. He appointed defense attorneys for each of the accused. For Chimal he appointed Perfecto Solís, the same attorney who two years earlier had distinguished himself with a vigorous defense of the killers of Manuel Rodríguez Solís.

Under the draconian law they chose, the whole affair had to be concluded in at most fifteen days. Things got more complicated, however. First an acting judge of the district court wrested the case from the chief of the Merida District. When the regular judge returned, he sent the case back.[9] That was a bad break for the defendants. No state court in Yucatan could impose the death penalty. That had been outlawed years before by the state legislature. The chief of the Merida District, however, would act under a federal law that required, after brief inquiry (if any), that he promptly execute them. The jurisdictional dispute hinged on typical, torturous interpretations of precedent and, more clearly, on an interpretation of just what the Indians were doing when they attacked Xuxub. The federal constitution expressly abolished the death penalty for anything that might be called a political offense—even assaulting settlements, and robbing, injuring, or murdering their inhabitants, so long as it was done for political reasons. (A sensible provision crafted by revolutionaries turned lawmakers and lawmakers who might yet revolt.) The Law of Highwaymen and Kidnappers did not suspend that constitutional article. If the Indians who assaulted Xuxub acted for any reason that might be called political, then the prisoners were not subject to that harsh law. If they destroyed Xuxub for a cause, then the prisoners would live. The judge who first wrested this case from the district chief of Merida may have favored that tack. The attack on Xuxub was a political act, or an act of war, or an act of revolutionary violence, none of which could be punished by death under either state or federal law. The judge could even have viewed the case as consisting of simple acts of murder as defined by state law, acts that, again, he could not punish with death. Apparently the new judge, who sent the case back to the chief of the Merida District, rejected all of those options out of hand. The district chief would handle this matter as a crime under the Law of Highwaymen and Kidnappers, and for that crime, the accused must die.

Before the district chief could move the case along, new obstacles arose. Two of the three attorneys for the accused declined their appointments. As they explained in a leading city newspaper, once the district chief had relinquished the matter to the courts, he could not again accept jurisdiction without a finding by superior authority, the Federal Supreme Court. They must strictly observe such formalities, since a special law was being applied and the lives of the men hung in the balance.[10]

The acting district chief wanted to press on. He put an advertisement in the Merida newspapers inviting any lawyer to step forward and defend the accused.[11] Within a few days it became clear, however, that the Supreme Court had to resolve the dispute over jurisdiction. The acting district chief referred the matter to Mexico City and surrendered his chair back to Andrés Urcelay.[12] Meanwhile José Chan, Perfecto Chimal, and Encarnación Cahum waited in the city jail.

José Chan was twelve years old. His parents had been captives sent to work as slaves on the farm of Bernardino Cen. When Chan's parents died, Cen took the boy into his home. The boy continued serving Cen even as the general fled from Santa Cruz and wandered north to meet his fate. Armed only with a machete at Xuxub, Chan guarded female prisoners and the booty piled up for the day of departure. When the larger number of the invaders left Xuxub on the morning of 13 October, Chan remained behind. His master still slept in a hammock in the big house. Now the skinny boy, his forehead marred by an old wound, unable to speak Spanish, sat terrified in a cell in the capital of the people he had been taught were merciless, evil-doing enemies.[13]

At thirty-eight, Perfecto Chimal was no boy. Rebel Indians had captured Chimal in his youth and raised him around San Antonio Muyil. He assimilated, and by the time of the Xuxub raid they trusted him to fight like the rest, though the only weapon they gave him was a machete. Just what he had done at Xuxub he would never say, nor why he remained behind with General Cen rather than departing earlier with the bulk of the men he knew from San Antonio Muyil.

Then there was Encarnación Cahum, the only one of the three who could speak Spanish. The swarthy man with the light mustache was aged beyond his years. He looked forty, though he was only twenty-eight. Originally from the barrio of Santa Ana, of the city of Campeche, Cahum had somehow or other wound up working at Miguel Pifarré's sugar estate, Dzaptun. In 1871 he had fled Dzaptun with two other workers and made his way south into the territory of San Antonio Muyil. What he had done at Xuxub (and earlier, guiding raiders against Kantunilkin) was well known. None asked why he had stayed behind on the morning of the thirteenth and where he had spent the hours before his capture the next day.

The proceedings against Chan, Chimal, and Cahum remained suspended until the Supreme Court rendered a decision. Consul Lespinasse continued taking depositions to support the accusation of official complicity in the destruction of Xuxub. He even made the long trip out to Holbox Island to depose some residents who had vital information to offer, like the fisherman Gasca who'd warned of the invasion a day before it happened. All the while Lespinasse's own fate was being decided in Washington. The governor of Yucatan had lodged a lengthy, formal complaint against the consul, and a Mexico City newspaper had published the complaint and issued a statement of support for the governor, while calling upon the federal government to resolve this matter in favor of the dignity of the nation. Meanwhile the new Mexican minister in Washington waited for the State Department to review the matter and respond to Mexican concerns.[14]

Minister Mariscal of Mexico and U.S. Secretary of State Fish sat down to resolve the Lespinasse affair the first week of the new year. Mariscal again pointed out that the governor of Yucatan wanted Lespinasse decertified as consul, a step the Mexican government was reluctant to take. For his part, Fish referred to the youth and inexperience of Lespinasse, and he reminded Mariscal that Lespinasse was a personal protégé of famed Judge O'Conor of New York. That old man lay even then "between life and death" (though O'Conor had years of life still in him), and it would pain the old fellow to learn Lespinasse had been removed as consul. Mariscal understood perfectly, and the two gentlemen struck a compromise. The State Department would rebuke Lespinasse in terms calculated to "soothe the wounded feelings of the governor of Yucatan."[15]

The Lespinasse affair was the least of Mariscal's worries. Mexican President Lerdo had declared his intention to seek reelection in 1876. Over the previous four years he had certainly accumulated enemies, despite the liberal and progressive character of his regime. None of those enemies was more vicious, less consolable, than the press, which enjoyed unprecedented freedom under Lerdo and which wielded that freedom to bring him down. Lerdo was constantly lambasted as a despot and tyrant for having interfered in the rights and governance of states (anarchic states like Yucatan), and journalists faulted him for the slow pace of economic growth and development. They attributed it to Lerdo's indolence and corruption, ignoring the enormous obstacles to growth and Lerdo's reasons for caution toward American investment in Mexico. Above all else, of course, the politicians and the militarists whose cause the press advanced had simply waited long enough for their day in the sun of public office. In March, Porfirio Díaz declared himself in revolt. Díaz was a hero of the resistance to French intervention. He was a perennial revolutionist who lost to Lerdo in the 1872 election, revolted, was defeated, and accepted Lerdo's humiliating offer of amnesty. Now proclaiming the cause of no reelection, Díaz called for the overthrow of Sebastián Lerdo and the press joined in the chant. (In victory Díaz would cure the press of the ills of freedom and open doors wide to American investment.)

In his next several meetings with Fish, Minister Mariscal did not again raise the Lespinasse problem. Rather he advised Fish of the revolution brewing in Mexico. He wanted American authorities to monitor Díaz's movements and activities north of the border. He wanted the U.S. to disarm rebels operating from American territory. And, as the situation grew more disturbing, Mariscal sought to get the United States military to preserve the neutrality of their common border.[16] To all such requests Fish gave only lukewarm encouragement.

Fish instructed Minister Foster back in Mexico City to wrap up the Lespinasse affair.[17] Since Foster had last discussed Lespinasse with his Mexican counterpart, Foreign Minister Lafragua had died and been replaced by Juan de Dios Arias. Foster explained to the new minister how the previous November he had personally disavowed the conduct of Consul Lespinasse. Now Foster could inform the Mexican foreign minister that the government of the United States disapproved of the objectionable remarks the consul made to the governor, and it disapproved of Lespinasse's "disregard of customary observances and courtesy."[18] On behalf of his government Arias "accepted with pleasure the manifestation made through the honorable medium of Your Excellency." He assured Foster Mexico would not expel Lespinasse.[19]

That hardly soothed feelings back in Yucatan. Mexican Foreign Minister Arias wrote to the governor of that state, rather curtly telling him that the U.S. government had disapproved of the conduct of its consul, that the consul had erred due, surely, to his lack of experience and ignorance of Mexican law, and that the matter was thereby resolved to the satisfaction of federal government and the government of the state of Yucatan.[20] Governor Ancona had to swallow that. Lespinasse wouldn't let it go. After receiving his rebuke, he responded to the department in Washington. He had only done what he thought proper. He was convinced authorities had a hand in Stephens's death, and "unless a person is on the spot where this event has occurred he can but form a very restricted idea of the prejudice which exists against foreigners, and unless strongest measures are adopted the lives of American citizens and respect which is due to the flag of the U.S. will be set at defiance. . . . I respectfully beg leave to state that if I have extralimited my power in the discharge of any duty I can only say in defense of my conduct that I did so being persuaded that I was defending a just cause and seeking retribution for the murder of an American citizen whose murderers remain up to this moment unpunished in the prison at Merida."[21]

With his testy reply Lespinasse enclosed several affidavits—not the statements taken from Xuxub workers, but sworn testimony from residents of the islands of Holbox and Isla Mujeres who had seen and heard things that would implicate Commander Montilla in the destruction of Xuxub. Lespinasse's superiors remained unimpressed and lectured their young consul, "To entertain a charge that the savages in the vicinity of Mr. Stephens' plantation were incited to attack it and that a road was made by the authorities in order that this might more easily be done, would require it is conceived proof much stronger than that which has been offered." As consolation, however, it was noted, "your decision, energy and promptness on the occasion of Mr. Stephens' calamity, however, deserve commendation."[22]

In late January the Supreme Court ruled on who should try the three men captured at Xuxub. The judges had all too fresh in their minds the torturous case of the killers of John L. Stephens and the diplomatic tensions it caused. They voted unanimously that the chief of the Merida District could apply the Law of Highwaymen and Kidnappers against Chan, Chimal, and Cahum.[23]

Once that decision reached Yucatan, the prisoners should have had only days to live. That federal law empowered the local district chief to execute the accused "highwaymen" seized out at Xuxub after only a brief inquiry, or none at all. For reasons never explained, they enjoyed a temporary reprieve. The political authority appointed to dispatch the accused may simply have been distracted by inklings of revolution in the state. In January, disaffected and ambitious militarists and politicians in Oaxaca declared themselves in revolt against the presidency of Sebastián Lerdo, and they named Porfirio Díaz to lead their fledgling army. Early in February armed bands began to act in various parts of Yucatan against Governor Ancona and in support, they claimed, of Porfirio Díaz. One place where the gathering national revolt had echoes was in tiny Puntachen. Residents there took Comandante Montilla prisoner and loaded him in a boat. They were intercepted, however, on their way to join revolutionaries elsewhere in Yucatan, and Montilla was freed again. Though the revolution on the Yucatan Peninsula did not gather steam until later in the summer, in March, Díaz forces seized the northern Mexican border town of Matamoros, and, despite several battles in Oaxaca, the federal army could not stamp out the growing fire there.[24]

Sometime during the early months of 1876, Domingo Evia replaced Andrés Urcelay as chief of the Merida District. It would be a while before Evia could get around to disposing of the case that had at least mildly vexed his predecessor.[25]

Authorities may also not have wanted to destroy their prisoners until they could see just what Mary Stephens and Ramón Aznar would say in the claims they had been preparing to file against the government of Mexico. Those claims were each lengthy narratives (prepared by attorneys) of life's course from the time Mary Stephens married Robert Stephens (establishing her economic interest in his demise, thereby) or the time Ramón Aznar became a naturalized American citizen (establishing his right to seek U.S. intervention). Each claim described how Robert Stephens and Ramón Aznar entered into partnership, how Xuxub prospered under the management of Mary's husband ("ever a loyal citizen of said United States and in every respect faithful in his allegiance to its government"), and how the Urcelays looked on with growing envy until they resolved to destroy Xuxub. Both claims told how Andrés Urcelay got himself named chief of the capital district, had the Xuxub area transferred to that district, and appointed as comandante Baltazar Montilla, "a man of bad character, being a fugitive from justice, unscrupulous and unprincipled in every respect."[26]

With each telling of their stories of outrage and woe, they drifted ever further from what anyone knew had really happened. So in their claims, long in the drafting, one would read of how, at the behest of the Urcelays, Comandante Montilla led two raids against "a notoriously wild dangerous revengeful and warlike tribe of Indians, known as the Maya Indians." The purpose of the raids was to incite those Indians, and cause them to seek revenge against the perpetrators. By passing through the Xuxub plantation and by cutting a path through "the dense woods and impenetrable undergrowth peculiar to Yucatan," Montilla led those Indians to believe that the raids had been launched from Xuxub. For good measure, the story now went, the Urcelays secretly sent information to the Indians through Cosme Cob "of the great amount of plunder which said plantation would afford to them should they make a raid against the same." In Aznar's version of events, not only were the Indians told of the plunder awaiting them at Xuxub, but "the said Montilla as comandante aforesaid in still further execution of said designs and of said conspiracy did agree with and promised said Indians that neither he nor the forces under his command would molest them during their raid against and work of destruction, robbery and murder upon my said plantation."

Then of course came the sad events of 12 October. Reading Mary Stephens's claim, one learned how Comandante Montilla tarried in going to the relief of Xuxub:

> The said Indians remained upon said plantation, pillaging, murdering and committing excesses thereon as aforesaid for 24 hours, during all which time the said Montilla as comandante aforesaid . . . willfully, cruelly, maliciously neglected and refused to afford to my said husband or to his property or employees any protection or assistance whatever. And this the said Montilla did solely for the purpose of giving to said Indians ample opportunity to murder my said husband and his employees and to destroy the property upon said plantation. By this neglect and refusal to send assistance and rescue the

said plantation as aforesaid, the said Montilla, as comandante aforesaid, simply executed the plot which the said Andrés Urcelay as Jefe
Politico aforesaid, by reason of his jealousy aforesaid, planned against
my said husband and his property, having been paid in money therefore by said Urcelay.

Both claims faulted Montilla for not pursuing the Indians who had already departed Xuxub, taking prisoners and booty with them, even
though, as Aznar's claim pointed out, those Indians were then only seven
miles away. Mary Stephens's claim stressed the callousness of Montilla
who, "though earnestly requested so to do, cruelly refused to allow his men
to take from the water where it had been thrown by said Indians the dead
body of my said husband until he was promised to be paid in money
therefor." Aznar dwelt on the further property losses occasioned by Montilla's own looting: "Yet the said Montilla as comandante aforesaid, though
earnestly requested so to do, refused to pursue said Indians or to make any
attempt whatever to recover the property they had taken as aforesaid from
my said plantation or rescue said prisoners from their hands, but instead
thereof commenced to steal and carry away all the effects belonging to my
said plantation as had escaped destruction or conversion at the hands of
said Indians." In sum, Mary Stephens's claim related that she was left "entirely destitute and with no one in the world to whom I may look for even
the bare necessities of life, nor have I any means whatever to educate my
said daughter Evangeline now aged seven years or to cloth and keep her
until she shall have attained her majority. . . . I find myself pressed with
wants and can see no prospect for relief. I have suffered and am still suffering the keenest anguish of spirit from this most cruel deprivation of my
husband."

By means of this claim she sought her government's help in getting
Mexico to pay thirty thousand dollars in damages. As for Aznar, he figured that he lost not only five thousand dollars in property destroyed outright, but the entire value of the Xuxub plantation, as "by reason of the
said Indian depredations so as aforesaid occasioned and the great and universal terror it inspires it is now impossible to procure employees to cultivate my said plantation and the same is on that account useless and
valueless." Aznar expected Mexico to pay eighty thousand dollars.

Whether they realized it or not, Mary Stephens and Ramón Aznar
appealed for redress under international law. It was an accepted premise of

international law that aggrieved persons like Stephens and Aznar should first exhaust local remedies before appealing for diplomatic intervention. Mexican citizens with serious complaints against their authorities could take those complaints to criminal or civil court, and courts did sometimes punish abusive or negligent officials. Though aliens in Mexico, Mary Stephens and Ramón Aznar enjoyed equal access to Mexican courts under international law and bilateral treaties. They had, for sure, tried local remedies, to little avail. The state government had declined to provide extra protection to Xuxub though warned that danger was imminent. The state court had declined to punish Montilla after conducting only a superficial, and certainly tardy, investigation of the complaints against him. The chief of the Merida District still had not tried or punished the three members of the raiding party whom they had captured. Whether all of that could be deemed "denial of justice," none could predict what an international tribunal would say.

Mary Stephens surely did not know, or likely Aznar either, that as individuals they were not proper subjects of international law. Nations were. International law concerned only the rights and responsibilities of nations toward one another, not relations between states and individuals. For the troubles of Mary Stephens and Ramón Aznar to become subjects of international law, the harm they suffered must first be construed as harm done to the nation of which they were citizens.[27] The wealth of American citizens was destroyed at Xuxub, and that constituted a loss to the wealth of the United States. An American lost his life at Xuxub, and that constituted at least an embarrassment to the government of the United States, whose only reason for being was to protect the lives and properties of its citizens. The United States and Mexico signed agreements concerning, among other things, how the nationals of one would be treated in the other. When terms in such treaties were violated, a state might consider itself aggrieved and offended. Were these harms done but nicks on the pride of the United States, minor offenses over which friendly neighbors should not quarrel? Or did they rise to the level of an "outrage," an offense so severe that it had to be repaired? Only in the latter case should representatives of that nation consider seeking indemnity from the offending state, Mexico.

In the past the seriousness with which American officials viewed the misfortunes of its citizens in Mexico depended upon whether they wanted something more from Mexico and whether outrage would help them get it. The murder of Americans could simply be the unfortunate, inevitable outcome of a certain amount of lawlessness in the neighboring republic, something Americans should consider before choosing to reside there. Throw in some lust for Mexican land, minerals, or whatever (Mexico had no money in its treasury, so they would have to give up something else in reparation), and such misfortunes loomed larger, became intolerable, evolved into grave offenses against the dignity of the United States, the rights of man, the very foundations of civilization.[28]

Timing is everything. Almost. When the claims of Mary Stephens and Ramón Aznar arrived, the American appetite for bits of Mexico had long ago been sated. The highest-ranking American diplomat in Mexico, John Foster, was inclined to consider the events of Xuxub as a regrettable but minor affair. Foster had wearied of American claims. He'd won little pressing them, and he had much else he wanted to accomplish during his tenure in Mexico City.

But the detailed, at times even exaggerated, stories of the Xuxub conspiracy contained in the formal claims of Mary Stephens and Ramón Aznar caught the attention of Secretary of State Fish in Washington. Mary's persistent, emotional pleading likely influenced him, too. The secretary had a heart. "Oh Dear their is nothing on earth More Plaine More Truer than that they cut a road throu our land to the well of the Indians to Molest them so that they Might come to Murder us," Mary wrote this time in her own words from Yucatan:

> Oh My God this day if you all knew how I am heir to day with My sick child you would all enterceed and Make them pay Me Some thing for the death of My Dear husband. Their we lived happy for fore years and in that time why did not the Indians come. Oh no the road was not Made for them before those two bad Men employed by the government was the cause of it all. One of them was Mr. urcelayes effe politica [jefe político, district chief] the other is Mr. Montilla as Military commandant and indeed I must say that they ar two the worst men in all yucatan. Oh My Dear Sir what I say heir and in all My steatments it is as true as their is a God in heaven. Oh it wont bring back My Poor husband to Me but the truth Must be. Mr. Montilla was heir in Prison and in the Chaingan for Murder and robing. That every one knows heir in Merida and they all say that it is to bad to have sich men to govern Poor hard working honest men in their own

Places. My husband met Mr. Montilla and his men when they returned from the well and he asked him where he was and why he went throu his land without his Permishon and he told him he don verry rong Indeed to molest the Indians and he told him that they was quietet in their Place and now they May come and Murder Me and My family. Mr. Montilla answer My husband verry cross Indeed and said it was government orders and he would do what he liked and he said he never saw American blood and I hope I soon would. Oh My Dear sir, that Made My husband verry angry Indeed and I saw it, and Mr. Byrns and I Persuaded him to the house for I was afraid of Montilla My self. My husband sat down and wrote to Merida to the governor and to the American Consul telling them that they must see about it and for them to write to Mexico. That was the third letter we wrote to them. Oh My Dear sir My husband did not want to leve his Place or his fore years hard labor for he had envested all his Money to inprove it More and More every year. I wish that you could see the Splinded field of Sugar cane and corn. Oh it is a sin Indeed to see it going to loss. I can not get now one to grind it for Me. They ar all afraid of thoes Men. Oh May Amighty God this day loock down upon Me. I have no husband now or Father Mother Brother or Sister no one in this world but two daughters and they cannot do any thing for Me. But I will hope and trust to God and to you Dear Sir Please pleed for Me. . . . But oh I can not see to write it all from the tears in My eyes, and I hope that you will excuse the writing and Mistakes.[29]

In a long dispatch to John Foster in Mexico City, Fish summarized the story of Xuxub. Comandante Montilla raided the camp of the "warlike, dangerous and revengeful tribe of Indians known as the Maya Indians," which was only seven miles from Xuxub. Montilla cut a path through the "dense forest or chaparral that served as a protection to the estate from the incursions of marauding Indians." His troops committed "great excesses and exasperated the Indians that when the attack was over, and the savages were found in this angry and revengeful mood, Urcelay and Montilla incited them to an attack on Mr. Aznar's plantation, telling them that Aznar was their enemy, that he [Aznar] had induced the authorities thus to make the raid on them, and the same time assuring the Indians that in any attacks they might make on Aznar's property and employees, they would not be molested by Montilla or his troops, and pointing out to them the new path through the chaparral, by which they could with greater facility reach the plantation."[30]

Fish considered the claims "supported in all the material facts by the depositions of seven of the surviving employees [or so that's who he thought they were] who were witnesses of the outrages, and also by the testimony of Mrs. Mary Ann Stephens." In Fish's opinion if those facts bore up under further scrutiny, then what happened out at Xuxub was "a very gross outrage upon the rights and immunities" of Americans residing peaceably abroad. Mexico would have violated its treaty obligations with the United States, which required that each nation provide citizens of the other equal protection under the law. In that case, the government of Mexico would be "justly accountable to that of the United States for the outrages and wrongs thus inflicted on two of its citizens." Foster was instructed to bring the claims to the attention of the government of Mexico, and to also see "That suitable measures may be adopted to bring the perpetrators and instigators of those outrages to justice."[31]

Whether the United States considered itself "outraged" was for Fish to decide, and he had. But outrage can pass, and Fish signaled that blood would go far towards settling the score: the last part of his letter meant, at least kill the prisoners taken at Xuxub.[32]

It was just coincidence. The same day that Secretary Fish wrote with some evident outrage to Foster in Mexico City, the new chief of the Merida District finally disposed of the matter of Chan, Chimal, and Cahum. Two days earlier Domingo Evia had reviewed case documents and invited attorneys to present their defense.

None could dispute what the accused did. Two were caught at Xuxub. They admitted that they took part in the invasion. Cahum was captured the next day, but he had confessed as well and was implicated by witnesses. Robert Stephens was not Manuel Rodríguez Solís. The accused had not been his workers. He had not abused them. Attorneys could not argue that the prisoners had been driven to commit this crime.

The only hope for the accused was that their attorneys could spare them from application of the Law of Highwaymen and Kidnappers. The defense argued that the law could not be applied because authorities had taken too long to apply it. According to article three of the congressional decree that created that law: "Highwaymen and kidnappers caught *in flagrante* shall receive capital punishment, with no more requirement that the drafting of an act by the commander of the force that captured them. . . . Those who were not caught *in flagrante* will be tried summarily and verbally by officials whose agents made the capture. . . . A decision shall be reached no later than the period, absolute and unextendable, of fifteen days."

That deadline had passed months ago, so that the law no longer applied, and the district chief had lost jurisdiction in the matter, attorneys argued. The case should revert to the courts of Yucatan. Attorneys for the defense also argued that the law in question mandated capital punishment, but the legislature of Yucatan had outlawed capital punishment. Therefore the law could not be enforced in Yucatan.

District Chief Evia did not budge. A band of men invaded Xuxub for the purpose of robbing, killing, and taking captives. The three accused belonged to that band. They were captured there and confessed. They had violated the Law of Highwaymen and Kidnappers. The long delay should not spare the accused. After all, defense attorneys had raised questions about jurisdiction and caused the whole matter to be sent to the Supreme Court, thus causing the long delay, Evia argued not quite accurately. Besides, he reasoned, the longer the delay, the better for the defense, who had more time to prepare. Evia also brushed aside the challenge to the death penalty, the only penalty provided for by that law. The Law of Highwaymen and Kidnappers was, after all, a federal law, and all citizens of Mexico were subject to federal law.[33]

Evia promptly declared José Chan, Perfecto Chimal, and Encarnación Cahum guilty and condemned them to be executed within twenty-four hours. First, however, as provided for by law, the condemned men could seek a pardon or commutation of their death sentences from the governor of Yucatan, the same who had called upon the accused to be punished with all the "cruelty and rigor that they deserve."[34]

The condemned men had no friends in Yucatan, no family, no political allies, nobody who identified with their cause. No one would bribe or cajole authorities into sparing them from execution. The lot of the condemned men was hopeless.

Or almost so. Some in Yucatan did step forward on their behalf in the name of a higher principle. The day Chan, Chimal, and Cahum were sentenced to death, forty-two Yucatecans petitioned the governor to spare the lives of the three. "We who wish for the well-being and happiness of our fellows," their petition went:

we who believe in the injustice of the death penalty, because we are persuaded there can never be reason sufficient to violate natural law, we find ourselves impelled to appeal to you demanding clemency in favor of the prisoners sentenced to the ultimate punishment as kidnappers and armed assailants in rancho Xuxub. We will not enter into the details of the process, which has been conducted with much justice and reason by the defense attorneys. . . . We only want to remind you of the inhumanity of the act, plainly opposed to the civilizing current of the times in which fraternity should be the olive branch of peace for peoples. And if you want to punish the crime, the enormity of it never gives one the right to destroy the existence of a rational being, only his creator may do that. What lesson will follow from the death of the prisoners? Will some benefit be had from the terrible execution of the sentence? Never! Blood that is shed calls for more blood to cleanse it, and the continuation of such terrible events plunges society into a bottomless abyss.[35]

The following day defense attorneys sought mercy from the governor's council, whose recommendation concerning sentencing the governor would follow. Rogenio Aguilar Andrade pleaded for the boy José Chan. Attorney Aguilar had tried to convince the district chief to spare Chan's life. Chan was a minor and wasn't responsible for his actions at Xuxub. Evia wouldn't listen. He said the law allowed no exceptions and condemned the boy to death. In a dig back at Evia, Aguilar suggested to the governor's council that the law must always be subject to logical interpretation for its proper application. To suppose otherwise was to suggest judges lack intelligence.

Besides, Aguilar pointed out, Chan was the child of slaves of Bernardino Cen. When Chan's parents died, he fell under the complete power of that man. General Cen obliged the boy to accompany him to Xuxub, expecting him to carry booty. "What sort of malice could Chan conceivably have?" asked Aguilar. "For there to be a crime, say the most wise, there must be a free, voluntary, malicious infraction of a law." Chan had no free will and no malice against the law. Therefore he could not have committed any crime. In punishing Chan, intoned Aguilar, they punished not the crime, but only innocence and the lack of free will. To do that was repugnant to the principles of equity and justice.[36]

Attorney Aguilar succeeded. Partly. He believed Chan had committed no crime at all. The governor's council recommended only that Chan be spared the death penalty. Instead they sentenced the boy to six years confinement in General Hospital of the City of Merida.

The attorney for Perfecto Chimal took a similar tack. First, Chimal had been captured as a youth by the rebel Indians and raised among them. Secondly, at Xuxub he was only a second-class soldier, armed with a machete, and did not actually hurt anyone. Thirdly, the law that condemned him did not allow for a normal judicial process in which the truth could be discovered. It was instead "a blind sword that wounded without purpose and without mercy." As soon as the Supreme Court decided that the district chief should try this case, Chimal's fate was sealed. Chimal would die not for what he had done, but only because they applied that vile law.[37]

The governor's council itself came up with a better reason—or a more palatable reason—for sparing the life of Perfecto Chimal. Because Chimal had been captured as a youth and raised among the savages since then, he had naturally acquired their habits and customs. He was deprived of the benefits of civilization. That made him less responsible for what happened at Xuxub than . . . well, the council would shortly pronounce upon the fate of Encarnación Cahum. As for Chimal, they commuted his sentence to twelve years in the fortress prison of San Juan de Ulua off the coast of Veracruz.

That left only Encarnación Cahum to satisfy the Americans and vindicate Mexico. To save Cahum's life his attorney could only feebly invoke for the governor the "sacrosanct memory of your beloved and venerable parents to whom you always showed the most tender affection and reverence."[38] Would the governor be moved to clemency by mention of his own dead parents? Fat chance. The governor's council rejected any clemency for Cahum. He had once lived in the midst of a civilized people, the council declared, and yet voluntarily he left to reside among the barbarians. He was a repeat criminal, having not only participated in the sacking of Xuxub but the invasion of Kantunilkin three years earlier. At Xuxub he helped guard Robert Stephens and accompanied the small group that executed him. For all of that, Cahum must die.

On the morning of 31 May Cahum learned that he would be executed at five that afternoon. Cahum's attorney made one more plea for the life of his client. At ten that morning, before the Superior Court of Yucatan, Cahum's attorney got right to the point. The crimes of which Cahum stood accused were ordinary crimes punishable by state law. The federal constitution prohibited federal government involvement in such cases. Therefore the application of the federal law was unconstitutional (not only in Cahum's case, but in all cases). Cahum's lawyer requested an urgent, temporary stay of the imminent execution.[39]

Within hours the court issued its decision. Cahum's attorney was right, they judged. Under the federal constitution clearly only states could legislate laws against such crimes as assault and kidnapping. The Law of Highwaymen and Kidnappers was plainly unconstitutional. Unfortunately only federal courts could resolve conflicts between the federal government and the states. Since the state superior court had no jurisdiction in such a dispute, it could not stay the execution. Only a federal court could do that. But there was no time left for an appeal to the federal circuit court.

An agent of the court let Cahum know that his time was up. On schedule, at five that afternoon, they put him to death. As the official newspaper announced to the public two days later:

> the prisoner Encarnación Cahum, one of the principal authors of the assault and murders at rancho Xuxub, went before a firing squad in the jail of the state. The law has treated him inexorably, and it made him pay with his life for his crimes. No circumstance could attenuate the responsibility of this disgusting man: He voluntarily left the benefits of civilization to find in the excesses of barbarity satisfaction for his depraved instincts; he served several times as guide for the savages; and finally, in the events at Xuxub, he was one who most distinguished himself by his cruelty. A sad social necessity took the life of this unhappy man. May we never have to inform our readers again of an event like that which motivated this execution![40]

The governor informed the Ministry of Foreign Relations that Cahum was dead. The minister informed John Foster. John Foster informed the secretary of state.[41] And the world was made right.

14 October

Fourteen men and boys and two women, one with two children, staggered into Puntachen on 14 October, captives who had survived the massacre in the savanna. Meanwhile, someone took the corpse of Robert Stephens over for burial on Holbox Island.

Two days later Montilla assembled some men again and returned to Xuxub. After a raid, frontier commanders were supposed to send men out to explore. They needed to make certain that the raiders had gone and weren't just lurking nearby preparing to strike again. They needed to look for stragglers, or captives who might have slipped away from the raiders. They needed to look for the bodies of their families and neighbors to give them decent burials.

At desolate Xuxub Montilla and his men found the bodies of fifteen enemy dead still lying where they had fallen. Montilla sent most of his men twelve miles beyond into the savanna. There they counted thirteen bodies of Xuxub workers, along with four more enemy dead. But where were the rest of the men, women, and children of Xuxub? Before disaster struck, Xuxub was home to a hundred or more people. Only twenty or so had reappeared. Montilla's men found only thirteen dead. They surely overlooked the bodies of children, or of people wounded in the massacre who managed to stagger off to die elsewhere. As for the rest? One report later suggested that four women and one child from Xuxub were living in rebel territory. Maybe still other men and women of Xuxub escaped the rage of their captors/liberators and kept on walking, to new lives free of masters, debts, and whips. No one ever inquired much into their fates. They just vanished, forgotten to posterity along with so much else of what transpired at Xuxub. They probably preferred it that way.[a]

While most of his men pursued their grim exploration of the savanna, Montilla and a few others busied themselves at Xuxub, loading canoes with whatever casks, utensils, paper, and furniture remained. When the others returned, they were surprised to learn they'd have to walk the whole way home. Montilla had no room for them anymore; no more need for them, either.[b]

Nine

Worldly Satisfaction

I N THE WEEKS AFTER XUXUB FELL, PEOPLE GIRDED themselves as usual for the Indian raids that a new year must spawn. A few days before the invasion of Xuxub, seventy men from Santa Cruz took several people captive in southern Yucatan and scouted the ground for a larger invasion to come. The following month Santa Cruz received a large shipment of weapons and ammunition from British Honduras. The supplies were for a big invasion of Yucatan to be launched next August. Then Santa Cruz forces and their allies in Campeche would overrun the garrisoned frontier towns of Peto and Tekax and drive on deep into Yucatan, as far as Izamal, at least. While the beleaguered people of Yucatan awaited their executioners, great events elsewhere caught their attention. Revolution in Mexico forced President Lerdo into exile, leaving the palace to General Porfirio Díaz.

People didn't notice the quiet that descended over the frontier until the new year brought no Indian raid. Neither did the next. Instead, finally, came news unimaginable before. Santa Cruz would attack Yucatan no more. With his belligerent colleague dead, Crescencio Poot no longer had to make war against whites. The death of the volatile General Cen had finally made peace possible.[1]

Poot flirted with peace, but could not firmly grasp it after decades of war. The new president of Mexico offered generous terms. Rebel Maya could keep the territory they occupied. Only men of their own race would govern them. Their domain would stay independent of the states of Yucatan and Campeche, against whom they had warred so many years. They'd only be answerable to the federal government.[2] Initial peace talks went well. Then suddenly Poot sent his men to raid the frontier again. It had been just an error: British authorities had told him Mexicans were preparing to attack. When the threat proved false, Santa Cruz again stood down, but permanent peace remained elusive.

Poot's tolerance of Yucatan angered some young subordinates, who chafed as well at the way Poot controlled commercial contacts with the outside. Those men matured, grew stronger, and eventually dared to challenge the rule of the aging general who seemed, like Cen, to have angered God. "Thus then my very beloved, ye Christian villagers," God spoke to his Maya children, "whichever of my engendered leaders will fulfill my holy commandments, his life will be extended, his life will have no end with God. Whoever is not obeying them, his life will be used up quickly, his soul will go where fire is never extinguished even a bit.... What is the reason that ye are not obeying those, my holy commandments, ye Christian villagers? Is there perhaps another God in the world for you, or because there should be? Tell me, because I am the Lord of Heaven and Earth."[3]

Poot couldn't defy both God and rivals forever. From her grave, the former captive Josefa managed to tilt the balance against him.

When Josefa returned to Yucatan as a free woman in early 1875, she settled in her murdered husband's house in Merida. There she remained in seclusion the rest of her tortured life, leaving an attorney to handle her affairs and fight her battles. He managed to thwart any efforts by the daughter of the mistress of Josefa's husband to get part of the estate. He forced the killers of Manuel Solís to labor for Josefa upon release from prison (they still owed money, after all). And he slowly bilked her fortune so that when Josefa died in 1881 at the age of forty-five, most of her inheritance was gone. A sum remained, though, tidy enough to spark some mischief back in Santa Cruz. Apart from small amounts bequeathed to faithful attendants, Josefa had left everything to her sister, Encarnación, still held captive near the capital of the rebel Maya. In her will she directed that all steps be taken to redeem her sister, paying whatever necessary to that end. If her sister died in captivity, then all that was left of her inheritance must go for Gregorian masses sung for the souls of Josefa's mother and father, of her mother-in-law and father-in-law, of her husband Manuel and her daughter Eulalia, and of Encarnación, abandoned by Josefa in hasty flight six long years before.[4]

Encarnación's husband, Francisco Avila, had made at least a tardy attempt to get his wife out of captivity. In 1879 he gathered up what money he could and set out for the rebel Maya capital of Santa Cruz. In earlier years none would dare make that trip. But word was out about Crescencio Poot's pacific policy toward whites. Ten months after Encarnación's husband walked into the forest, newspapers reported that the barbarians had killed him. In fact, Avila was alive, but there was a problem. General Poot accepted the money as sufficient only for Avila to remain with his wife in captivity. To free the woman, more money was needed, and where was Avila to get that?

When he heard that his sister-in-law had passed away, Avila hurried back to Yucatan hopeful that from the dead woman's estate would come money enough to free his wife. Josefa had grown wary of her sister's husband. Her will declared that funds from the estate could go only directly to Encarnación, not to anyone who "may have and allege legitimate right to represent her"—like Francisco Avila. Avila implored the judge handling the deceased's affairs, however, to give him money to free Encarnación. Josefa had willed that her sister be redeemed. "Who better than the husband of the captive lady," argued Avila before the judge,

> can undertake with perfect and full willingness such a delicate, even dangerous, mission? Who better than that husband, who for no other purpose than to achieve that desired result has made the greatest and most costly sacrifices, the most tiring journeys by sea and land, and spent everything to the point of having destituted himself, he grasps for the last to which a man has recourse; he remembered that he still had life and with rare selflessness he risked it going to Santa Cruz, headquarters of the barbarous Indians, where though he managed to live some time with his wife, it was not possible for him to save her, because he lacked the necessary means that for that were indispensable.[5]

Avila got the money, thirty-five hundred pesos, all that was then available from the partially liquidated and still much-litigated estate. For good measure, General Teodosio Canto, acquaintance and debtor to Josefa's husband and President Díaz's principal negotiator with the rebel Maya, stepped forward and pledged to make good on the money should Avila abscond.

Avila returned to Santa Cruz with money in hand, but it was too late. Encarnación had survived over twenty years of captivity. She died there with freedom in sight. Oddly, her husband Avila stayed on at Santa Cruz. He had gone there not only to free his wife. General Canto recruited him to help the effort to conclude a peace treaty with Crescencio Poot. Avila was to ply the Maya general with money and report back on how things stood at Santa Cruz. Avila played the part well. Too well, it seems, becoming in time less an agent for Canto than an assistant to Crescencio Poot, traveling around in rebel territory selling alcohol produced from Poot's establishments.

Poot's rivals for power at Santa Cruz, growing stronger as the aged general grew more feeble and fond of drink, viewed Avila as an ally of Poot's and therefore a nuisance. Yucatecan newspapers reported in August of 1883 that both Avila and Poot had been assassinated. They had subsequently to correct that false news, but something was afoot. Again, a few months later, an escaped captive reported that Avila had been murdered.

This time it was true. Avila had gone peddling alcohol for Poot in Chun Pom. Men there seized him, garroted him, hung his lifeless body from a tree, and burned it. Then they turned on the aging general who'd let this white man wander among them. Led by a brazen young commander named Aniceto Dzul, upstarts rebelled against the rule of Crescencio Poot. They withdrew from Santa Cruz down the trail that Cen had taken a decade earlier, to Chun Pom and Tulum. Poot dispatched his trusted general, Juan Chuc, to crush the rebels, but battle went against Chuc. Dzul and his men killed General Chuc, seized Santa Cruz, and a few days later tracked down Poot and murdered him, too.

As one of his first acts as the new ruler of Santa Cruz, Aniceto Dzul raided the frontier at the same point Bernardino Cen once did in defiance of the doomed leader Dionisio Zapata. That was the last raid ever against Yucatan, but with it, the chance for permanent peace expired. Over the next decade and a half, Mexico slowly organized the final campaign of the war, convinced that the Mayas would never submit to anything less than arms. After months of battling their way through the forest, building a broad road all along the way, in May of 1901 federal troops marched into Santa Cruz and declared their interminable struggle against the enemies of civilization to be over.

Josefa couldn't free her sister, but from the grave she had her revenge against Santa Cruz. Mary Stephens, too, sought to wrest worldly satisfaction from those she held responsible for the death of her loved one. She and her husband's partner, Ramón Aznar, filed their claims against the Mexican government early in the year following the destruction of Xuxub. Then Mary left Yucatan after hearing from Aznar she'd get no money from him. True, he and her husband had a partnership. But that partnership dissolved upon her husband's demise. Even if he then put Xuxub up for public auction, nobody would buy it, because nobody could get anyone to go work there anymore. Aznar owed her husband no money. On the contrary, over the three years her husband supervised Xuxub, Aznar gave him almost fifteen hundred dollars for expenses and the like, and Aznar expected that Mary would one day reimburse him that amount. Anything that remained at Xuxub had been bought with Aznar's money, so it belonged to him. So too the house lot in Puntachen. From Aznar Mary would get nothing but a ticket home and the desperate hope that her claim would bear fruit.[6]

Hope was all she had. Secretary of State Fish instructed Minister Foster to present the claims of Aznar and Stephens to the Mexican government, but months later Foster had done nothing, claiming he had received no instructions from Washington. Then Foster commenced a long leave of absence in the United States. The chargé d'affaire at the U.S. legation did finally present the claims and waited for a Mexican response. The Mexican government was already teetering under the strain of armed revolt in the countryside and intrigue within the administration, but a new foreign minister managed, two months later, to draft a brief reply. He reported that the president of Mexico rejected the claim of Ramón Aznar. Under Mexican law Mexicans who became naturalized citizens of another nation, but who again took up residence in Mexico and displayed every intention of remaining there, lost their foreign citizenship and became Mexicans again. That was clearly the case with Ramón Aznar, so the United States had no business pressing a claim on his behalf. As for the claim of Mary Stephens, the Ministry of Foreign Relations had evidence in its files proving that her accusations were false. So her claim, too, was rejected.[7]

That response disturbed the American chargé d'affaire. Certainly Mexico could not strip an American citizen like Ramón Aznar of his American citizenship. As for the claim of Mary Stephens, they had hardly addressed it at all. He sought instructions from Washington on how to proceed.[8]

He never received any instructions. Fighting in Oaxaca between federal forces and rebels lead by Porfirio Díaz ended the presidency of Sebastián Lerdo de Tejada, who a few days later fled Mexico City for exile in New York. Meanwhile after a bitterly contested presidential election in the United States, a new administration prepared to seat itself in Washington. From West Hoboken, Mary Stephens wrote plaintively to the outgoing Secretary Fish in January 1877. She had heard nothing about her claim, and was "anxious to learn something that will satisfy me for you do not know how badly I and my children are situated. Here in this country unprovided and without means to pass a winter although born in this country we have always been away from it at this season of the year. So you can form an idea of how we will be able to do so, without our Country does what it can in order to gain redress for a widow and two fatherless children."[9]

Now Fish had nothing to offer, except a dour note: "The condition of affairs in that country is far from favorable for negotiation upon any sub-ject." Mexico was even then struggling to meet its first annual payment on money due from claims settled under the 1868 Claims Commission. The United States was still far away from even recognizing the government of Porfirio Díaz, come to power by the violent overthrow of a constitution-ally elected president. The troubles of Mary Stephens could not be ad-dressed under such circumstances.[10]

The new head of the State Department, William Evarts, hardly had settled into his office when Mary Stephens tried anew. She wrote Evarts about how her husband had been murdered and pleaded with him to "con-sider this case a little." Evarts took scant interest in the case and did not bother to look at the claims papers. If Mary had legal proofs of all she claimed, then Mexico could be held accountable. Otherwise, she could ex-pect no amends. Unless, he added as an afterthought, there were another general settlement of claims between Mexico and the United States, an agreement like that back in 1868 to resolve all outstanding demands against one or the other nation. "This must take place sooner or later," it seemed to Evarts, "but when is at present quite uncertain."[11]

Inspired by the chill of yet another winter, Mary tried again the fol-lowing January. This time Secretary Evarts actually looked at the claims documents. It seemed to him that though the people who killed her hus-band were "in one sense" Mexicans, "in point of fact they were savage Indi-ans." Two of them (Evarts had not read so carefully) had been punished, and the Mexican government had subsequently rejected the claim. On the other hand the State Department was not, upon further reflection, really satisfied with the reasons given for the rejection. He would send new in-structions to the American representative in Mexico.[12]

Unfortunately for Mary, that representative was still John Foster, an able, honest, diligent minister, but one decidedly, often rightfully, averse to the claims of American citizens against the government of Mexico. Foster just believed that Americans should seek redress for their grievances in the courts of Mexico, a position he asserted was consistent with American policy since the founding of the Republic. Besides, Foster was less interested in picking such small disputes with the new regime than he was in resolving the larger, more dangerous problems then plaguing U.S.-Mexican relations: Indian raids; banditry; possible international conflict on the northern border; formal recognition of the regime of Porfirio Díaz (which in Foster's estimation offered extraordinary promise of maintaining order and promoting trade and prosperity); and removing other pretexts for war with Mexico, a war some Republicans were then promoting in the U.S. for reasons of domestic political and economic gain. In any event, instructed to seek the Mexican government's "proofs" regarding the falsity of Mary Stephens's claim, Foster, again, did nothing at all.[13]

The following winter brought no letter from Mary to the State Department. She did not write, either, the winter after that. Instead, with the turn of that new year, 1882, she bought a plot in Holy Name Cemetery in Jersey City, and over it had erected a crucifix inscribed on its block base:

IN MEMORY OF
My Husband
ROBERT STEVENS
DIED OCT. 12 1876
AGED 44 YEARS
May His Soul Rest In Peace

She remembered the year wrong and changed the spelling of her husband's name. It must already have seemed so long ago. As for her claim and the hopes of money and justice for the murder of her husband, the time had come to let go. Meanwhile that household filled with women—Robert Stephens's aged and senile mother, his widow Mary, daughters Evangeline and Catherine, and Catherine's two school-aged daughters—managed as well as they could, supported only by the income of Catherine's Cuban husband employed as a cigar maker in a local factory.[14]

The consul Lespinasse had done the best he could. Had he gained a better grasp of why Xuxub was wasted, it wouldn't have helped Mary Stephens. Her rescue lay in the American government making guilty Mexicans pay. Lespinasse saw it the same. He was led to that view by principals—first Robert Stephens and then repeatedly by Ramón Aznar who became so influential with the consul that he was appointed vice consul himself. (The appointment fell through when Aznar wouldn't pay the bond that the appointment required.) The lack of forthcoming answers made sense to Lespinasse, all too familiar with the corruption and shenanigans of his own New York political machine, and with the resentment and even envy he encountered south of the border. For the still-green American, that explained it all. He didn't think to talk to Josefa. She could have shown him that the Indian Cen was no tool of white men, not even the Urcelays. He didn't get to talk to the Indian prisoners. Maybe they did know something about the Urcelays. But men like Cen, they would have told the consul, obey only the commandments of God. At least they always had—until General Cen had measured himself against God and brought sure ruin on them all. Lespinasse spoke to some of the workers of the late Robert Stephens. He recorded their words, but didn't listen to what they said. The raiders didn't come down Montilla's road. They walked across the savanna, and no worker shouted an alarm. The workers had been expecting them.

That was more than young Lespinasse ever wanted to hear. He would not interview any more workers, only residents of the island of Holbox who didn't like the Urcelays and who repeated in unison the praises of Robert Stephens. "I first met Mr. Robert L. Stephens four years ago," said a blacksmith, "and I can attest from the time he founded the Xuxub farm until his death nobody harbored anything but gratitude toward him for his charitable and equitable conduct towards all." "I can attest," assured a Holbox man who had helped Stephens install equipment at Solferino, "the said Mr. Robert L. Stephens from the time he settled at Xuxub made himself liked by all because of his charitable and generous conduct towards all without distinction." From Xuxub's own workers the best praise the consul could extract was acknowledgment that the enterprise was growing more prosperous every year. They should know; their labor made it so. As for the character of their dead master, the consul declined to ask.[15]

After the execution of Encarnación Cahum for the crimes at Xuxub, Lespinasse began to plot his escape from Yucatan, surely sooner than he'd imagined upon arrival not two years before. Early in 1877 he was on leave in New York City. He hoped not to have to return to Mexico. Lespinasse got another bevy of New York merchants to nominate him for a consular position on Spain's Costa del Sol. He didn't get the post and had to return to Yucatan, but a few months later he was back in the States and avoided returning to Merida until late in August. Lespinasse wanted out, permanently. A year and a half later he was on long leave in Paris receiving treatment, he reported, for his chronic indigestion. When late in the year his bosses denied a request for an extended convalescence in France, Lespinasse still avoided returning to his post. Finally, in February of 1880 the State Department requested his resignation.

The new U.S. consul in Merida, a New Yorker himself, had never met Lespinasse. From the look of things in the consulate, however, it was clear that his predecessor lacked enthusiasm and energy. At least that's what he told Washington, not knowing that Lespinasse had begun brimming with youthful vigor. Lespinasse never grasped what had happened at Xuxub, but the trying changed him, and sent him yearning for a world just as corrupt but more familiar.

Epilogue

Truth, Guilt, and Narrative

BEFORE MIGUEL AND I LEFT CHIQUILA THEY TOOK US
to hear the story. A wizened, nearly blind neighbor of our launch-
men could tell us what really happened at Xuxub. A storekeeper
cautioned us, though. That old man's stories were so many and long, we'd
tire of listening before he was done.

Xuxub was worked by slaves under the tyrant Roberto Stephens, the
old man gladly declared. One day for some minor infraction Stephens
gave a man twenty-five bloody lashes. To spice the pain he had salt rubbed
in the wounds. You will pay for this, the defiant slave spit back. In their
quarters and in the fields, the brave soul appealed to his brothers and sis-
ters in bondage. Help me escape. From your rations set aside the food I'll
need for a long journey on foot. I will go in search of the Indians. I will
find them and bring them back, and then we shall taste revenge. His
neighbors did as he asked, and before long he commenced the long, slow,
dangerous trek into unknown forests south.

The fugitive from Xuxub walked on and on, until one day in the thick
of the woods he heard a cock crow, and next, an axe against wood. A village must be near. Weary from so many days walking, and fearful of Indians, too, he cautiously announced his presence. The Indians received the
traveler belligerently, but once he explained why he had come and displayed his still-raw wounds, they took him in, fed him, and applied heal-
ing herbs to his back. They passed the visitor on from group to group ever
further along the trail south, until finally he reached a village called Chun
Ox.[1] The Indians of that place were well armed with bows, arrows, and
spears. They sympathized with the runaway's plight and decided to follow
him to wreak vengeance upon Xuxub.

From the old man's tale we learned nothing of the long march back,
how many Indians came, who led them. In the next utterance of his story,
the fearsome Indians simply appeared crossing the Turbio River, approaching doomed Xuxub from the east, just like the fisherman said. As

they reached the cane fields, they set them on fire. Master Stephens ordered his slaves to extinguish the flames consuming all his profits. But Stephens was no longer their master, and the people refused. Led by the runaway slave, Indians found and seized Stephens. The story's hero then reminded the tyrant Stephens of his angry oath—Stephens must pay for his cruelty. Stephens promptly forfeited his head. Soldiers eventually came from Puntachen and drove the drunken Indians off, but Xuxub at least was free of the likes of Robert Stephens.

People remember such stories for a reason. Not everything that happens gets inscribed in collective memories, and without grasping motives behind recall, old men can seem to select details in a random manner. The story of Xuxub remains vividly told not just for what happened there in 1875, but for what happened afterward, too.

Despite his predictions to the contrary, after Xuxub was destroyed, Ramón Aznar convinced men to labor out there again. They returned to planting and harvesting sugarcane, and turning it into rum and sweetener, until flames finally accomplished what Maya rebels and the Urcelays had not. Fire swept through Xuxub in May of 1880, devastating the cane fields and reducing the sugarhouse to ashes. (Was that the fire that our old man recalled?) Aznar quit the place for good.[2]

That left the Urcelays kings of the frontier, and all who remained in Puntachen became their indebted workers. They had no choice. Petitions for land to farm routinely failed. The fabled wealth of the east was not for little men.[3] Some years later someone raided the Urcelays' warehouse at Chiquila and plundered their logwood camps, too. They must have been local men, bandits, or someone who just did not like the Urcelays.[4] Whoever they were, they couldn't loosen the Urcelays' grip on the land and labor out there. Only death and debt could. Manuel Urcelay died of an aneurysm in 1883, leaving an estate heavily mortgaged to Merida merchants. His son had to sell Solferino. Five years later Nicolás Urcelay passed on, leaving his children little to show for all those years of struggle on the frontier—a couple of thousand pesos, a pile of salt awaiting a market, a few house lots in Progreso, and some nearly worthless lands without laborers. Fortunately for the children of Manuel and Nicolás, both had thought to purchase insurance polices from New York Mutual Life, whose agent in Yucatan was old Ramón Aznar.[5]

The Urcelays passed so quietly from the scene that memory of them soon vanished from the minds of the common people who had once re-

sented them. Afterward came other powerful men to dominate that eastern frontier. They too succumbed, though in ways less dramatic than the
fall of Robert Stephens. With the triumph of a revolution fought elsewhere in Mexico, the peons of eastern Yucatan could respectfully petition
for lands and, after many years of trying, receive parcels to farm around
the ruins of Solferino, Xuxub, and other former sugar estates along the
frontier. Their grandfathers labored as slaves, petitioners told federal
agents, and yes, an Urcelay was among many masters named. But with the
turn of a new century none loomed so large as Robert Stephens, a scourge
from which they freed themselves in their own perilous and heroic action.
They planned and sacrificed and rose against the master, not in plaintive
petition, but with machetes, aided by some shadowy allies known as "the
Indians" who were kind enough to leave and never come back again.[6]

For my companion Miguel, of course, those Indians were not name-
less. The name of one he knows like his own, and since childhood he's listened to stories of the great deeds of that man and other wartime leaders.
Miguel is one of their distant progeny, and he's accepted their charge as an
officer in the Maya church, devoted still to worshipping before those
crosses that inspired Cen and others. "The spirit, the great general, Don
Bernardino Cen," as men like Miguel refer to him, spoke with God. Cen
got his orders from True God, Miguel explained as we drove along the
highway home from Chiquila. So long as he followed those orders, Cen
could never lose. But success got to Cen, who came to think himself as
great as God. Eventually God recoiled at the thirst for blood his favored
general displayed. Cen didn't take prisoners. All fell before the machete he
kept tightly strapped to his forearm so that wet with blood his grip still
would not slip. He'd kill men, women, children, even those who'd already
surrendered and who on their knees begged for mercy. Among Miguel and
his colleagues, Cen is most admired. But they shake their heads when re-
calling the strange brutality of the man. In any event, God told Cen to
stop such senseless slaughter. It was too late, however. Cen had grown too
large and bold to listen even to God. "You gave me the power," he dared to
tell his Lord. "I'll do what I have to do."

For Miguel, his friends and neighbors, Bernardino Cen epitomized
how powerful they could be when they acted decisively, concertedly, and in
accordance with God's will. Cen's fall at Xuxub epitomized, too, the consequences of human foibles, the bane of egotism, the punishment for
hubris, the fate that awaits all who so readily stray from the path God

commands. In the decades since their defeat at the hands of the Mexican military, Maya like Miguel have had repeated occasions to ponder the paradox of their great deeds and their defeat, of how they could win their battles and yet lose the war, of how they could be God's chosen people and yet merit his abandonment. The summer Miguel and I ventured back to Xuxub was just one more such occasion. A hurricane the year before had ruined their corn crops. Drought this year had razed the seedlings. Hunger loomed. Miguel's commander held it as a sign that the world had grown too old. It yearned to be young again. The world pained to be reborn a child, the aged officer explained to me. It wanted to start over, to have as many years again as it has already had. God has just been waiting for this old world to ripen well, before the harvest and the dawn of a new day. It might only be a few more months, he thought. Village folk had already sold all that they owned, just to buy corn to eat. Rich town folks, those wealthy pigs with voracious appetites, would never give a little to the poor. Well then, the poor would just have to take it, if necessary with guns, just like their distant predecessors did. Even today they could easily overrun the towns, the commander suggested to me. Their various Maya centers had already made written agreements to come to each other's aid if "something" should start near the one or the other.

When such talk of war begins, Cen's name is usually uttered. Cen will return, many have said. Other dead leaders are also named, but none so often as Cen. The leader returned will be young and strong; he'll not be old, or bloodied, or wizened. Still, people will recognize him for who he is, since he'll know all the stories of the past times, of the war Mayas fought, of all the past leaders and battles, of places like Santa Cruz and Xuxub. When that fallen general returns, wayward Maya rebels will drift back to the fold, and the peace with whites will expire.[7]

They've awaited that day a long time. Some years the waiting seemed close to an end; other years, like it had all been in vain. Of course it's not the man who died at Xuxub whom they're waiting for. They're waiting for themselves. They're waiting for that day prophesied when they'll again seize control of their own destinies. Since their conquest five centuries ago, that's meant taking up arms against the whites. Their prophets have proclaimed that they must do that again in the ripeness of time. Still, the ones I know, though they believe that to be true, shrink from the sacrifice, suffering, and cruelty they understand war entails. As a peaceful people, they recoil at the hubris of murdering fellow human beings. Stories of

General Cen's triumph in battles evoke an image of the war that in each generation some Mayas have said must be fought. The story of Cen's fall at Xuxub evokes, in counterpoint, both his humanity and their own.

Though so prominently remembered among his own, Cen's name means nothing to whites on the peninsula of Yucatan. Whites have told and written their own stories about other leaders of the Maya rebels. To some they've erected statues to promote ethnic reconciliation and to appropriate the Maya rebellion to a more universal struggle for social justice (the advancement of which Mexico's long-ruling revolutionary party still claimed it was the vanguard). Monuments celebrate the bellicosity of early leaders like Jacinto Pat and Cecilio Chi. A memorial plaque in the former rebel Maya capital of Santa Cruz (now named Felipe Carrillo Puerto) applauds the embrace of former enemies and the end of hostilities. But for Bernardino Cen, once so feared by his enemies in Yucatan, whites could, for many years, offer only a puzzled query—Who?

Cen wasn't just forgotten by his former enemies. The most prominent historian of the Indian war, Serapio Baqueiro, helped his students to forget. Baqueiro was an astute witness to the war, and he authored the most detailed, still fundamental, volumes on the conflict. He alone among historians displayed curiosity and interest concerning the identity, personality, and capacities of the men who led the Maya rebellion. In addition to his lengthy books on the war, Baqueiro published a biographical sketch of Crescencio Poot in 1887, two years after Poot's death.[8] Baqueiro undertook to rehabilitate the Maya leader whom earlier he had characterized as brutish, bloody, and savage. The man at least fought for a cause, unlike most of the whites, Baqueiro noted, whose rebellions had plagued Yucatan almost constantly since independence. According to Baqueiro, Poot was a tireless warrior who put his own life at risk, time and again, with calm and even humor. Eventually Poot was properly rewarded for his unceasing effort with supreme command of his people. Poot was a universal hero in this new imagining of Baqueiro, "if by that is meant he who by his valor or his victories has earned the renown of posterity," and who earned that renown "not shedding the blood of his brothers and his people, but sacrificing himself to the last."[9]

According to the white historian, Poot earned his position as leader of Santa Cruz on the strength of his energy and character, his loyalty and his sacrifices to the cause, and "never was it known of him that he had discord with the principal leaders, much less that he contested for power."[10]

Baqueiro knew that was not true; he falsified history in which he was himself involved. Baqueiro was a friend, he acknowledged, of the brother-in-law of Josefa Romero de Rodríguez. He knew what had transpired between Cen and Poot over the ransom of Josefa. He knew of the bloody struggle between the two that left Poot as supreme ruler at Santa Cruz. In Baqueiro's public recollection, Francisco Avila went to the noble Poot and freed his wife from captivity, though Baqueiro knew that too was false—that Encarnación died in captivity and his good friend Avila was murdered at Chun Pom.[11]

Why so many contortions of the truth to avoid raising the specters of Bernardino Cen, Josefa, the Americans at Xuxub, and more? Fear, perhaps. Baqueiro didn't earn his living as a journalist and chronicler, but rather through the patronage of powerful others who gave him a position as a judge here or a magistrate there. In still other seasons he toiled happily in the governor's palace or as a state statistician, whatever work there was for a politically connected man. Even his grand historical project, a multivolume history of the War of the Castes, was financially supported by the state. Writing about turmoil in Yucatan, Baqueiro slipped up twice. Parts of the first volume of his grand chronicle of revolution and race war on the peninsula, *Ensayo Histórico sobre las Revoluciones de Yucatán*, were published in 1866 by none other than Eligio Ancona. In the introduction, Baqueiro expressed the hope that from those pages "those who govern us" might learn much. After only a few installments, however, publication ceased. Maybe that was just because the publisher went out of business, but Baqueiro cryptically asserted that he stopped in order to avoid "passing on inexactitudes to posterity." That would seem to mean someone powerful objected to what the historian had to say. Baqueiro issued a revised first volume in 1872, but that one, too, quickly faded from circulation, again due to objection from on high. It was four years before he could reissue the work and move on to other volumes.[12]

While forgetting who he was, whites retained Cen's broken skull. Collected from his body in Xuxub back in 1875, it had been sent to Merida and deposited in the Regional Museum of Yucatan, along with the man's earring, other captured Maya artifacts, and the skulls of two or three other illustrious (white) Yucatecans. Eventually it was transferred to the osteological collection of the regional center of the National Institute of Anthropology and History. Across the top of the yellowing skull someone long ago telegraphically inscribed: "Gen. Cen muerto en Xuxub 13 de Octubre 1876," "General Cen killed at Xuxub 13 October 1876." The date of course was wrong, and I never did learn the significance of the large black "A" drawn on the forehead.

The contemporary keepers of the skull didn't know who Cen was, or how the relic had come into their hands. That changed when a Merida newspaper published some of my research into Cen's career and death at Xuxub. That reintroduction to Bernardino Cen occurred even as scholars and officials were commemorating the 150th anniversary of the start of the War of the Castes with a conference at the state university and public addresses in various parts of Yucatan. Now that the skull had a name, and the man an important history, officials of the Institute decided it should be returned to the land from which Cen had come and be closer to those who kept Cen's memory alive.

Months later, the artifact arrived home. The skull would rest in a museum in the town of Tihosuco, the final siege of which Cen had commanded. To inaugurate the macabre exhibit, local, state, and federal authorities and an audience of interested outsiders gathered there. They viewed the skull on its new pedestal in the local museum and made or listened to speeches about the significance of the moment. Peace was the message authorities then wished to convey, as the nation roiled from the revolt of Mayas in Chiapas and from the crises of the presidential succession of 1994. The town mayor, himself Maya, delivered the most ironic statement that by celebrating the return of Bernardino Cen, they celebrated peace. Cen and the other leaders of the rebel Maya, the mayor told his audience, fought to improve the lives of their people. They took up arms and led the people in struggle only with the intention of making things better for everyone. Today the Mayas no longer go for their guns. Instead, they follow the path of dialogue. They send their children to school, they employ their resources peacefully, they walk toward a new horizon, all with the goal of improving their lives and the lives of their children. It is no longer necessary to take up arms, and they are not doing so, the mayor intoned. As for the return of the skull of Bernardino Cen, he declared it had a mystic significance for the Maya Zone, as the heartland of the once rebel Indians is sometimes called. The mayor fumbled to state just what that significance was, before he yielded the podium to the governor of the state.

The governor also used the occasion to denounce violence, even while his well-armed bodyguards scanned the crowd before him. The struggle of the Maya, the struggle that Cen once led, said the governor, continues in pursuit of greater liberty and prosperity. It is no longer a violent struggle. Instead, in an alliance of Mayas and government all work together to ensure the success of development programs. The governor trailed on discussing what the state had already done for that town and region, not imposing anything upon anyone, but orienting people and supporting people in their quest for betterment.

The governor brought a Maya priest to offer his perspective upon this occasion. The man spoke in Yucatec Maya, so few in the audience of outsiders could follow what he said. Even for those who could understand, the priest spoke so lightly into the microphone that his amplified voice was almost inaudible as he fumbled for direction in his remarks. Finally he found his tempo and tone, however. Back then we were fewer, he said, in reference to the time of the war against slavery. I did not see it, it's a story, but if you want to hear it. . . so went the usual formulas that Mayas offer when talking about things they have not witnessed themselves. We . . . that war . . . we did that. We managed that. We did not have much literacy, but we could think, could figure out how to do things. Jacinto Pat, Cecilio Chi, the other great leaders, Bernardino Cen, they directed things here. We did it ourselves. Only God knows what he will send to us, but we know how we shall live, how to live, how to make a living from the land, from the forest. We can't ask someone else to tell us how to make a living. It belongs to us alone to see how we shall live. A governor can give us an orientation, but we must decide for ourselves.

What the governor heard in that was a message of self-help consistent with his own theme—that the government helps, but that people have to work hard to make a better life for themselves. They must collaborate, and from that alliance of government and citizenry, progress will emerge. The priest was making a different point. When they speak of Cen, they speak of their destiny, it has seemed to me. The priest didn't want to talk much that day about the late general. Rather, he cut directly to the point that they, the Maya, must live their own lives as they see fit. To free people that sounds banal. To a conquered people like the Maya that quiet message can stir emotion. Long Live Mexico, the priest shouted in conclusion.

Most people who spoke that day were concerned more with the recent uprising in Chiapas and tumultuous national politics on the one hand, and very local politics on the other, than with Bernardino Cen, whose feats and fate remained largely unknown to the speakers and audience there. On the margins of the small crowd stood some who actually knew the name of Bernardino Cen, who from childhood in their Indian villages had heard the stories of Cen's triumphs and of his fall, and who had heard as well of his prophesied return. At best the skull left under glass in Tihosuco mutely testifies to the fact that the stories they had heard were not all lies. The man did once exist. Perhaps then it is true that he will come again.

Mexicans and Americans once hotly debated why Xuxub was destroyed, who was to blame, who should pay. The historian Baqueiro effaced Xuxub from the pages of Yucatecan history, but other records survived. Reams of paper about Xuxub trickled into the official archives of each nation. The original dispatches of Montilla, the Urcelays, and Governor Ancona survived; so too most diplomatic exchanges over the case; the plaintive missives of Mary Stephens and her daughter to the highest officials of their government; the voluminous claims filed on behalf of the aggrieved; memorials and analyses of the case in terms of international law; even a lone letter from Robert Stephens to his wife, expressing optimism in the wake of the first storm to wrack his estate. Many of these disparate records would have been lost had they not been gathered together in an ungainly collection known as the Claim of Mary A. Stephens.

Mary had seemed to bury her claim when she bought that grave for her husband back in 1882. Yet her claim didn't die, thanks largely to new troubles for Ramón Aznar in Yucatan. Aznar believed that powerful rivals had plotted to destroy Xuxub. A decade later he came to suspect that new rivals plotted to ruin his other landed concern, a cattle hacienda called Chablé, in western Yucatan. Harassment by local officials out there, armed invasions of his property, incessant cattle rustling, and threats against his Cuban supervisor (who unlike the fatefully stubborn Robert Stephens did flee the state with wife and family in tow) all prompted Aznar to protest anew before the U.S. consul in Merida and to file another claim against the government of Mexico. Aznar tried plaintively to enlist former (and future) president Grover Cleveland to champion his cause stateside. Republicans, it seemed to Aznar, were soft on Mexico, unwilling to defend American interests there. Democrats like Cleveland, on the other hand, were not afraid to get tough with their southern neighbor, of course for the good of that neighbor.[13]

Unfortunately, back in Yucatan Aznar no longer had an impressionable consul like Lespinasse whom he could guide down appropriate paths.

After making two trips out to Chablé to investigate the goings-on, Consul Edward Thompson concluded for his superiors that while Aznar had suffered all the damages alleged, authorities in Yucatan were generally trying to do the right thing by him. The real problem, Thompson reported, was Aznar himself, "by intention an upright man, but one hasty in temper and lacking in discretion, given to making statements that cannot be proved and to unwarranted actions. These facts have caused him to become very unpopular in the region wherein his plantation is situated."[14]

Aznar soon found a buyer for his beleaguered property, while his claim against Mexico went nowhere.[15] But Aznar's protests inadvertently spurred descendants of Robert Stephens to renew their search for justice in the old case of Xuxub. In 1891 Mary Stephens's son-in-law Joseph Duff took charge for the aged widow and contacted the State Department, Alphonse Lespinasse, then working in New York, and John Foster, who had relinquished his Mexican post in 1880 to become U.S. Minister to Russia and later Minister to Spain. When Duff reached him, Foster had returned to private practice in Washington.

Duff pressed his offensive armed with a new affidavit from Ramón Aznar in which he offered yet another rendition of the whole sad story of Xuxub. Over the years in the mind of that much-vexed man, ambiguity and uncertainty faded while damning evidence shined more brightly through. The workers of Xuxub *did* see the Indians coming on that fateful day in October, but they thought those were peaceful Indians from Kantunilkin. General Cen had no intention of harming Robert Stephens until the Urcelay brothers ordered him to kill his prey. The runaway worker who had guided the Indians to Xuxub, Encarnación Cahum, came from the Urcelays' Solferino. He was not captured by Montilla's men but simply presented himself, announcing that he had fulfilled his mission. He was surprised to find himself then arrested, taken to Merida, and held incommunicado until permanently silenced by execution. After their defeat at Xuxub the Indians held a council to decide the fate of the other fugitive worker who had served as a guide, Cosme Cob. He protested that *he* had been deceived by the promises of the Urcelays and Montilla, "but they placed no value on his words and killed him."[16]

Despite the crystal clarity of Aznar's damning recollections. the Stephens claim went nowhere. When John Foster soon became Secretary of State, Duff wrote to him impatiently: "Mrs. Stevens (my mother in law) is a poor old woman, incumbent on me and taking up her claim from any legal point of view it is just and honest and she certainly is deserving of every dollar, but it seems for some reason or other the matter is continually left, dropped, or no attention is paid to it. If it is for the want of money we would like to know it. I am satisfied to pay for any favors any one does me but I don't feel inclined to give up $5,000.00 for fun. Knowing as you do the exact circumstances, being minister at the time, sitting at your desk the very hour when he was murdered . . ."[17]

Duff ranted, and he insulted Foster by alluding to an open secret. Between diplomatic assignments Foster made a lucrative career as paid legal counsel to foreign legations in Washington. Under present-day American law he may well have had to register as a foreign agent or lobbyist for Mexico, many other Latin American nations, Russia, China, Spain, and more. Despite his former aversion to American claims, in private practice Foster championed the claims of Americans who could pay well. More than one American newspaper openly protested Foster's appointment to head the State Department precisely because he served too many other masters. The *New York Times*, for example, wryly commented, "Foster has been as prosperous in diplomacy as most commercial men have been in trade of a different kind." So Duff was not embarrassed now to offer Secretary of State Foster five thousand dollars for his help. Perhaps for that reason Foster left it to a subordinate to reply tersely, "Mrs. Stevens' claim was presented to the Government of Mexico in 1876 and by it disallowed. After this delay of sixteen years it will be much more difficult to establish the responsibility of the Mexican Government."[18]

When Aznar's attorney, Grover Cleveland, was elected president of the United States, Duff tried again hopefully to elicit interest in the case. "It does seem very hard and unjust to us not to get any redress, where the facts in the case are so clear," Duff wrote the president, blaming inaction on the unwillingness of Republicans to help Democrats like himself (and the new president).[19] Unjust it may have seemed, but the new secretary of state said too much time had passed to take up that old claim now.[20]

Duff gave up, but his wife Evangeline pushed on. She'd been active in the women's suffrage movement in New Jersey, helped organize the first Women's Democratic Caucus in that state, and could call upon a congressman to look into the matter. The congressman received the same answer as had everyone else. Mexico rejected the claim, and it was too old to take up again. Evangeline also petitioned the president, now Roosevelt, but elicited the same refrain. Evangeline had just started her campaign;

her mother's death soon ended it. Mary's daughters buried her in their father's empty grave and let the claim rest, too.[21]

Deep in the archives of the State Department, the claim would have remained forgotten but for the turmoil, destruction, and carnage of the first of the twentieth century's great revolutions. The revolt that brought Porfirio Díaz to power back in 1876 had frustrated the efforts of Mary Stephens to have her claim heard fully. The revolution that removed the dictator from power in 1910 revived her claim again, as to it were added thousands of other claims from Americans whose lives or property were affected by the new upheaval, and from thousands of Mexicans who suffered at the hands of the American troops that intervened at points during the civil war. In 1924, by agreement between Mexico and the United States, Special and General Claims Commissions began meeting to slog through the mountains of protests and tales of woe that flooded the foreign ministries of each country. Each nation established an agency to prepare and present their cases to three commissioners—one chosen by the president of Mexico, one by the president of the United States, and one neutral commissioner chosen by agreement of the two countries or, if they could not agree, by an official of the Permanent Court of Arbitration at The Hague. Each nation would plead its case, back and forth, before the commissioners, who would then decide the matter up or down on the basis of "international law, justice and equity." Only once all filed claims were disposed of would monetary awards be distributed.[22]

The work of receiving, preparing, and arguing claims proceeded at a snail's pace. After meeting occasionally over seven years the General Claims Commission disposed of only 148 claims. That left over 3,000 cases pending. The American agent briefly handled the claim of the late Ramón Aznar. It had ballooned to three hundred thousand dollars for damages at Xuxub and his other hacienda, Chablé. However, when his children in Yucatan learned that the claim had been revived, they insisted it be dropped. According to one of them, Julian, then a prominent attorney in Merida, he was already under attack from local authorities for being involved in any such claim against his own country.[23] As for the claim of Mary Stephens, the American agency filed her case with the commission in 1925 and wrote to Evangeline, the last relative with whom any official had had contact. Their letter went to the former workplace of her by-then deceased husband, so naturally the letter was returned, "Addressee not found." The Americans moved on to other cases.[24]

A decade after their initial agreement, Mexico and the United States decided to accelerate procedures for disposing of remaining claims, and American officials again, this time successfully, contacted Evangeline Stephens about the Xuxub matter.[25] Within a few weeks, and fifty-eight years after the facts, the U.S. agency formally filed its memorial, "The United States of America on Behalf of Mrs. Mary A. Stephens vs. The United Mexican States."

Officials no longer sought to discover truth. Each agency sought only to present its case in the most favorable light possible. They aimed to produce resolution, one way or the other, and at the end of the day to have cleared their dockets of all such festering problems. Along the way, of course, they needed to keep an eye open to the impact of their arguments and judgments upon international law and their own careers.

In preparing Mary Stephens's case the American agency had to fashion the disparate fragments of the various recorded versions of the Xuxub tale into a single, coherent, and compelling narrative about how a foreign nation wronged an American citizen. They chose a tale of official malfeasance, emphasizing how powerful men in Yucatan, some of them officials of the government, actively conspired to harm Robert Stephens. The American craftsmen of that story took care to suppress the prior judgments of American diplomats either that there had been no such malfeasance or that the evidence for such was weak. (Those documents were consigned to a file of "evidence not used.") After all was said and done, weak evidence was all they had, and it would have to do.

According to the Americans, Robert Stephens had been "willfully harassed and disturbed by the political and military authorities of the district in the enjoyment of his property and the management of his plantation." In addition, those authorities, and by extension the government of Mexico, failed to provide Stephens with reasonable protection against Indian depredations, even though they had been warned an invasion was likely and even though authorities had promised to protect him.[26] Montilla opened a road on the Xuxub estate, and marauding Indians came down that road. Without Montilla's road, the Indians could not have penetrated the bush to reach the estate. The Holbox fisherman Gasca swore that he told Montilla about the impending invasion a day before it occurred. Even after receiving positive news that Xuxub had fallen, Montilla willfully delayed another day in responding to the attack. As yet further evidence of the neglect of Mexican authorities, after liberating

Xuxub Montilla failed to pursue the main body of Indians, with their prisoners and plunder, then only seven miles away. As for the three prisoners Montilla did capture, only one received adequate punishment. The other two received light sentences, which, the Americans asserted, it was not even certain they actually served.

The failure of Mexican authorities to provide reasonable and promised protection, their failure to respond to the invasion in a timely fashion, and their failure adequately to punish the invaders constituted violations of Mexico's obligations towards other nations under international law. As a consequence, the Americans contended, Mary Stephens and her two daughters "were deprived of their means of support, and of the love, affection, companionship, association, advice, protection and counsel of a devoted husband and father. The widow and daughters moreover suffered great mental anguish and sorrow by reason of the violent severance of family ties."

The American agency sought for Evangeline ten thousand dollars for the harm she had suffered in her own right as a child who lost her father, and half of the thirty-thousand-dollar award that would have been claimed for her mother.[27]

In its written response the Mexican agency contested virtually every premise of the American position, starting with the right of the United States to present that claim at all. Evangeline Stephens was born in Cuba, and they therefore assumed, no adequate proof to the contrary having been offered, that she was a citizen of Cuba. The United States could not present the claim of someone who was not a citizen of the United States. As for Mary Stephens, no proof of her citizenship had been offered, either. In any event, the Mexicans argued, the damages claimed for her were "moral" damages, and moral damages could not be bequeathed to others. Whatever outrage and pain she had suffered for the loss of her husband, the right to compensation died with her back in 1907.

Beyond that the Mexican agency disputed most of the facts of the Xuxub case. Robert Stephens was not co-owner of Xuxub, only an employee of Ramón Aznar. What difficulties there had been between Aznar and Stephens on the one hand, and local authorities on the other, were due entirely to the "arrogant" characters of Aznar and Stephens, especially Aznar, "who being a Mexican naturalized in the United States claimed undeserved prerogatives with no other basis than his supposed North American nationality." Montilla had not molested Xuxub. He was diligently doing his job when he investigated signs of Indian movements in the area, and when he entered Xuxub that summer of 1875 he did so at the invitation of Robert Stephens. Rather than thanking Montilla for his diligence, Stephens berated and threatened him, to which treatment Montilla did not respond. Aznar and Stephens, however, took malicious advantage of that incident to increase their attacks on local authority and to initiate a newspaper campaign against it. They further abused the trust and good faith of the American consul in Merida, who unfortunately believed their story and was thus led in error to address himself in an offensive manner to the governor of the state. Mexico called for the withdrawal of the consul but desisted once the United States disavowed his conduct. As for the invasion of Xuxub, as soon as Montilla received word of the attack he commenced to assemble the weapons and men necessary to respond. He then liberated Xuxub, killed nineteen of the invaders, and captured three, among them Encarnación Cahum, a renegade worker from that very place. Cahum was tried and executed, and the two other prisoners had their death sentences commuted for good reasons, especially the boy José Chan. When a judicial commission did finally reach Xuxub to investigate the original complaint of Robert Stephens, it found that complaint to be baseless, especially the false allegation that Montilla had opened a road or a path.

In summary, the Mexican agency argued, Robert Stephens chose to live and work out on that frontier. He did not want protection, supposing his own resources adequate to defend Xuxub. He made himself, thereby, ultimately responsible for his own demise. As for the more general principle of international law involved in this case, governments are not responsible for the damage to foreigners caused by "rebels, insurgents, revolutionaries or any kind of group of armed men who are temporarily beyond the control of the established government or who defy its authority, especially when, as in the present case, said government has exercised particular diligence and care both to suppress the rebellion, insurrection or revolution, and to prevent damage, even against the wishes of the victim, and has besides inflicted a very severe punishment on the band of evil doers."[28]

In support of that point the Mexican agency cited a long roster of treaties, arbitration commission reports, texts in international law, and the like, and could correctly assert that the United States itself had consistently denied responsibility under similar circumstances in the past.[29]

Those were just the opening gambits of the American and Mexican side. Each side had one more opportunity to make its case at greater length still. The American brief that came in next ballooned with citations of evidence in response to the Mexican position, and even more with extended discussion of relevant precedents under international law and preceding decisions of the sitting claims commission. At stake was not only an award for the claimant, but the reinforcement, interpretation, or revision of international law and the likely disposition of other claims further down the docket. The Mexican response ballooned as well. Neither side budged much in its position. The Americans did shift the weight of their argument a bit, placing less emphasis on the malfeasance of Mexican officials—their deliberate attempts to harm Stephens—and more on their nonfeasance—their failure to prevent and respond quickly to the Indian invasion and their failure adequately to punish the Indians. The Mexicans, for their part, shifted emphasis accordingly, while still questioning the adequacy of evidence of the nationality of the claimants. Indians had invaded Xuxub for reasons of their own, and local authorities had properly responded to the invasion, inflicting severe punishment upon the marauders.

The long arguments were in vain. A year later the Claims Commissioners had to report that they could come to no agreement on the eternal dispute. The secretary of state so notified Evangeline, offering that only further diplomatic negotiations with Mexico could settle the matter and that "the Department will use its best endeavors to bring about the most expeditious and advantageous solution of the claims that may be practicable."[30]

It was June of 1943 before Evangeline heard from them again. An agreement with Mexico had been reached, the Claims Convention of 19 November 1941, which included settlement of the Stephens' case. Ten thousand dollars would be coming her way, blood money to still the pens, to let the story of Xuxub die as it should have long ago.

So full round spun the wheel of blame and guilt. Robert Stephens blamed the Urcelays. The Urcelays blamed the Indians. The Indians blamed the workers. The workers blamed Robert Stephens. Mary Stephens gave the wheel yet another spin. Listen, she said, to what the fisherman Gasca had to say. Montilla was too cowardly to kill her husband himself. So Montilla sent for the Indians to do it. He knew the day before the attack that the Indians were near, but he sent no warning to Xuxub.

Though Puntachen was only three or four miles from Xuxub, he waited a full day before going there. He wanted to make sure they had time to kill her husband. He wanted to be sure they'd left before he came. They killed her husband, and most Indians had left before Montilla sauntered in. As it was, according to Mary Stephens, Montilla found only "a few miserable drunken wretches unable to help themselves," and those he ordered butchered."[31]

"This is the truth, and nothing but the truth," Mary avowed, and she could prove it all. But so could the others prove what emerged from their little eddies of truth spun off from the grand whole. Montilla and the Urcelays; General Cen and his men; fugitive laborers like Cob and Cahum, and other men and women still in bondage; even Aznar and Robert Stephens, too: each in their way prepared the fall of Xuxub. Little happened quite as any intended. Still, each contributed to the whole and earned a right to his own truth as certain, like Mary said, as that there was a God in heaven. Apostles and poets mocked that faith in worldly truth: "let God be true, but every man a liar." A fitting epitaph for Xuxub.

Acknowledgments

Much of the research for this book was conducted at Yale University. My thanks to the interlibrary loan librarians of that institution for their willing and able fulfillment of my many requests. My thanks as well to the personnel of the Archivo General del Estado de Yucatan, especially the archive's director, Dr. Piedad Peniche Rivero, and Candy Flota García, for their interested and professional assistance over the years. Finally, I am grateful to Dr. Miguel Antochiw of La Universidad del Mayab, who generously provided me with copies of a number of interesting documents; to Chris Gill who tipped me off more than once to things I'd find in the archives; to Jason Vanasse for helping locate wills and deeds in Hoboken; to Mr. George Schreck for providing me with a copy of the burial record for Robert Stephens and a photo of the memorial stone from the Hudson and Bergen County Catholic Cemeteries; and to Ueli Hostettler, Allen Wells, and Paul Eiss for their comments on earlier drafts this work.

Abbreviations

U.S. Consulate General, Mexico City
   Miscellaneous Letters Received   Mlr
U.S. Embassy, Mexico City
   Notes to the Mexican Foreign Office   NtMFO
   Notes from the Mexican Foreign Office   NfMFO

PERIODICALS

The Merchant's Magazine	*MM*
New York Herald	*NYH*
New York Daily Tribune	*NYTrib*
New York Times	*NYT*
El Espíritu Nacional	*EN*
El Espíritu Público	*EP*
La Nueva Epoca	*NE*
La Revista de Mérida	*LRdM*
La Razón del Pueblo	*LRdP*
La Unión Liberal	*UL*

Notes

Chapter 1: Promises of Quiet

a. The hurricane of 1873 is described in Robert Stephens to Mary Stephens, 2 October 1873, Claims. This may be the same storm mentioned in "Tizimin," *LRdM*, 26 October 1873. According to Stephens the storm destroyed vessels all along the coast of Yucatan and Campeche.

1. Concerning Lespinasse's background and application for office, see "File of Alphonse J. Lespinasse." Applications and recommendations for appointment to the Consular and Diplomatic Services, 1901–24, Box 141, RG 59, National Archives. That he was a protégé of Judge O'Conor is mentioned in Fish Diaries, entry of 6 January 1876. Concerning O'Conor, see: Charles E. Fitch, *Memorial Encyclopedia of the State of New York*, vol. 1 (New York: American Historical Society, 1916), 295–97. "Charles O'Conor," *NYH*, 24 October 1869. Concerning Murphy, Arthur, and Bliss, and the difficulties Hamilton Fish had resisting attempts to use American foreign service posts as dumping grounds for entitled incompetents, see Allan Nevins, *Hamilton Fish: The Inner History of the Grant Administration* (New York: Dodd, Mead and Company, 1936).

2. Concerning the history of occupancy of that post see "List of U.S. Consul Officers, 1789–1939," M587, roll 12, RG 59, National Archives.

3. Marlin Hatch to William Hunter, 1 November 1873, Con. Merida, roll 1.

4. The best discussion of the slow revival of export agriculture after the worst ravages of the Indian rebellion is that found in Lawrence Remmers, "Henequen, the Caste War, and the Economy of Yucatan, 1846–1883: The Roots of Dependence in a Mexican Region," (Ph.D. diss., University of California, Los Angeles, 1981), chapter 6.

5. Rankings were calculated from data provided in, "Statement showing the number of vessels and passengers arriving at and departing from the following ports of Mexico during the year ending June 30, 1875," p. 47 of Julius Skilton's annual commercial report dated 16 December 1875, Con. Mexico, roll 8.

6. Lespinasse to Hunter, 10 December 1874, 20 January 1875, and 24 September 1875, all from Con. Merida, roll 1.

7. Information that James Stephens, born in the 1780s in Ireland, was a gardener comes from the 1850 census, Township of Hoboken, M432 roll 452, p. 551. That he worked for the Stevens family is an inference—he was a gardener, he lived on the

edge of the Stevens property, and the Stevens family employed large numbers of such people to tend their estate. Concerning the latter point, from 1831 there is this observation in the diary of Philip Howe, edited by Allen Nevins in 1936: "The Messrs. Stevens have a large number of men employed laying out the grounds in a very tasteful manner, and erecting a large, light airy building, which is to be called by the classic name of Trivoli." Notes by Basil M. Stevens, microfilm edition of the Stevens Family Papers, roll 45. That James Stephens named his son after the famous lord of the Stevens domain at that time, Robert L. Stevens, who was also the boy's godfather, strengthens the case further. See below.

8. Concerning how the Stevens family acquired and developed their property, see microfilm edition of the Stevens Family Papers, especially notes by Basil M. Stevens, roll 45.

9. The Knickerbockers started playing there in the 1840s according to Irving Leitner, *Diamonds in the Rough* (New York: Abelard-Schuman, 1972), 33.

10. George P. Schreck, great-grandchild of Robert L. Stephens, letter to author, 26 March 1998.

11. For descriptions of Hoboken and Jersey City in these years I rely upon Daniel Van Winkle, *History of the Municipalities of Hudson County, New Jersey, 1630–1923*, vol. 1, *Historical-Biographical* (New York: Lewis Historical Publishing Company, 1924); John Barber and Henry Howe, *Historical Collections of New Jersey: Past and Present* [1868; reprint, New Jersey State Library, 1966]; Brian Danforth, "Hoboken and the Affluent New Yorker's Search for Recreation, 1820–1860," *New Jersey History*, 95(3),133–44 (1977); and "Resources and Manufactures of Jersey City," *MM*, 15(6), 597–98 (December 1846). The only source concerning Robert Stephens having joined a surveying expedition is a statement by his aide in Yucatan, Joseph Byrne, who asserted that "Stephens was in the U.S. Service as civil Engineer or similar capacity engaged in the Survey of the Southern Atlantic coast under I believe then commander Cunningham—probably about 1845 or 6—He was a very skillful marine Engineer + draughtsman . . . ," Joseph Byrne to Alphonse Lespinasse, 21 October 1875, Con. Merida, roll 1. That James Stephens's house was called the "Bolivar House" is attested to by the affidavit of Andrew J. Kenny, 10 June 1935, Claims, and the previously cited communication from George Schreck to the author, in which he recalled that his great-grandfather and great-grandmother were part owners (with James Stephens?) of the "Balover House," Elysian Fields. The Bolivar House was ordered razed by the Executive Committee of the Hoboken Land and Improvement Company in 1897. Basil M. Stevens notes, microfilm edition of the Stevens Family Papers, especially notes by Basil M. Stevens, roll 45.

12. I rely here on Kerby Miller's in-depth study of the backgrounds and attitudes of pre-famine immigrants toward emigration: *Emigrants and Exiles: Ireland and the Irish Exodus to North America* (New York: Oxford University Press, 1985), especially chapter 6.

13. Many sources attest to Stephens being in Cuba during most of the period 1850 to 1870. Only one source states clearly what he was doing there. Based on first- or secondhand information, Nestor Rubio Alpuche wrote in "La emigración extran- jera," *LRdM*, 26 September 1875, that Stephens had been occupied "en Cuba en montar los grandes trenes para elaborar el azúcar . . ." Concerning the need for foreign machinists and their ubiquity, see Laird Bergad, *Cuban Rural Society in the Nineteenth Century* (Princeton: Princeton University Press, 1990), 121–22. That most of those for- eign machinists were Americans is asserted in William Robertson to William Marcy, 7 October 1855, in Con. Havana, roll 30.

14. The meeting in Jersey City is described in *NYH* 28 August 1851, p. 1.

15. Regarding the plight of American engineers in that area, there is: Richard Gibbs to H. R. La Reintrie, 2 January 1869 and 25 January 1869, Con. Havana, roll 52; "Correspondent from Nuevitas," *NYH*, 17 January 1869; "Cuba," *NYH*, 5 March 1869; "Cuba," *NYH*, 13 March 1869; and "Cuba: American Reports from the Field of Revo- lution," *NYH*, 8 May 1869.

16. Napoleon Arango had a plantation named El Destino, according to *NYH*, 5 June 1869, p. 4. That while in Cuba Stephens graduated from engineer to estate ad- ministrator comes from Nestor Rubio Alpuche, "La emigración extranjera," *LRdM*, 26 September 1875. It seems almost certain that Stephens worked for Arango. How else does an American engineer become the intimate of a member of the Camagüey elite?

17. The involvement of the brothers and their father in past independence upris- ings is mentioned in Fermin Peraza Sarausa, *Diccionario biográfico cubano*, vol. 8 (Coral Gables, Florida, 1967), 56; "Cuba: Particulars of General Arango's Assassination," *NYH*, 13 February 1869; and "Names of Persons Arrested at Puerto Príncipe by Order of General Manzaro," *NYH*, 3 March 1855. Napoleon Arango appeared among the names of people not arrested because they were then "fugitive."

18. Concerning the views of the Arangos, particularly Napoleon, see: "Cuba," *NYH*, 23 January 1869; "Cuba," *NYH*, 25 February 1870; "Cuba," *NYH*, 9 April 1870, (paraphrasing Napoleon Arango's "Address to the Cubans"); and Ignacio Agramonte, "Proclama denuncia de la traición de Napoleón Arango," 17 March 1869, reproduced in Juan Jiménez Pastrada, *Ignacio Agramonte: Documentos* (Havana: Editorial de Cien- cias Sociales, 1974), 125–28.

19. The arrest of Robert Stephens is alluded to in "Cuba," *NYH*, 8 May 1869, based upon a letter dated 26 April from their Nuevitas correspondent. That source referred to Stephens as "an American named Robert Sterms, an intimate friend of Jo- rango." Other sources that more clearly identify the American arrested with Napoleon Arango as Robert Stevens (as his name was alternatively spelled) are: "For- eign News: Cuba," *NYTrib*, 29 April 1869; and "Cuba," *NYH*, 5 June 1869, p. 4.

20. "Cuba," *NYH* 5 June 1869, p. 4.

21. In response to his defection, rebels destroyed the estate of Napoleon Arango in April 1870: "Cuba," *NYH*, 7 May 1870, p. 5. Concerning the near-capture of Arango's

family, see "The Cuban Shiloh," *NYH*, 3 February 1870, p. 3. Concerning his having been offered the command of the rebel army, which hardly seems plausible but not impossible, given the desperate straits of the rebel cause, see "Cuba," 5 March 1870. Concerning Arango's defection to the Spanish side, see the following articles from *NYH*: "Cuba," 21 March 1870, p. 7; "Cuba," 31 March 1870; "Cuba," 9 April 1870; "Cuba," 30 April 1870, p. 3; "Cuba," 7 May 1870, p. 5; "Cuba," 19 May 1870; "Cuba," 5 July 1870, p. 5; also see "Cuba: Reported Surrender," *NYTrib*, 18 April 1870, p. 1. Concerning the defection of other rebels, see "The Cuban Revolution," *NYTrib*, 4 March 1870, p. 1. Concerning the execution by their comrades of rebels who wanted to accept Spanish officers of amnesty, see "Foreign News, Cuba," *NYTrib*, 8 April 1870, p. 1; "Cuba," *NYTrib* 12 April 1870, p. 5; "Rebel Atrocities on the Island," *NYH*, 21 February 1871, p. 5. Focusing as I have on the activities of the Arango brothers, I have not had occasion to cite important book-length sources on the war written by Cubans who long ago consigned Napoleon Arango to the niche of traitor of the revolution, though in hindsight reasonable men could argue that he was neither a traitor (in the sense of having betrayed any of his colleagues to the enemy) nor wrong in his judgment of the prospects of the revolution. Those book-length sources, which were very helpful in providing an overview of the long conflict, included: Ramiro Guerra, *Guerra de los 10 años*, 2d ed. (Havana: Editorial de Ciencias Sociales, 1972); Fernando Figueredo, *La Revolución de Yara* (Havana: Instituto del Libro, 1969); Vidal Morales y Morales, *Hombres del 68* (Havana: Editorial de Ciencias Sociales, 1972); and Emilio Soulere, *Historia de la insurreción de Cuba*, 2 vols. (Barcelona: J. Pons, 1879–1880). As Ada Ferrer convincingly argues in *Insurgent Cuba: Race, Nation, and Revolution, 1868–1898* (Chapel Hill: University of North Carolina Press, 1999), though the 1868–1878 insurrection ended in what most rebels considered failure, the long struggle did commence to change race relations profoundly and undermine the viability of slavery on the island of Cuba.

22. Byrne to Lespinasse, 21 October 1875, Con. Merida, roll 1. Early on, the Novelty Iron Works may have been Stephens's employer in Cuba, since they also built sugar-milling machinery for the Cuban market. Concerning such work done at the Novelty Iron Works at that time: "Work at the Machine Shops," *NYH*, 4 August 1861, and "The Novelty Iron Works," *NYTrib*, 30 December 1869. Concerning their sugar-mill work for the Cuban market, see Robert Greenhalgh Albion, *The Rise of the Port of New York* (New York: Charles Scribner's Sons, 1939), 178.

23. "Jersey City: Another Chapter in the History of Our Neighbor," *NYT*, 21 August 1870.

24. In the 1860 census, the occupation of James Stephens was given as porterhouse—I assume he was serving ale, not steaks. Census of the United States, 1860, M653, roll 694, Weehawken Township, Post Office Hoboken, 244. That he might have done so out of the Bolivar House is suggested by the recollections of Andrew Kenny, recorded in 1935: "[W]hen a boy in West Hoboken, I often went down to the Hudson River and knew old Poppy Stevens, of the 'Boliver House', as it was called, at

the northwest corner of the Elysian fields, where he sold sweetmeats to hungry boys who had a few pennies to spend." Affidavit of Andrew J. Kenny, 10 June 1935, Claims.

25. The real-estate transactions are recorded in the following libers of the Hudson County Register's Office in Jersey City, New Jersey: liber 228, p. 38; liber 225, p. 533, liber 244, p. 186. Stephens's arrival at Sisal, Yucatan, on 27 April 1871 is mentioned in "Puerto de Sisal," *LRdM*, 30 April 1871. In 1870, 70 percent of all adults in that village of four thousand were foreign born. A quarter of those were Germans, and another quarter, Irish. (These statistics are calculated from the 1870 Federal Census, M-593, roll 865, Township of West Hoboken.) That mix of German and Irish sometimes proved explosive down in the meadow of Hoboken, as thousands of German weekenders from New York would battle with their Irish counterparts over slights real or imagined. In West Hoboken, early on a favorite alternative site for German picnickers, however, they lived in peace together.

26. That Castro contacted a New York firm to hire an engineer for the pier construction, and that it was Robert Stephens whom they sent, comes from Nestor Rubio Alpuche, "La emigración extranjera," *LRdM*, 26 September 1875. That it was Moller and Thebaud who recruited Stephens comes from Mary Stephens to Ulysses S. Grant, 3 December 1875, Misc. Letters, roll 453.

27. That the pier was too short comes from Lawrence Remmers, "Henequen, the Caste War, and the Economy of Yucatan, 1846-1883: The Roots of Dependence in a Mexican Region," (Ph.D. diss., University of California, Los Angeles, 1981), 653. Andrés Urcelay held the contract: "Indice de escrituras del oficio Núm. 6 de la propiedad de Manuel Avila Maldonado," AGEY Justicia, Caja 86-D.

28. *LRdM*, 7 May 1874, quoted in Remmers, ibid., 636. The characterization of prosperity in Yucatan in the early 1870s, because of increased henequen exports and prices, also comes from Remmers. See pages 719ff, especially p. 736.

29. Palmero's petition for vacant land on which to found Xuxub is communicated in Ministro de Fomento to the governor, 15 November 1869, AGEY Ejecutivo, Caja 173 (one of two dispatches that day). His divorce and money problems—his ex-wife sued for support—are described in "Diligencia de amparo de pobra solicitado por la Señora Manuel Tonzum," AGEY Justicia, roll 83, 1870.

30. My sources for this genealogy of Ramón Aznar include: José María Acosta, *A través de las centurias*, vol. 2 (Merida, 1926), 112-13, 128-30; and "Testamentaria de Dolores Pérez de Aznar [mother of the Aznar brothers]," AGEY Justicia, Caja 155-D, 1886.

31. Concerning Salsipuedes and the Aznars in the Laguna de Terminos, I rely upon: "Testamentaria de Dolores Pérez de Aznar," ibid.; "Protest of Ramón Aznar," 17 May 1890, and the accompanying affidavit of Pablo Garcia dated 20 May 1890, in Misc. Letters, roll 828, 1891; Tomás Aznar [this is not Tomás Aznar of Salsipuedes] and Juan Carbó, *Memoria sobre la conveniencia, utilidad y necesidad de erigir constitucionalmente en estado de la confederación mexicana el antiguo distrito de Campeche. . . .* (Mexico:

Imprenta de Ignacio Cumplido 1861) (especially, Censo de población del Estado de Campeche en 1861, published therein); Louis Fernando Sotelo Regil, *Campeche en la historia*, vol. 2 (Mexico, 1964), 255 (regarding Aznar as 2nd alcalde of Carmen in 1858); Pedro Lavalle, "Establecimientos de campo, propietarios, sirvientes y sus deudas," 1869, in ibid., p. 262 (at that time only eight establishments in all of the state of Campeche had more workers than Salsipuedes); Justo Acevedo, *El Partido de Carmen* (Mexico: Compaña editorial nacional, 1910); John M. Rouse to secretary of state, 9 December 1866, from Con. Carmen, roll 1 (whose account of the movements of García's army lends support to Aznar's later claim to have hosted the insurgents with the resources of Salsipuedes); José del Rosario Gil, 20 September 1852, "Descripción estadística y noticias del distrito de la comandancia military de la Isla de Carmen," reproduced on pages 39–51 of Miguel Civeira Taboada, *Crónicas de la Isla del Carmen* (Campeche, 1968); Arturo Shiels, *Boletín de la Sociedad Mexicana de Geografía é Estadística*, 2a época, tomo II, 1870, republished on pages 51–71 of Civeira Taboada, *Crónicas*.

32. My knowledge of his activities as an importer and retail merchant comes mostly from those newspaper announcements of shipments and sales. That he was among the wealthiest men in Merida—a cut below the top rung, for sure—I conclude from several lists of forced loans of the sort the state imposed on businessmen from time to time to raise funds for revolutions and the war against the Indians. Ramón Aznar usually was required to pay much less than the top four or five wealthiest individuals in the state, but more than most others on those lists. For those lists of forced loans, see: "Nomina de los señores prestamistas que han sido cuotizados conforme al artículo 2 del decreto de 3 del presente," *LRdP*, 6 April 1872 (Aznar ranked 20); "Relación de los individuos á quienes la comisión prestamista ha pagado proporcionalmente un quince por ciento del préstamo que cada uno de ellos satisfizó conforme al decreto de 22 de junio del año próximo pasado," *LRdP*, 3 April 1868 (Aznar ranked 4 out of 120).

33. Aznar's purchase of the Chablé hacienda and his activities at the place are detailed in Protest of Ramón Aznar, 17 May 1890; Miscellaneous affidavits concerning the claim of Ramón Aznar, 2 June 1890; both from Misc. Letters, roll 828. For a description of the place under a previous owner, see "Intestado de Don José Dolores Zetina," AGEY Justicia, Caja 72, 1863.

34. Stephens's contract with Ramón Aznar is described in varying detail in the affidavit of Ramón Aznar, 6 April 1876, Misc. Letters, roll 462; and in Ramón Aznar to Mary Stephens, 3 March 1876, File of Evidence Not Used, Claims. In the latter document Aznar told Mary that though Palmero had approached him he didn't want to buy Xuxub since he had no one to manage it. Robert Stephens advocated a partnership so enthusiastically, however, that Aznar changed his mind.

35. Stephens was in Jersey City granting his wife power of attorney over all his affairs there on 27 June 1872, according to liber 246, p. 121, Hudson County Register's

Office, Jersey City, New Jersey. The text of that grant mentions that his father was already deceased. Affidavit of Ramón Aznar, 6 April 1876, Misc. Letters, roll 462, and affidavit of Mary Ann Stephens, 4 March 1876 (same source). Aznar said that Stephens started out at Xuxub on 31 July. Mary, however, recalled that her husband took up residence there on 5 July. In this matter I would trust the wife's memory.

36. For the census of Puntachen in 1869, Genera Cevera, "Estado que manifiesta el número de habitantes . . . ," 25 December 1869, AGEY Ejecutivo, Caja 173. The only description I have found of the place is Antonio Cisneros Cámara to the governor, 8 September 1881, in *LRdP*, 21 September 1881.

37. On maps the lagoon has often been called Laguna Yalahau, though recent maps of the Mexican Secretaria de Programación y Presupuesto label it Laguna Conil. Old maps sometimes labeled it Bahía de Conil. Most often they did not label it at all. In all of the documents I have consulted concerning the period about which I write, I only found that water named once, as Río Conil. So I'll call it Conil. Concerning the pre-hispanic background of Conil, see Anthony P. Andrews, "El antiguo puerto Maya de Conil," *Estudios de Cultura Maya* 22 (2002), 135–49.

38. Robert Stephens to Mary Stephens, 2 October 1873, Claims.

39. Ramón Aznar claimed that during the first three years Stephens managed the estate, the value of the farm increased 50 percent per annum, surely a rough estimate since it includes Aznar's estimation of the price he could receive for the property were he to sell it at that time. See the affidavit of Ramón Aznar, 6 April 1876, Misc. Letters, roll 462. As for Stephens sending his wife money and alcohol, see Robert Stephens to Mary Stephens, 2 October 1873, Claims.

40. The arrival of a mestizo majordomo is mentioned in Stephens to Stephens, ibid. The trip home is mentioned in Ramón Aznar to Mary Stephens, 3 March 1876, File of Evidence Not Used, Claims.

41. Stephens's intentions are revealed in Stephens to Stephens, 2 October 1873, Claims. That Stephens actually went to Belize City in December of that year is indicated in "Gacetilla: Noticias de Belice y Chan Santa Cruz," *LRdM*, 6 January 1874.

42. Byrne arrived at Xuxub on 15 March 1875. Byrne to Aznar, 1 November 1875, Con. Merida, roll 1. The only hint of what Byrne actually did for a living at Xuxub comes from Joseph Duff to John Foster, 26 July 1892, Misc. Letters, roll 844. Duff therein referred to Byrne as the bookkeeper at Xuxub. By August drought appeared to guarantee poor harvests of cane and corn that year, though some areas got rain that alleviated their concerns somewhat. See "Correspondencia del interior, Tizimin," *LRdM*, 4 October 1875; "Las lluvias," *LRdP*, 30 July 1875; and "Aristófanes," *LRdP*, 17 August 1874. In fact around Tizimin the harvests turned out poor after all. See "Caña dulce," *LRdM*, 23 December 1875; and "Aristófanes, Correspondencia del interior, Tizimin," *LRdP*, 6 February 1876. Concerning their expectations of the value of Xuxub and amounts invested, see the affidavit of Ramón Aznar, 6 April 1876, Misc. Letters,

roll 462; Ramón Aznar to Mary Stephens, 3 March 1876, File of Evidence Not Used, Claims; other sources could be cited, though regardless of their putative authors, they appear to have been prepared by Ramón Aznar.

CHAPTER 2: A DANGEROUS PATH

a. Gasca related all of this to the American consul Lespinasse weeks after the raid on Xuxub. I infer that Gasca went back to Holbox after his rejection by Montilla, because in his deposition, events up to the rejection are related in the first person, while events after the rejection are not, suggesting that Gasca was no longer on the scene in Puntachen on 11 and 12 October. Affidavit of Ramón Gasca, Holbox, 18 January 1876, Misc. Letters, roll 462. A slightly different version of this affidavit is found with Con. Merida.

1. Stephens to Lespinasse, 29 June 1875, Con. Merida, roll 1.

2. Regarding the National Guard at Puntachen, and Montilla's appointment as commander, see: "Batallon 17 Guardia Nacional, Partido de Sisal, Estado que manifiesta la fuerza que tiene el expresado . . . 21 December 1870," *LRdP*, 28 December 1870; "Batallon 2 Núm 17 de Seguridad Pública, Estado que manifiesta la fuerza que tiene el expresado . . . ," *LRdP*, 27 December 1871. "Diligencias practicadas en comision del H. Tribunal Superior de Justicia contra el C. Baltazar Montilla . . . , Juzagado 2 del crimen," AGEY Justicia, Caja 110, 1876. The last source discusses, in retrospect, the bases of Montilla's military authority, concluding that although he was chosen on 15 May 1875, he actually became a commander of the National Guard some days or weeks later, since his selection had to be communicated to and approved in Merida. Thus, when he undertook military actions in May, he would have done so as a civil official acting under appropriate regulations governing the security of settlements, etc. Upon that issue hung the question of who should investigate the complaint against Montilla—a civilian court or the military.

3. Baltazar Montilla to the governor, 23 June 1875, in *LRdP*, 9 July 1875. The route taken by the exploratory party is mentioned in Tribunal Superior de Justicia, Yucatan, "Fallo de las diligencias practicadas en comision del H. Tribunal Superior de Justicia contra el C. Baltazar Montilla," 30 December 1875, Annex 30, Mexican Reply Memorial, Claims. Though Montilla and Mexican investigators would always later claim that that party did not cross through Xuxub, numerous statements taken in conjunction with a subsequent incursion mention that Montilla's men twice passed through the estate, several weeks apart.

4. That Montilla requested armed workers from Xuxub, and Stephens's response, are given in Mary Stephens to Ulysses S. Grant, 3 December 1875, Misc. Letters, roll 453.

5. Accounts of what transpired during this second expedition out of Puntachen are found in: Montilla to the governor, 23 June 1875, in *LRdP*, 9 July 1875; Mary

Stephens to Grant, ibid.; Tribunal Superior de Justicia, "Fallo," 30 December 1875, Annex 30, Mexican Reply Memorial, Claims; Montilla to Andrés Urcelay, n.d., reproduced in Ancona to Lespinasse, 9 October 1875, Con. Merida, roll 1; affidavit of Cesario Arguelles, 30 January 1876, Con. Merida, roll 1 (it was Arguelles who provided the detail that the road or wide path that was cut was cut in reverse—not going to the well, but coming back); Stephens to Lespinasse, 29 June 1875, Misc. Letters, roll 462; Mary Stephens to John J. Cadwalader, 24 February 1876, Misc. Letters, roll 453; Mary Stephens to William Evarts, 4 April 1877, Misc. Letters, roll 483; Byrne to Aznar, 1 November 1875, Con. Merida, roll 1. No two sources (not even from the same individual) give the same account of events. Robert Stephens was too brief in his account. Montilla lied. Questioned by Mexican authorities, some sources said one thing, when questioned by Americans, another. Mary Stephens appears to have telescoped events, putting into one encounter things that probably happened on different days.

6. Concerning Montilla's aliases and criminal past, see: "Exhorto del C. Juez de 1a instancia de Campeche relativo á la causa seguida á Miramón Montilla por hurto," AGEY Justicia, roll 92, 1872; A. Mendoza to Comandante militar del estado, n.d., AGEY Ejecutivo, Caja 66, 1870; Ramón Aznar to Sr. Redactor de *La Revista de Mérida*, 11 October 1875, published within Nestor Rubio Alpuche, "Los medios de defensa," *LRdM*, 12 October 1875; Bartolomé Heredia, Secretario del Juzgado de lo criminal de este departamento judicial, 2 April 1869, copied by Thomas Casasus, Belgian Consul in Campeche, 12 February 1876, and by A. Garcia Buela, Secretario del H. Ayuntamiento de esta capital [Merida], 14 March 1876, both found in Misc. Letters, roll 462. Had Montilla really been in jail for murder, it seems likely that one of the above-cited sources would have said so. That rumors circulated to that effect, however, I conclude from something Mary Stephens once wrote: "Mr. Montilla was . . . in the Chaingan for Murder and robing. That every one knows heir in Merida," Mary Stephens to John Cadwalader, 26 February 1876, Misc., roll 458. The Urcelay payments to Montilla are mentioned in the affidavits of Adolfo Correa, 11 December 1875, and Ramón Gasca, 18 January 1876, both from Misc. Letters, roll 462. Gasca was a reliable informant on this matter. He had worked many years for the Urcelays and had on two occasions transmitted Montilla's receipt of payment to the judge in Holbox.

7. They were children of José Nicolás Urcelay Canton and Rita Peniche Sabina, who had yet another son, Enrique. The latter, however, does not figure in any of the events with which this book is concerned. For an outline of the Urcelay family history I rely upon José María Valdes Acosta, *A través de las centurias*, vol. 2 (Merida, 1926), 502–7.

8. Concerning the prewar land grab, see Robert Patch, "Decolonization, the Agrarian Problem, and the Origins of the Caste War, 1812–1847," in *Land, Labor and*

Capital in Modern Yucatan: Essays in Regional History and Political Economy, eds. Jeffery Brannon and Gilbert Joseph (Tuscaloosa: University of Alabama Press, 1991), 51–82; and Terry Rugeley, *Yucatán's Maya Peasantry and the Origins of the Caste War* (Austin: University of Texas Press, 1996). The best source concerning the colonial-era transition towards commercial agriculture is Robert Patch, *Maya and Spaniard in Yucatan, 1648–1812* (Stanford: Stanford University Press, 1993).

9. For this general perspective upon the elite of Yucatan in the wake of the War of the Castes, I rely principally upon Lawrence Remmers, "Henequen, the Caste War, and the Economy of Yucatan, 1846–1883: The Roots of Dependence in a Mexican Region," (Ph.D. diss., University of California, Los Angeles, 1981), chapter 6; Pedro Bracamonte y Sosa, *Amos y sirvientes: Las haciendas de Yucatán, 1789–1860* (Merida: Universidad Autónoma de Yucatan, 1993); Hernán Menéndez Rodríguez, *Iglesia y poder: Proyectos sociales, alianzas políticas, y económicas en Yucatán (1857–1917)* (Mexico: Editorial Nuestra América and Consejo Nacional para la Cultura y las Artes, 1995); Allen Wells, *Yucatán's Gilded Age: Haciendas, Henequen and International Harvester, 1860–1915* (Albuquerque: University of New Mexico Press, 1985); and Allen Wells and Gilbert Joseph, *Summer of Discontent, Seasons of Upheaval: Elite Politics and Rural Insurgency in Yucatán, 1876–1915* (Stanford, Stanford University Press, 1996). The only Urcelay of prominence at the turn of the century appears to have been Carlos Urcelay Martínez, a major henequen exporter and son of Juan Antonio Urcelay Peniche.

10. F. Gil, "El partido de Cozumel," *El Constitucional*, 23 February 1863. For a discussion of the sugar scarcity in Merida markets and the causes of that scarcity, see "El Azúcar," *EP*, 1 March 1861.

11. Manuel Castilla to Jefe Superior de las Armas, 20 February 1863, AGEY Ejecutivo, Caja 137; Felipe de Jesús Moreno to the governor, 28 December 1862, AGEY Ejecutivo, Caja 127, 1861; José M. Iturralde to the governor, 22 December 1862, AGEY Ejecutivo, Caja 131, 1862.

12. That San José Majas belonged to Urcelay by March 1868 I surmise from Santiago Medina to the governor, 26 March 1868, AGEY Ejecutivo, Caja 172. The document in question reports that some fugitives found their way to San José Majas in order to ask Nicolás Urcelay to assist them in turning themselves over to authorities. A comprehensive report on various disputes in the Puntachen region, which appears to date from October 1868, more directly indicates that Nicolás Urcelay was then the owner of San José. See Olegario Molina to the governor, [October] 1868, AGEY Ejecutivo, Caja 169. That San José was a cattle ranch, not a sugar estate, I infer from its description in "Autos de juicio de intestado del C. Manuel Urcelay, 1883," AGEY Justicia, Caja 138, 1883.

13. Regarding that property, Yohaltun, see "Testamento de Pedro José Campos, 1872," AGEY Justicia, Caja 94, 1872.

14. Their petition is detailed in Ministro de Fomento, Mexico City, to the governor, 15 November 1869, AGEY Ejecutivo, Caja 173 (one of two dispatches on the same

date). Seven years earlier Manuel and Nicolás had done much the same thing—petition for unoccupied lands out east on which to establish a plantation. They argued that their operations on that stretch of deserted coast would bolster the security of the eastern frontier from the threat of hostile Indians and would "serve as vanguard to extirpate that barbarous race or reduce it to order and to obedience and respect for legitimate authority." But the Urcelays already owned so much land in Yucatan and others had their eye on the stretch of coast they sought. That time they weren't successful. See Manuel Urcelay to the president of Mexico, 15 July 1862, AGEY Ejecutivo, Caja 130; and Manuel Castilla to the governor, 26 September 1862, AGEY Ejecutivo, Caja 132.

15. Such was the opinion of chief of the Tizimin district. See M. Sierra Arce to the governor, 13 October 1868, AGEY Ejecutivo, Caja 172.

16. The death of Urcelay's wife in 1870, the number of his children, and their ages in 1883 are documented in "Autos de juicio de intestado del C. Manuel Urcelay . . . ," AGEY Justicia, Caja 138. Since Manuel wouldn't be living at Solferino after all, he hired a manager to run the place in his absence, just as Ramón Aznar would do with Xuxub. See "Juicio ordinario por el apoderado de Don Juan Froilan Saenz contra el intestado de Don Manuel Urcelay Peniche," AGEY Justicia, Caja 142-B.

17. Concerning the mishap at the Progreso docks, see the complaint of Wenceslao Miguel Encalada against Andrés Urcelay, c. November 1872, AGEY Justicia, Cajas 94 and 92. The court rendered a split decision in the case. They held the boat owner responsible for the loss of the boat, since no one employed violence to force him to load, and then not to unload, the boat. On the other hand, once the boat was loaded, it was technically "in navigation"—on its way, that is—and the verbal contract between Encalada and the Urcelays stipulated, the court believed, that while in navigation Encalada would be responsible for any damages sustained by the boat, but not by the cargo. Mention of a dispute between Stephens and the Urcelays regarding the machinery he installed is found in the affidavit of Adolfo Correa, 11 December 1875, Misc. Letters, roll 462 (Correa, who helped Stephens install the equipment, said it worked fine); Byrne to Aznar, 18 October 1875, Min. Mexico, roll 53; Mary Stephens to Ulysses S. Grant, 3 December 1875, Misc. Letters, roll 453.

18. Such complaints against the Urcelays are found in O. Molina to the governor, [October] 1868, AGEY Ejecutivo, Caja 169; and M. F. Rosado to the governor, 23 October 1877, AGEY Ejecutivo, Caja 200, 1877.

19. "Juicio verbal seguido por el C. Benito Pérez, contra el C. Ramón Aznar, por suma de pesos, Juzgado 4 de Paz, Inicio el 29 de Octubre 1879," AGEY Justicia, Caja 121-A.

20. Complaints are mentioned in O. Molina to the governor, [October] 1868, AGEY Ejecutivo, Caja 169. See also dispatch 119, L. Yrigoyen to the governor, 26 July 1878; and M. Romero Ancona to Consejo de Gobierno, both from AGEY Ejecutivo,

Caja 203, 1878. As for Stephens having been called upon to help locals, see Lespinasse to Julius A. Skilton, 4 November 1875, Con. Merida, roll 1.

21. The terms of the peace agreement, both preliminary and final, are detailed in: Simon Medina to the governor, 28 July 1859; and José Antonio Garcia and Juan José Villanueva to the governor, 2 August 1859 (which included translations from Maya to Spanish of José María Pérez, Jacino Moguel, Perfecto Sánchez, and Carlos Alaya to the governor and Jefe Político of Tizimin, 3 August 1859 [a mistake for 3 July 1859]), both from AGEY Ejecutivo, Caja 120. See also Pedro Acereto and Vicente Marin to the governor, 3 October 1859; and Pedro Acereto, Vicente Marin, and Teodoro Villanueva to the governor, 2 October 1859, both from El Constitucional, 10 October 1859. For a description of Kantunilkin at the time the peace agreement was signed, see Nicanor Contreras Elizalde to the governor, 18 October 1859, El Constitucional, 21 October 1859.

22. Their protests against the Urcelays are mentioned in O. Molina to the governor, [October] 1868, AGEY Ejecutivo, Caja 169; and M. Sierra Arce to the governor, 13 October 1868, AGEY Ejecutivo, Caja 172. Persistent concerns about the loyalty and peacefulness of those Indians is found in sources such as Sierra Arce to the governor, 2 October 1863, AGEY Ejecutivo, Caja 136; Molina to the governor, [October] 1868; Sierra Arce to the governor, 4 November 1867, AGEY Ejecutivo, Caja 168; Sierra Arce to the governor, 13 October 1868; and José de Vargas to the governor, 22 August 1871, in LRdP, 11 September 1871.

23. For a summary of the expedition see Don Dumond, The Machete and the Cross: Campesino Rebellion in Yucatán (Lincoln: University of Nebraska Press, 1997), 317–19. That Andrés Urcelay carried the orders to recruit volunteers there is mentioned in Cipriano Rivas, "To the Editor of La Revista de Mérida," LRdM, 26 July 1872. That Andrés led them on to Kantunilkin, and that Nicolás brought his workers, is mentioned in Juan de la Cruz Valle to the governor, 30 July 1872, in LRdP, 4 September 1872. A day-by-day account of the experiences of the expedition, including mention that deserters went back and attacked Kantunilkin itself, is provided in Nicolás Urcelay, "Itinerario de la marcha de las tropas sobre los indios bárbaros," 19 August 1872, in LRdP, 26 August 1872. Humanitarian assistance, namely two hundred pesos, was channeled to Kantunilkin through Nicolás Urcelay according to Vicente Mariscal and Eligio Ancona to the Comandante military of Kantunil, 31 October 1872, and Juan de la Cruz Valle to the governor, 12 November 1872, both in LRdP, 22 November 1872.

24. Concerning this episode in July 1873, known as Coronado's revolt, I rely upon primary documents, there being little published about it. Those documents include: Francisco Canton to the governor, 9 July 1873; and Francisco Canton, "Relación de los indígenas vecinos del pueblo de Chichimilá, que con sus familias se han presentado al Comandante de aquel punto," 9 July 1873, (both in LRdP, 14 July 1873); P. Osorio to the governor, 19 July 1873 (two dispatches that date, both in LRdM, 23 July 1873); F. M.

Cossa to the governor, 29 July 1873; Francisco Canton to the governor, 29 July 1873; and P. Osorio to the governor, 30 July 1873 (all three in *LRdP*, 1 August 1873); P. Osorio to the governor, 31 July 1873, and again on 2 August 1873, (both in *LRdP*, 4 August 1873).

25. The Catalan was Miguel Pifarré, and concerning him I rely upon: "Denuncia de José Pifarré contra el Juez de Paz de Puntachen," AGEY Justicia, Caja 92; and "Inventario de los bienes de D. Miguel Pifarré, 1879," AGEY Justicia, Caja 120, 1879. That Dzaptun was deserted as late as 1859 is recorded in P. Acereto to the governor, 28 November 1859, in *El Constitucional*, 2 December 1859. José Solar from Tizimin took over the ranch named Tejas, according to F. S. Pérez, "Correspondencia de *La Revista de Mérida*, Tizimin," 3 February 1873, in *LRdM*, 12 February 1873. Solar's Rancho Tejas is described in an advertisement announcing its sale in March, 1875, "Positiva ganga, venta del rancho Tejas," *LRdM*, 1 April 1875; and in M. Sierra Arce to the governor, 12 January 1872, in *LRdM*, 17 January 1872; and, at the time of its sale under a previous owner, in "Remate de los bienes . . . de . . . D. José Gómez, 4 January 1869," in *LRdP*, 6 January 1869. That Solar had a foreign partner in his logging operations comes from "Correspondencia del interior. Tizimin. 20 November 1876," in *LRdM*, 30 November 1876.

26. Concerning the size of Axnal, see "Testamentaria de Dolores Pérez de Aznar [mother of the Aznar brothers]," AGEY Justicia, Caja 155-D, 1886. Glimpses of what Tomás Aznar was doing out at Axnal are drawn from a set of letters, dated between 1842 and 1847, from Tomás to his brother or father in Merida, as well as from receipts of his transactions with others in the region, copies of which were kindly provided to me by Michel Antochiw. The letter from which I have quoted is: Tomás Aznar to Alonso Aznar, Axnal, 15 January 1847. Tomás Aznar's logwood work is also alluded to in Pedro Regil de Estrada to the Secretary of State, 15 January 1845, Con. Merida, roll 1.

27. Mexican historians have pointed out that as ubiquitous and important as was the office of jefe político, it remains little studied and, probably, little understood. My brief description of the powers and perquisites of the jefe político, or district chief, in Yucatan is not confined strictly to their legal duties and powers. Rather, I rely upon evidence concerning what district chiefs actually could and did get away with. That is not to say that the almost dictatorial powers of the district chief were never successfully challenged in particular cases in courts. One of the best discussions of the nature of the office in another Mexican state (with seemingly little applicability to Yucatan in the period about which I write, however) is Romana Falcón, "Force and the Search for Consent: The Role of the Jefaturas Políticas of Coahuila in National State Formation," in *Everyday Forms of State Formation: Revolution and the Negotiation of Rule in Modern Mexico*, eds. Gilbert Joseph and Daniel Nungent (Durham: Duke University Press, 1994), 107–34.

28. The sources for my brief history of the administration of the northeast are: F.

Gil, "El partido de Cozumel," *El Constitucional*, 23 February 1863; M. Sierra Arce to the governor, 2 October 1863, AGEY Ejecutivo, Caja 136; "Imperio Mexicano, Secretaria de la prefectura política del departamento de Yucatan, división territorial del departamento de Yucatan, propuesta por la Prefectura política y mandada observar provisionalmente por el Excmo. Sr. Comisario Imperial de la Península con fecha 6 del corriente . . . ," *Periódico oficial del departamento de Yucatán*, 25 September 1865; El Prefecto Político de Yucatán to Sr. Comisario Imperial de la 7a división, 29 September 1866, AGEY Ejecutivo, Caja 163; Secretaria general de gobierno del Estado libre y soberano de Yucatán, Notice, in *LRdP*, 28 April 1869, 1; Notice in *LRdP*, 26 January 1872, 1; Genaro Cervera to the governor, 24 June 1870, AGEY Ejecutivo, Caja 66, 1870; "Decree of the 5th Legislature of the Free and Sovereign State of Yucatan, Decree #50, 19 March 1875," in *LRdP*, 22 March 1875.

29. Ramón Aznar, more experienced and astute in the ways of real estate and worker recruitment, explained these other consequences in Aznar to Mary Stephens, 3 March 1876, File of Evidence Not Used, Claims.

CHAPTER 3: PROTECTION

a. The most detailed account of those moments and of events of the rest of the day is Byrne to the editor of *La Unión Liberal*, 22 October 1875, a copy of which was found in Con. Merida, and Byrne to Aznar, 18 October 1875, Min. Mexico, roll 53. The only other eyewitness accounts of those hours at Xuxub on 12 October are found in the affidavit of Pascual Koyoc, 7 December 1875, and the affidavit of Francisco Hernández, 7 December 1875, both from Misc. Letters, roll 462.

1. Record No. 5, New York Superior Court Record Bundle No. 63, New York Regional Office National Archives.

2. Peon Rivas y Peon to the governor, 20 December 1863, AGEY Ejecutivo, Caja Sin Número, Distintos Años, Sin Clasificar. The position of the U.S. regarding forced loans and extraordinary taxes in Mexico was complicated and shifting. See Frederick Dunn, *The Diplomatic Protection of Americans in Mexico* (New York: Columbia University Press, 1933), chapter 5. Dunn points out that the opposition of American officials to forced loans softened considerably when they favored the revolutionaries or regime in question (e.g., Benito Juarez). At other junctures, the U.S. representatives argued vigorously for immunity from forced loans for its citizens in Mexico. See Daniel Cosío Villegas, *The United States Versus Porfirio Díaz*, trans. Nettie Lee Benson (Lincoln: University of Nebraska Press, 1963), 121ff.; Donathon Olliff, *Reforma Mexico and the United States: A Search for Alternatives to Annexation, 1854–1861* (University, Alabama: The University of Alabama Press, 1981), 105ff.

3. Concerning Aznar's passport renewal, see Lespinasse to Skilton, Mlr, Volume of Correspondence for 1870 through 1876. Minister Foster responded to Lespinasse's query about whether he should renew Aznar's passport in Foster to Skilton, 12 July

1875, Mlr. In that note to Skilton, Foster said: "I would be very reluctant to issue passports to persons [naming Aznar and another] who have been naturalized as citizens of the United States, had left the country for many years, did not expect to return, and had all their property and interest in this [i.e., Mexico]. Such applications should not be encouraged. American citizenship involves burdens and duties as well as benefits." Several days later, however, Foster renewed Aznar's passport: Foster to Skilton, 16 July 1875; and Foster to Skilton, 19 July 1875, both from Mlr. With his claim of 6 April 1876, Aznar provided evidence of having matriculated with the Ministry of Foreign Relations on 14 July 1875. Ramón Aznar, affidavit of 6 April 1876, Misc. Letters, roll 462.

4. Lespinasse to Ancona, 12 August 1875, Con. Merida, roll 1.

5. Good summaries of the change of governments in Yucatan during this period are found in Serapio Baqueiro, *Reseña geográfica, histórica, y estadística del estado de Yucatán* (Mexico City, 1881), 155–56; Albino Acereto, "Historia política desde el descubrimiento europeo hasta 1920," in *Enciclopedia yucatanense*, vol. 3. (Mexico, 1947); and Laurens Ballard Perry, *Juarez and Díaz: Machine Politics in Mexico* (Dekalb: Northern Illinois University Press, 1978), 101–6.

6. Concerning the plagiarizing of Ancona's novels, there is "Eligio Ancona, Plagio," *LRdM*, 10 November 1891. My summary of Ancona's career comes from Edmundo Bolio, *Diccionario histórico, geográfico, y biográfico de Yucatán* (Mexico, 1945), 25–27. See also Ukib Espadas Ancona, "Eligio Ancona—Liberal integro (1836–1893)," *Boletín de la Escuela de Ciencias Antropológicas de la Universidad de Yucatán*, 14(84), 26–37 (1987). Concerning partial acquiescence of Ancona and other republican liberals to the imperial regime in Yucatan, see Menéndez, *Iglesia y poder*, 47–58.

7. Urcelay's appointment was reported in *LRdP*, 18 November 1874, p. 1. See also Ancona to Jefe político del partido de esta capital, 17 August 1875; and Ancona and J. Hubbe to Lespinasse, 17 August 1875; both in Con. Merida, roll 1. Various communications between Ancona and the administrator of the Customs House of Progreso also contain relevant information, dated 23, 25, 26, and 27 August 1875, from Claims, Contestación [Mexican Reply Memorial], Anexo 7, 8, 9, 10.

8. Sources for the shooting on 15 November 1870 at Komchen include: Yanuario Manzanilla to the governor, 17 November 1870; and Ignacio Gómez to the governor, 17 November 1870, both in *LRdP*, 18 November 1870. See also Gómez to the governor, 23 November 1870, *LRdP*, 25 November 1870; Manzanilla to the governor, 26 November 1870, *LRdP*, 30 November 1870. Sources for the Xluch dispute, and others involving the Urcelays in that neighborhood, are: "Juicio de revisión intentado por el Lic. D. Julian Carrillo con poder de Vicente Yam contra su amo D. Andrés Urcelay," AGEY Justicia, Caja 71, 1863; "Juicio verbal seguido por el agente defensor de naturales contra los SS. Don Manuel Urselay y su hermano Andrés por un solar de la propiedad de María Urzula Pecha . . . ," 19 July 1865, AGEY Justicia, Caja 77-A, 1865; Manzanilla to the governor, 17 November 1870; Gómez to the governor, 17 November

1870; Gómez to the governor, 23 November 1870; Manzanilla to the governor, 26 November 1870; "Diligencias de aprobación de la mensura de las tierras de la hacienda San Ysidro y su anexa Dzontilá de Don Manuel Urcelay," AGEY Justicia, Caja 80-A, 1866; parts of various files concerning the conflict between Juan Peon (later Andrés and Manuel Urcelay) and residents of Noh Luch, AGEY Justicia, Caja 61, 1859; "Juicios seguidos por los heredores de Pablo Pacab y Rosa Chan sobre la propiedad del rancho Noh-luch," AGEY Justicia, Caja 87, 1870; "Autos de la mensura de las tierras de la hacienda Xcanantun de la propiedad de Don Andrés Urcelay Peniche, 1859," AGEY Justicia, roll 38; "Juicio ordinario promovido por los CC. Manuel y Andrés Urcelay sobre propiedad del rancho Noh Luch, 27 April 1868," AGEY Justicia, roll 38; "Artículo promovido por el apoderado del Lic. D. Juan Peón á fin de que los vecinos del rancho Nohluch le presten los servicios á que esten obligados . . . ," AGEY Justicia, roll 38.

9. The matter of the unwanted worker and a plot either to kill Stephens and/or burn down the estate is very sketchily recounted in Mary Stephens's 3 December 1875 letter, cited above; more fully, but many years later, in Ramón Aznar's somewhat confused affidavit of 1892 (Ramón Aznar, affidavit, January 1892, Misc. Letters, roll 832; and most contemporaneously, "D. Roberto Stephens," UL, 23 October 1875, Con. Merida, roll 1.

10. Mary Stephens to Ulysses S. Grant, 3 December 1875, Misc. Letters, roll 453.

11. Ibid.

12. Nestor Rubio Alpuche, "La emigración extranjera," LRdM, 26 September 1875, and the continuation of that editorial on 30 September 1875.

13. "Respuestas á la prensa," LRdP, 8 October 1875.

14. Ancona to Lespinasse, 9 October 1875, in Con. Merida, roll 1. There is a bit of confusion over the date of this letter. In most copies of the governor's communication, it was dated 9 October; when published in the official press, however, it was dated 12 October. It appears that 9 October is the correct date.

15. Nestor Rubio Alpuche, "Los medios de defensa," LRdM, 12 October 1875.

16. Ramón Aznar, letter to the editor of La Revista de Mérida, 11 October 1875, in LRdM, 12 October 1875.

17. "D. Ramón Aznar," probably from La Unión Liberal, probably 13 October 1875, a clipping of which article was found among Con. Merida, roll 1.

18. Lespinasse to Ancona, 13 October 1875, Con. Merida, roll 1.

19. "La Cuestion Stephens," LRdP, 15 October 1875.

20. Baltazar Montilla, "Letter to the Editor," 8 October 1875, in LRdM, 17 October 1875.

CHAPTER 4: BETWEEN STRENGTH AND WEAKNESS
a. Montilla's version of what he knew, and when he knew it, is contained in Baltazar Montilla to the governor, 15 October 1875, in LRdP, 20 October 1875. He stated

that "around 11 a.m. I received positive news that an armed force of rebel Indians had taken possession of Rancho Xuxub, arriving up to Puntatunich, putting this settlement in great alarm." Others suggested that Montilla had been told earlier that morning, which is not inconsistent with his own statement—i.e., that only around eleven o'clock did he receive "positive" news. Ramón Gasca, in his affidavit cited above, stated that Montilla was informed between nine and ten that morning by a worker who fled Xuxub. That would appear consistent with the report of Adolfo Correa that while he was in Chiquila, some miles west of Puntachen, a boy who came from Puntachen told him at around eleven o'clock that Xuxub had been invaded; (affidavit of Adolfo Correa, 11 December 1875, Misc. Letters, roll 462). That Justice of the Peace Morales had gone out that morning to Xuxub and returned to Puntachen carrying news of the invasion is mentioned in only one source: Domingo Sierra to (?), 19 October 1875, in *LRdP*, 22 October 1875. Sierra's report is second- or thirdhand, conveyed to him by men on a customs patrol of the coast. Still, that Commander Montilla declined to mention just who had provided him with "positive news"—reports of frontier invasions were usually very specific in that regard—inclines me to believe it was Morales and that Morales's trip out to Xuxub that morning was somehow awkward for Montilla.

b. The rebuffed pleas to rush to aid Xuxub are mentioned in the affidavits of Manuel Alvarez and Adolfo Correa, both of Holbox, taken by Consul Lespinasse on 11 December 1875, Misc. Letters, roll 462, accompanying Ramón Aznar's affidavit and claim dated 6 April 1876.

1. Lespinasse to Ancona, 19 October 1875; Ancona to Lespinasse, 20 October 1875; both from Con. Merida, roll 1.

2. Byrne telegraphically describes his combat career in Byrne to Lespinasse, 21 October 1875, Con. Merida, roll 1. The list of battles he participated in is consistent with records of the regiments in which he said he served, for which I consulted Frederick Phisterer, comp., *New York in the War of the Rebellion 1861 to 1865* (Albany: Weed, Parsons and Company, 1890).

3. Byrne to Lespinasse, 21 October 1875, Con. Merida, roll 1.

4. "D. Roberto Stephens," *UL*, 23 October 1875, Con. Merida, roll 1.

5. Joseph Byrne, "To the Editor of *La Unión Liberal*," 22 October 1875, found with dispatch 19, 13 November 1875, vol. 2, consular dispatches from Merida. (Microfilm copies of the Merida dispatches do not include the complete copy of this article.)

6. "*La Unión Liberal*," *LRdP*, 27 October 1875.

7. That may be why Lespinasse's first communication to Skilton concerning the Stephens matter was never included in subsequent compilations of records of the case. Lespinasse had been so indiscreet as to acknowledge that he had, upon the consul general's instructions, collected $12.50 each for two passport renewals and forwarded the money to the consul general's "lady." That for those same passports

Skilton turned in only $10.00 each comes from Foster to Skilton, 19 July 1875, Mlr, vol. 1870-1876.

8. Skilton's impressive record of corruption in office is detailed in: Foster to Thompson, 7 July 1877, Min. Mexico, roll 56; Foster to Skilton, 1 March 1880, Min. Mexico, roll 65; Foster to Evarts, 12 June 1879, Min. Mexico, roll 63.

9. Foster to Skilton, 11 September 1875, Mlr, vol. 1870-1876. It was with little urgency that back at the end of August, Consul Lespinasse had communicated with his superior about the problems of Robert Stephens. To a dispatch otherwise dealing with the routine matter of a passport renewal, Lespinasse appended the protest of Robert Stephens and copies of the related communications he'd already had with the governor of Yucatan. Lespinasse to Skilton, 31 August 1875, Mlr, vol. 1870-1876.

10. For Foster's life prior to his occupying the Mexican Legation, I rely upon John Watson Foster, *Diplomatic Memoirs*, 2 vols. (Boston: Houghton Mifflin Co., 1909). The quote is from vol. 1, p. 4. A good overview of Foster's life and career is provided in the only biography written of the man: Michael J. Devine, *John W. Foster: Politics and Diplomacy in the Imperial Era, 1873-1917* (Athens: Ohio University Press, 1981).

11. Good discussions of this shift in American designs on Mexico can be found in J. Fred Rippy, *The United States and Mexico* (New York: Alfred A. Knopf, 1926), especially chapters 14 and 15; and James Morton Callahan, *American Foreign Policy in Mexican Relations* (New York: Macmillan Company, 1932), chapter 9.

12. The only biography of Lerdo, in any language, is Frank Knapp's *The Life of Sebastián Lerdo de Tejada, 1823-1889: A Study of Influence and Obscurity* (Austin: University of Texas Press, 1951). Lerdo's maxim is quoted on page 203 of that book, whose author argues that Lerdo was less concerned about American military aggression than overbearing commercial and economic influence.

13. John Watson Foster, *Diplomatic Memoirs*, 2 vols. (Boston: Houghton Mifflin Co., 1909), 1:13-14.

14. Gadsen's views are discussed, and the relevant dispatch quoted, in Frederick Dunn, *The Diplomatic Protection of Americans in Mexico* (New York: Columbia University Press, 1933), 72-74. Dunn explains that Gadsen's exasperation with American claims was partly alleviated when he realized that by pressing claims America could acquire territory.

15. Concerning the prior history of U.S.-Mexican claims see J. Fred Rippy, *The United States and Mexico* (New York: Alfred A. Knopf, 1926). When it finished its work in 1876, the Joint Claims Commission (established in 1868) disposed of over 1,000 claims of Americans against Mexico and almost 1,000 filed by Mexicans against the United States. It rejected most of those 2,000 claims, making only 168 awards in favor of Americans, and 167 in favor of Mexicans. The balance was far less favorable to Mexico than it seems. In terms of monies awarded, successful American claims against Mexico were valued at 4.25 million dollars; successful Mexican claims against the United States at only 150 thousand dollars. See Daniel Cosío Villegas, *The United*

States Versus Porfirio Díaz, trans. Nettie Lee Benson (Lincoln: University of Nebraska Press, 1963), 15. Not long after the Claims Commission concluded its work, Mexico presented convincing evidence that two of the successful American claims were entirely fraudulent, and in value they amounted to almost a quarter of the entire American award. Years down the road Mexico hired none other than John Foster to press the case for nullifying the awards and returning the million dollars to Mexico. Foster labored at it for over twenty years, with the case going back and forth between the U.S. Congress, the Supreme Court, the Court of Claims, and the executive branch, before the U.S. decided the only remedy was to reimburse Mexico directly out of the U.S. Treasury (i.e., the fraudulent claimants got to keep what they had already received). See John Watson Foster, *Diplomatic Memoirs*, 2 vols. (Boston: Houghton Mifflin Co., 1909), 2:282–85.

16. Foster to José María Lafragua, 11 June 1873, attachment thereto of "a copy of the remarks which I propose to address to His Excellency," NtMFO, vol. 9.

17. David Watkins to Foster, 4 March 1874, enclosed with Foster to Fish, 7 March 1874, Min. Mexico, roll 50.

18. Foster to Fish, 7 March 1874, Min. Mexico, roll 50.

19. Fish to Foster, 25 March 1874, Instructions, roll 115.

20. Foster to Fish, 15 April 1874, Min. Mexico, roll 50.

21. Isaac Sisson to William Hunter, 6 July 1874, Con. Mazatlán, roll 4.

22. Foster to Lafragua, 11 August 1874, NtMFO, vol. 9.

23. Fish to Foster, 8 September 1874, Instructions, roll 115.

24. Governor of Jalisco to the Ministry of Foreign Relations, 27 July 1874, enclosed with Foster to Fish, 2 September 1874, Min. Mexico, roll 52. Governor of Jalisco to the Ministry of Foreign Relations, 9 December 1874, enclosed with Lafragua to Foster, 18 December 1874; and Corte Suprema de Justicia de los Estados Unidos Mexicanos, 29 May 1875, enclosed with Lafragua to Foster, 5 June 1875, both from NfMFO, vol. 1874–1875.

25. Lafragua to the Supreme Court of Mexico, 3 October 1874, AGN, Suprema Corte de Justicia, Tribunal Plena, Caja 271, Leg. 3-1a Pte, Arch 650–761, Exp. 157–268, #220, "Amparo promovido por José María Hernandez y socios contra el Alcalde 1 de Ahualulco que los condenó á muerte por el asesinato de John Stephens."

26. Supreme court circular dated 5 October 1874, enclosed with Lafragua to Foster, 5 October 1874, NfMFO, vol. 18.

27. Lafragua to Foster, 26 November 1874, NfMFO, vol. 18.

28. Information about the attack and subsequent developments in and around Acapulco derive from: John A. Sutter to Skilton, 27 January 1875, enclosed with Foster to Fish, 9 February 1875; Sutter to Foster, 3 February 1875, enclosed with Foster to Fish, 15 February 1875; Sutter to Foster, 14 February 1875, enclosed with Foster to Fish, 27 February 1875; all from Min. Mexico, roll 51. Foster's communication with Lafragua is described in Foster to Fish, 30 January 1875, Min. Mexico, roll 51.

29. Foster to Fish, 15 February 1875, Min. Mexico, roll 51. Fish to Foster, 23 February 1875, 2 March 1875, and 8 March 1875, all from Instructions, roll 115. Dunn commented upon the similarity (and temporal coincidence) of the cases of the murdered American missionaries in Mexico and the murdered Mexican shepherds in Texas, and he suggested that Fish's temperate response to the one was shaped by his having rejected a claim in the other. See Frederick Dunn, *The Diplomatic Protection of Americans in Mexico* (New York: Columbia University Press, 1933), 285–86.

30. Lafragua to Foster, 24 August 1875; Decisions of the Mexican Supreme Court dated 29 May 1875, enclosed with Lafragua to Foster, 5 June 1875; Decision of the Mexican Supreme Court dated 24 September 1875, enclosed with Lafragua to Foster, 14 October 1875; all from NfMFO, vol. 18.

31. Lafragua to Foster, 27 October 1875, NfMFO, vol. 18.

32. Foster to Lafragua, 30 October 1875, NtMFO, vol. 9.

33. Lespinasse to Skilton, 4 November 1875, Con. Merida, roll 1.

34. Lespinasse to Ancona, 29 October 1875, Con. Merida, roll 1.

35. Ancona to Andrés Urcelay, 20 October 1875, Mexican Reply Memorial, Annex 16, Claims. The law in question was the "Ley de Salteadores y Plagiarios" of 3 May 1873, renewed for one year on 28 April 1875. Manuel Dublan and José María Lozano, eds., *Legislación Mexicana. Colección completa de las disposiciones legislativas expedidas desde la independencia de la república*, vol. 12 (Mexico, 1882), 443–44, item 7169. I will have more to say about the application of this law below. Urcelay to Ancona, 20 October 1875, *LRdP*, 1 November 1875. "Los prisioneros," *LRdP*, 22 October 1875. "Proceso," *LRdM*, 24 October 1875. The intervention of the district judge is mentioned in a brief newspaper clipping found with the article "Robert L. Stephens," newspaper unknown, Con. Merida, roll 1, and more clearly in Juan de Dios Espinosa, Jefatura política accidental de Merida, to Ancona, 26 October 1875, *LRdP*, 1 November 1875.

36. That rebel prisoners were sometimes murdered by their captors was not something officials usually reported openly in their dispatches. The governor of Campeche, Pablo Garcia, inadvertently admitted as much while defending himself against charges that he illegally sentenced rebel prisoners to hard labor on public works. In his defense Garcia asserted, "What [I] did was free them from the mortal reprisals they are usually subject to by our soldiers." Tomás Aznar Barbachano, "Pablo García. Apuntes biográficos" (1895), reprinted in Alejandro Negrín Muñoz, comp., *Campeche. Textos de su historia*, vol. 2. (Gobierno del Estado de Campeche y Instituto de Investigaciones Dr. José María Luis Mora, 1991). Historian Serapio Baqueiro noted concerning the fate of prisoners, "there were taken to our settlements so many prisoners that they died by the hundreds in the jails, or before arriving they met with an even more inhumane fate in the wilderness." Serapio Baqueiro, "Un estudio biográfico de Crescencio Poot," 1887, republished by Luis Millet Cámara in *Boletín de la E.C.A.U.D.Y.*, 16(96), 15–33 (1989). Some officials had no qualms reporting that they executed their prisoners in the field (e.g., Martin Peraza to General en Jefe de la Division Ampudia, 3 April 1855, in *El Regenerador*, 9 April 1855; same to same, 4 May 1855,

in *El Regenerador*, 11 May 1855. Martin Peraza to Comandante general del estado, 20 September 1856, in *Las Garantias Sociales*, 24 September 1856 (reporting the massacre by government troops of at least thirty prisoners). But such direct reference to the execution of Indian prisoners was otherwise rare, and one is left to infer their fate from such official oddities as: 1) The report of prisoners being interrogated, with no further word on what happened to them. 2) Final prisoner counts at the end of operations that add up to less than earlier counts of prisoners taken during the operation. 3) Reports of prisoners dying en route due to "starvation." (All of Hernández's prisoners, seven men and seven women, died of starvation, he claimed in Diego Hernández to Secretario General del Gobierno, 7 July 1853, in *El Regenerador*, 10 June 1853.)

37. Ancona to Lespinasse, 31 October 1875, Con. Merida, roll 1.

38. "La invasión de Xuxub," *LRdP*, 20 October 1875.

39. Lespinasse to Ancona, 2 November 1875, and Ancona to Lespinasse, 4 November 1875, Con. Merida, roll 1.

40. Aznar to Lespinasse, 2 November 1875, Con. Merida, roll 1.

41. Ancona to Ministro de Estado, México, "Desacuerdos entre los propietarios del rancho 'Xuxub' y las autoridades locales de 'Puntachen' . . . ," 4 November 1875, Annex 1, Mexican Reply Memorial, Claims; [Illegible] to the governor, 19 November 1875, AGEY Ejecutivo, Caja 73-A, Sección Gobernación.

42. William Hunter to Lespinasse, 6 November 1875, State-Consuls, vol. 80. Lespinasse's original request for instruction came in Lespinasse to Hunter, 20 October 1875, Con. Merida, roll 1.

43. "La carta de Mr. J. Byrns," *UL*, 1/4, 6 November 1875, Con. Merida, roll 1.

44. Fish Diaries, entry of 6 November 1875. The entry identifies Fish's visitor only as "General Butler." I infer that he meant Massachusetts Republican Benjamin Butler, then cooling his heels after electoral defeat the year before. Alan Nevins quotes the same passage and similarly identifies the speaker as Benjamin Butler, in *Hamilton Fish: The Inner History of the Grant Administration* (New York: Dodd, Mead and Company, 1936), 886. Concerning Butler see Howard Nash Jr., *Stormy Petrel: The Life and Times of General Benjamin F. Butler, 1818–1893* (Rutherford, N.J.: Fairleigh Dickinson University Press, 1969). Butler had his own claim against Mexico which he'd tried, unsuccessfully, to get Foster to support. *John Watson Foster, Dipliomatic Memoirs*, I:14.

45. Quotes are from letters Fish wrote to John Cadwalader and Edward L. Plumb, quoted in Nevins, ibid., 912.

46. Foster to Fish, 10 November 1875, Min. Mexico, roll 53, dispatch 350.

47. Lespinasse to José Jesús Castro, 4 November 1875, and Manzanilla to Lespinasse, 4 November 1875, Con. Merida, roll 1. Byrne's assessment of his interview by Judge Castro is mentioned first in a 1 November postscript to his 18 October 1875 letter to Ramón Aznar. Byrne to Aznar, 18 October 1875, accompanying Foster to Fish, 10 November 1875, Min. Mexico, roll 53, dispatch 350.

48. The reasoning of the court in referring the matter back to the district chief is

given in Yanuario Manzanilla to Editor of *LRdM*, 18 November 1875, which included
the text of the court's decision dated 4 November: "Juzgado de Distrito del Estado de
Yucatan—Merida 4 November 1875."

49. R. Aldana and Perfecto Solís, "To the Editor of *La Revista de Mérida*," 10 November 1875, in *LRdM*, 11 November 1875; and Francisco Rojas, "Escribano público del
estado y secretario en la causa que la Jefatura política sigue contra los prisioneros . . . ,"
8 November 1875, in *LRdP*, 10 November 1875.

50. The appeal in question was that of Epitacio Verastegui and Miguel Solís.
Their appeal had several aspects to it. That Verastegui won his appeal, while Solís
lost his, though both had experienced the same delay, indicates that the court rejected
that particular argument I mention. AGN, Mexico City, Suprema Corte de Justicia,
Tribunal Plena, Caja 270, Leg. 4, Arch. 1158–1697, Exp. 371–570, #456, 4 October 1875.

51. Lespinasse to Hunter, 13 November 1875, Con. Merida, roll 1.

52. Skilton to Lespinasse, 24 November 1875, Min. Mexico, roll 8.

CHAPTER 5: THE WILL OF GOD

1. Lespinasse to Hunter, 10 March 1876, Con. Merida, roll 1.

2. Hunter to Lespinasse, 31 March 1876, State-Consuls, vol. 81.

3. Byrne to Mary Stephens, 21 October 1875, Misc. Letters, roll 451. (The microfilm copy omits the first page of this letter. One has to consult the original paper
copy.) An edited version of Byrne's letter to Mary Stephens was in *NYH*. That was
based upon the original received by Mary's daughter, and I follow that letter when it
differs from the State Department copy. "Assassination of an American Citizen in Yucatan—Wholesale Butcheries by the Indians," *NYH*, 12 December 1875.

4. According to her eldest daughter, Catherine Vila, Mary Stephens left New
York by steamer on 26 October. That steamer was due to arrive in Progreso on 4 November. It came in a day late, on 5 November. Catherine Stephens Vila to Hamilton
Fish, 9 November 1875, Misc. Letters, roll 451. "Puerto-Progreso. Linea Neo-Yorkina
y Mexicana. El vapor americano 'City of Mexico'," *LRdM*, 4 November 1875. "Comercio de cabotaje," *LRdM*, 11 November 1875.

5. The record of the travels and findings of this commission are contained in a se-
ries of articles published in the official newspaper of the state government of Yucatan.
Only the first article concerns what they found at Xuxub. José M. Río, Puntachen, 13
November 1875, "Apuntes del secretario de la comisión judicial, sobre los acontec-
imientos del rancho Xuxub," *LRdP*, 22 November 1875. That the boat they took was
owned by Nicolás Urcelay comes from AGEY Congreso del Estado, Ramos Varios,
Caja 18, vol. 5, exp. 10, 1878, Datos estadísticos del partido de Temax, D. Canto,
Temax, 30 April 1878.

6. His last name was pronounced "ken." At the time, among his own people and
his enemies, Cen's first name was rendered in many different ways, partly thanks to
the absence of an "r" sound in Yucatec Maya. Documents refer to him variously as
Bernardino, Bernaldino, Bernadino, Bernabel, Bernabé, and Bel.

7. That the judge so ordered is mentioned in Río's account cited above. That the head arrived in Merida is mentioned in A. Barrera to the governor, 17 November 1875, AGEY Ejecutivo, Caja 73-A, Seccion Ayuntamientos, Series Elecciones/Correspondencia, Lugar Merida, Año 1875.

8. The best study of the causes of this long war is Terry Rugeley, *Yucatán's Maya Peasantry and the Origins of the Caste War* (Austin: University of Texas Press, 1996).

9. The fullest study of the half-century long War of the Castes is Don Dumond, *The Machete and the Cross: Campesino Rebellion in Yucatán* (Lincoln: University of Nebraska Press, 1997).

10. Much of what we infer about the religious devotions of nineteenth-century Maya comes from anthropological study of their twentieth-century descendants. Some more direct evidence is provided in the work of historians Nancy Farris, Terry Rugeley, and Matthew Restall. See Nancy Farris, *Maya Society Under Colonial Rule: The Collective Enterprise of Survival* (Princeton: University of Princeton Press, 1984); Terry Rugeley, *Of Wonders and Wise Men: Religion and Popular Cultures in Southeast Mexico, 1800–1876* (Austin: University of Texas Press, 2001); Matthew Restall, *The Maya World: Yucatec Culture and Society: 1550–1850* (Stanford: Stanford University Press, 1997).

11. José Maria Guerra, "Pastoral del Ilustrísimo Señor Obispo, Dirigida a los Indígenas de esta Diócesis" (1848), reproduced in Michel Antochiw, "Documents Printed in the Maya Language Addressed to the Insurgents of the Caste War," *Saastun: Revista de Cultura Maya*, o(1), 89–112 (1997).

12. Jacinto Pat to Father D. Canuto Vela, 24 February 1848, and Cecilio Chi and Jacinto Pat, et. al. to Domingo Bacelis and José Dolores Pasos, 19 February 1848, both reproduced in Serapio Baqueiro, *Ensayo Histórico sobre las Revoluciones de Yucatan*, vol. 1 (Merida, 1878), 592–96.

13. Quotes from rebel correspondence derive from, respectively, Timoteo Ek, Cacabdziú, to (?), 22 December 1849; Timoteo Ek and Juan Crisóstomo Chable to Venancio Pec, 27 December 1849; and Florentino Chan to the Generals, Commanders, and Captains in the North, 13 July 1850, all reproduced in translation in Fidelio Quintal Martín trans., *Correspondencia de la Guerra de Castas* (Merida: Universidad Autónoma de Yucatán, 1992), 56–57, 62, 84–85.

14. Written versions of the rebel Mayas' divine commandments can be consulted in Victoria Bricker, *The Indian Christ, the Indian King: The Historical Substrate of Maya Myth and Ritual* (Austin: University of Texas Press, 1981). Concerning the rise of the new religion, see also Lorena Careaga Viliesid, *Hierofanía combatiente: Lucha simbolismo y religiosidad en la Guerra de Castas*, (Chetumal: Conacyt y la Universidad de Quintana Roo, 1998).

15. "Relacion de los comandantes que tiene la fuerza de los indios sublevados en Chan Santa Cruz," Peto, 22 August 1862, reproduced in Leocardio Espinosa to the governor, 24 August 1862, in *EN*, 27 August 1862.

16. Only one source mentions this alleged coup, and perhaps the source is false. "Declaration of Andrés Alvino Canul," contained in Pedro Rosado Lavalle to Comandante en jefe de la division del estado, 23 July 1863, in *NE*, 27 July 1863.

17. Two sources mention Cen in connection with this October 1862 incursion: Dionisio Peniche to the governor, 2 November 1862, in *EN*, 5 November 1862; and F. Zavala to the governor, 10 November 1862, in *EN*, 14 November 1862.

18. "Statement of José de los Angeles Loesa," Corozal, 26 August 1861, AB, R. 74. Puc's words were reported in Seymour to Governor Darling, 13 March 1858, Foreign Office 39/5x/j 1901, Public Records Office, England.

19. "Proclamation of Juan de la Cruz," in Victoria Bricker, *The Indian Christ, the Indian King: The Historical Substrate of Maya Myth and Ritual* (Austin: University of Texas Press, 1981), 194.

20. General Dionisio Zapata, General Leandro Santos, and Gerardo del Castillo to the superintendent of Belize, 1 January 1864, Archives of Belize, R. 84.

21. Edmund Burke to George Berkeley, 25 January 1864, AB, R. 84; V. Panting to acting superintendent of British Honduras, 3 March 1864, AB, R. 84. General Dionisio Zapata, General Leandro Santos, and Gerardo del Castillo to the superintendent of Belize, 1 January 1864, AB, R. 84. The exact language of the letter was neither that of Zapata nor of Santos, but, rather, that of Castillo, who was a white captive in Santa Cruz. Separately, Castillo provided a slightly different account of the coup in Gerardo del Castillo, Santa Cruz, to Garcia Martinez [actually José María Martínez], Mexican Consul in British Honduras, 1 January 1864, AB, R. 84. See also Burke to Berkeley, 25 January 1864, AB, R. 84.

22. "Declaration of Julian Euan," contained in Juan Montalvo to the governor, 12 February 1864, in *NE*, 15 February 1864.

23. The assertion that Cen ordered the raid comes from "Declarations of Ramón Mendosa Fomas and Antonio Alcocer," reported in José Tejero to Prefecto político del departamento de Merida, 26 March 1864, AGEY Ejecutivo, Caja 140, Sección gobernación, Serie Subprefectura Peto. Dzonotchel was attacked, Peto was not, because rebels learned how strong the government garrison there was. That Zapata was not strong enough to resist those who wanted to launch the raid is stated in Burke to Berkeley, 5 March 1864, AB, R. 84.

24. Zapata's death is documented in, 4 April 1864; and Burke to Berkeley, 20 April 1864, both from AB, R. 84; Manuel A. Sierra de O'Relly and Pantaleon Barrera to Prefecto político del departamento de Yucatán, 13 June 1864, in *NE*, 24 June 1864. It was this latter source that attributed the killing of Zapata to men from Chan Cah Derepente who had been supporters of Venancio Puc. A list of names of white female captives, and the numbers of their children or younger siblings, was provided in Martinez de Arredondo, "To the Editor, 14 March 1864," in *NE*, 18 March 1864. He could not list or count those held at sites outside of the rebel capital.

25. That the ranch called Chan Cah Derepente "belonged" to Bernardino Cen is

mentioned in "Declaración de María Cocom y otros," *LRdP,* 29 March 1871; by "Declaration of Marcos Balam," in Moreno Navarrete to the governor, 6 March 1875, in *LRdP,* 8 March 1875; and by the statements of José Chan, communicated in Nestor Rubio Alpuche, "Invasión de Xuxub," *LRdM,* 21 October 1875. I am unable to determine how far back Cen's connection to that place went. Sierra and Barrera to Prefecto político, 13 June 1864, in *NE,* 24 June 1864; Burke to Berkeley, 20 April 1864, AB, R. 84.

26. Concerning the English characterization of Cen and his corulers, there is Burke to Berkeley, 4 April 1864, AB, R. 84. The principal source concerning Yucatecan peace overtures is Sierra and Barrera to Prefecto político, 13 June 1864, in *NE,* 24 June 1864. Concerning the intransigence of the new leaders, there is V. Panting to Acting Superintendent of British Honduras, 3 March 1864, AB, R. 84. A somewhat differently phrased statement of intransigence is found in "Declarations of Ramón Mendosa Fomas and Antonio Alcocer," reported in José Tejero, to Prefecto político del departamento de Merida, 26 March 1864, AGEY Ejecutivo, Caja 140, Sección gobernación, Serie Subprefectura Peto.

27. Sources at the time provided little information about who directed the rebel forces besieging Tihosuco. Later, mention appeared that Cen directed the siege in "Declaración de María Cocom y otros," *LRdP,* 29 March 1871. Newspaper commentary upon those declarations noted that the siege had established Cen as a leader "de sobresalientes dotes para la carrera de las armas." Contemporary Maya oral history in that area attributes the siege to Cen, though it is likely that an operation of that size and duration actively involved both Cen and Crescencio Poot.

28. Escaped captives gave varying reports over the years concerning who was the military leader of Santa Cruz, Poot or Cen. Three good sources, however, suggest Cen was in charge of the army and that Poot was second. The first source is the report of a British visitor to Santa Cruz, son of the rebel Mayas' most important official contact in that colony. He reported that Cen was "second chief" (i.e., after Novelo, head of the church) of Santa Cruz and that "he has command of the whole army of Santa Cruz which consists of 11,000 fighting men . . ." John Carmichael Jr. to J. R. Longden, 15 November 1867, AB. R. 93. The second is a communication from the magistrate of the northern district to the lieutenant governor of British Honduras, responding in part to a question from the latter concerning who was in command of the rebel army. The magistrate reported that Cen was in command of the army, and "associated in power with Crescencio Poot." Edwin Adolphus to J. R. Longden, 30 September 1869, AB. R. 105. The third source reported that Cen had been removed from command of the army and replaced by Crescencio Poot: "Declarations of María Cocom, et. al.," conveyed in Antonio Espinosa to the governor, 28 February 1871, in *LRdP,* 3 March 1871. My reading of the relative standing of Poot and Cen in the hierarchy of Santa Cruz differs from that of Don Dumond, *The Machete and the Cross: Campesino Rebellion in Yucatán* (Lincoln: University of Nebraska Press, 1997), 307–8,

374. Dumond concludes that Poot was superordinate, whereas I see their relative standing fluctuating back and forth over their years of joint rule.

29. That total does not include engagements between Santa Cruz allies in Campeche and government troops of that state. Though Santa Cruz was deeply involved in fomenting rebellion there, the subsequent battles were fought by locals, not forces from Santa Cruz.

30. The changing equilibrium of the war is described by contemporary observers in Serapio Baqueiro, "Remitido de Tekax," *El Periódico Oficial,* 5 December 1864, and Governor Cepeda to State Legislature, 27 August 1868, in *LRdP,* 28 September 1868.

31. My calculation of this rough average—which did not include some prolonged involvements, like their fueling of civil war in Campeche—is detailed in my article, "Para qué lucharon los mayas rebeldes?" See Paul Sullivan, *Para qué lucharon los mayas rebeldes, y Vida y Muerte de Bernardino Cen* (Chetumal, Quintana Roo: Universidad de Quintana Roo, 1998).

32. I provide evidence for this interpretation of frontier raiding as revenge in Sullivan, ibid.

33. It is difficult to estimate accurately losses that rebel Maya suffered on their raids. But estimate one must, if we are to assess the levels of sacrifice they endured to continue the war against Yucatan. As I explain at some length in Sullivan, ibid., I estimate that during their long offensive against the Yucatecan frontier (1853–1875), Maya rebels would seldom have suffered more than 12 percent killed and captured. In that article I provide a complete list of frontier raids and my estimates of the size of the raiding parties and their losses. These are, of course, very rough figures. The estimates of losses are based upon body counts after battle and reports of graves found at the site or along the path of the rebels' withdrawal. My estimates appear to be consistent with contemporary assessments that rebel Maya raiders adopted tactics to maintain low levels of casualties among themselves (i.e., not attacking well-defended places).

34. The sources concerning this raid are: "La Redacción"; Serapio Baqueiro, "Remitido de Tekax"; Juan Montalvo, "Relación de los muertos y heridos hechos por los indios sublevados en los ranchos Kakalná, Thuul y el pueblo de Tzucacab"; and others, all in *El Periódico Oficial,* 5 December 1864. See also Subprefecto político de Sotuta to Prefecto superior político del departamento de Yucatán, 2 December 1864; same to same, 3 December 1864; Francisco González to Prefecto superior del departamento de Yucatan, 1 December 1864; same to same, 12 December 1864; same to same, 14 December 1864; Juan Montalvo to Prefecto superior del departamento, 1 December 1864 [two dispatches that day]; same to same, 3 December 1864; J. Escalante to Prefecto político superior del departamento de Yucatán, 1 December 1864, all from AGEY Ejecutivo, Caja 140, Sección Gobernación.

35. The report of the chief of the Peto district comes from Montalvo's second dis-

patch to Prefecto superior del departamento, 1 December 1864. Baqueiro's observa-
tions come from his "Remitido de Tekax," *El Periódico Oficial*, 5 December 1864.

36. Concerning this raid, see "Crónica del estado," *LRdM*, 19 January 1870. See
also: Nazario Novelo to the governor, 16 January 1870; Manuel Cirerol to Nazario
Novelo, 18 January 1870; Manuel Galera to the governor, 18 January 1870; and Novelo
to the governor, 17 January 1870, all published in *LRdP*, 21 January 1870. At the time of
the attack it was thought that the invaders were likely from rebel communities in
Campeche. A subsequent report from a captive who escaped Santa Cruz suggests,
however, that the raiders were from Santa Cruz. See B.C., "Correspondencia de *La
Revista de Mérida*, 'Ticul," 12 January 1873, *LRdM*, 15 January 1873.

37. "Sermons of the Talking Cross," in Alfonso Villa Rojas, *The Maya of East Central Quintana Roo* (Washington, D.C.: Carnegie Institution of Washington, 1945), 163.
The quote comes from an addendum to that Maya manuscript dated 15 August 1887,
very near the second anniversary of the killing of Crecencio Poot and his second,
General Juan Bautista Poot.

38. Sources for the Xaya incident include: J. A. Cepeda Peraza to the governor, 19
December 1870; and Francisco I. Fuentes to Cepeda, 19 December 1870, both in *LRdP*,
21 December 1870; M. Díaz to the governor, 20 December 1870; Cepeda to the governor, 21 December 1870; and Manuel Galero to the governor, 21 December 1870; all
three in *LRdP*, 23 December 1870; Cepeda to the governor, 23 December 1870; and
Galero to the governor, 23 December 1870, both in *LRdP*, 26 December 1870; Crescencio Poot to Ignacio Chablé and María Uicab, 28 December 1870, published in
Spanish translation in *LRdM*, 1 March 1871; and José Díaz to the governor, 1 December 1871, in *LRdP*, 6 December 1871. It is not absolutely certain that the raiders who attacked Katbé were the same that Poot had commanded at Xaya. They would have
had time to double back and hit Katbé, and it would have made sense for them to
head south to their allies in the Chenes, rather than directly back to Santa Cruz, if
they were burdened with wounded and short on supplies. Finally, the scant damage
done and haste of the rebels at Katbé inclines me to believe they were just passing
through (i.e., returning from raiding), not heading out on a raid.

39. An official report of the battle counted only four Yucatan soldiers were killed
at Xaya, certainly not the 179 that Poot claimed. J. A. Cepeda Peraza to the governor,
19 December 1870, in *LRDP*, 21 December 1870. That Poot's losses were higher than
the two score he admitted is suggested by an unsigned, undated report from Belize,
"Al Señor General Don Guillermo Palomino en respetuosa prueba de admiracion,"
Collections of the Latin American Library, Tulane University. (Copy provided me by
Michel Antochiw.) Comparing this document to "Informe que en obsequio á los pa-
trióticos deseos del ilustre Sr. General Don Jesús Lalanne . . . ," also at Tulane, one can
conclude that they had the same author, José María Muñoz, a Mexican soldier who
defected to the Maya rebels in Campeche and some years later drifted to the English

colony. In the unsigned report, which appears to date from the 1870s (because Bernadino Cen has been removed from government, but there is no mention of his death), the author states that "General" Pedro Dzul was killed in action in 1871 in an engagement in which Santa Cruz also lost eighty-four men. This must refer to the battle at Xaya in December 1870. Muñoz was still living among Poot's Campeche allies when Poot's raiders passed through in January 1871, limping home after their loss at Xaya. Both of the Tulane documents have recently been reproduced in Terry Rugeley, editor, *Maya Wars: Ethnographic Accounts from Nineteenth-Century Yucatan* (Norman: University of Oklahoma Press, 2001), 95–102.

40. John Carmichael Jr. to J. R. Longden, 15 November 1867, AB, R. 93.

41. Crescencio Poot, et. al., to the governor, Tibolon, 1 July 1869, in *EP*, 27 July 1869.

42. Crescencio Carrillo y Ancona, *Historia Antigua de Yucatán* (Merida: Gamboa Guzman y Hermano, 1883), 537–39; Joaquin Hübbe, *Belice*, (Merida, 1880), 114; "Gacetilla. Sobre los bárbaros," *LRdM*, 4 May 1879.

43. "La guerra de castas y la última excursión," *LRdP*, 29 March 1871, reprints an article that appeared earlier in *La Voz del Oriente*.

44. I discuss all the evidence concerning the killing of José Antonio Muñoz in "La Vida y Muerte de Bernardino Cen," in *Para qué lucharon los mayas rebeldes, y Vida y Muerte de Bernardino Cen* (Chetumal, Quintana Roo: Universidad de Quintana Roo, 1998). As I point out in that discussion, several reports confirmed that Muñoz was killed for courting the wrong woman. One source alleged that the woman was the mother of General *Felipe* Cen. Santa Cruz never had a general named Felipe Cen, nor do documents mention any general whose first name was Felipe. Hence, the suspicion that Bernardino Cen was meant.

45. Edwin Adolphus to James Longden, 1 December 1869, AB, R. 105.

46. "Declarations of María Cocom et. al.," contained in Antonio Espinosa to the governor, 28 February 1871, in *LRdP*, 3 March 1871.

47. Ibid.

48. A defector from the rebel Maya community of Chun Pom reported back in October 1869 that rebels planned to assemble near Tulum for attacks upon Chemax, Kantunilkin, and Puntachen. Therefore the general plan for such a northeast offensive went back some years before Tulum was destroyed. "Declaration of Feliciano Canché," in Santiago Medina to the governor, 6 November 1869, AGEY Ejecutivo, Caja 175, Sección Milicia.

49. The Kaua raid and its casualties are documented primarily in: C. Moreno Navarrete to the governor, 14 January 1873 and 18 January 1873, in AGEY Ejecutivo, Caja 69; same to same, 25 January 1873, in *LRdP*, 29 January 1873; José Anastasio Aguilar, "Letter to the Editor of *La Revista de Mérida*," 14 January 1873, in *LRdM*, 17 January 1873; Francisco Canton to the governor, 18 January 1873, in *LRdM*, 26 January

1873. More details of the raid emerged in the weeks and months following as captives wandered back to their homes.

50. The report that Poot had told his Chenes allies to be prepared is contained in "Declaration of Martin Beltran," in R. Bolio to the governor, 30 June 1873, in *LRdM,* 4 July 1873. The report that Santa Cruz was partially destroyed by fire is contained in "Correspondencia, Flodoro, Valladolid," in *LRdP,* 5 August 1874. Reliable reports that Poot led the raid against Dzonotchel in July 1874 come from "Extracto de la declaración de Mónica May," in Juan Carbó to Jefe de la Colonia militar del Sur, 1 August 1874, in *LRdP,* 5 August 1874; and "Declaration of José Luciano Cahum," in Nazario Novelo to the governor, 26 February 1879, in *LRdP,* 3 March 1879. Concerning reports in late 1874 of a still-to-come joint offensive against Yucatan, see "Declaration of Pedro Uc and Carolina Pantí," in Rafael A. Pérez to the governor, 11 December 1874, in *LRdP,* 16 December 1874. Regarding Cen's plan, there is a report from a captive who escaped servitude on Cen's farm: "Declaration of Nazario Cutís," contained in Fernando Piña to the governor, 19 February 1875, in *LRdP,* 24 February 1875.

CHAPTER 6: HUBRIS

a. Joseph Byrne, "To the Editor of *La Unión Liberal,*" 22 October 1875, found with dispatch 19, 13 November 1875, vol. 2, consular dispatches from Merida. (Microfilm copies of the Merida dispatches do not include the complete copy of this article.)

1. Growing British concerns about the insolence of the rebel Maya is reported in Antonio Mathé to Gardiner Austin, 12 August 1867, AB, R. 96; Edwin Adolphus to James Longden, 17 August 1868, AB, R. 102; same to same, 1 December 1869, AB, R. 105; James Longden to Governor Grant, 29 January 1870, AB, R. 98.

2. Detailed census figures for this period are woefully scarce. The 1861 census of British Honduras determined the population of Corozal and surrounding areas, up to a few miles out, to be 10,700. Belize City and environs, including the Belize River, had a population of 7,400. Census of British Honduras, 1861, a copy of which is included in Con. Belize, roll 1. That there were about 400 houses in Corozal comes from Manuel A. Sierra de O'Relly and Pantaleon Barrera to Prefecto político del departamento de Yucatán, 13 June 1864, in *NE,* 24 June 1864.

3. The best discussion of the transformation of the Corozal region is found in Angel Cal, "Rural Society and Economic Development: British Mercantile Capital in Nineteenth-Century Belize" (Ph.D. diss., University of Arizona, 1991).

4. John Carmichael Jr. to J. R. Longden, 15 November 1867. AB, R. 93, reproduced in Terry Rugeley, editor, *Maya Wars: Ethnographic Accounts from Nineteenth-Century Yucatan* (Norman: University of Oklahoma Press, 2001) pp. 82–87. The fact that John Carmichael Jr. was allowed to stand among the rebel Maya was derived directly from the esteem in which they held his father, who for years served as principal go-between

for the rebel Maya on one side and British Honduran authorities on the other. Concerning the father, see Paul Sullivan, "John Carmichael: Life and Design on the Frontier of Central America," *Revista Mexicana del Caribe*, 5(10), 6–89 (2000).

5. Bonifacio Novelo, Bernardino Cen, and José Crescencio Poot to the "governor" of Belize, 9 January 1868, AB, R. 97; same to same, 7 May 1868, AB, R. 102 (referring back to the Maya original, I have modified the translation of this letter).

6. English concern regarding the change in leadership at Santa Cruz is expressed in R. H. Mitchell, "Report called for by his Excellency W. W. Cairns, in a minute dated 4 October 1872 addressed to the Colonial Secretary, on the state of the Northern District and on other points detailed in said minute," 26 October 1872, AB, R. 111.

7. Probably with exaggeration, a Yucatecan newspaper reported that at Christmastime in 1872 British authorities at Corozal entertained one thousand rebel Indians with "gifts and refreshments," even as those Indians were planning their major upcoming assault on the Yucatan frontier at Kaua (January of 1873). "Guerra de bárbaros," *LRdM*, 9 November 1873.

8. Josefa's appearance in Corozal and what transpired there are related in: Edwin Adolphus to acting colonial secretary, 26 December 1874; same to same [second dispatch], 26 December 1874; Adolphus to officer commanding detachment 2nd West Indies Regiment [Lieutenant James Wilkin], Corozal, 26 December 1874; Wilkin to Adolphus, 26 December 1874; Wilkin to officer commanding the troops in British Honduras, Orange Walk [Captain G. D. La Louche], 27 December 1874; Adolphus to Crescencio Poot, Bernardino Cen, and the other commandants, 27 December 1874; Adolphus to acting colonial secretary, 28 December 1874; same to same [second dispatch], 28 December 1874; La Louche to acting colonial secretary, 28 December 1874; attorney general of Belize to lieutenant governor, 30 December 1874; Sub-Lieutenant J. Davy to acting colonial secretary, 2 January 1875; Adolphus to acting colonial secretary, 2 January 1875; Thomas Graham to officer commanding the detachment, 2 January 1875; Crescencio Poot to [Adolphus], 7 February 1875; Adolphus to acting colonial secretary, 15 February 1875; all of the above from AB, R. 114. I calculate Josefa's age back from that given when she dictated her last will and testament in 1878: "Will and Inventory of the Estate of Josefa Rodríguez Romero," AGEY Justicia, Caja 130-A, 1881.

9. A Tunkas captive who later escaped, Anastasio Durán, reported this ritual of pardon and rebaptism. He was not entirely clear whether only Indians were rebaptized, or Indians and the white women, too. My interpretation of his words is that all who were spared underwent this ritual. Durán, by the way, was one of the white men who passed himself off as Indian. Nazario Novelo, "Noticias que emite el C. Anastasio Durán á esta jefatura, de su prisión en Tunkas por los indios bárbaros, conducción y permanencia en Santa Cruz . . ." 26 August 1862, republished in *EP*, 12 September 1865.

10. Concerning the distribution of captives among rebel officers and their subsequent employment on farms, citing only sources from after 1860 that derive from reports of people who escaped their captivity, see: A. Sandoval, Peto to the governor, 14 February 1862, in *EN*, 19 February 1862. Leocardio Espinosa to the governor, 24 August 1862, in *EN*, 27 August 1862; Juan I. Montalvo to the governor, 12 February 1864, in *NE*, 15 February 1864; José María Martinez de Arredondo, "To the Editor of the *Nueva Epoca*," in *NE*, 18 March 1864; "Declaración de Pablo Encalada," 12 August 1867, in *EP*, 24 and 27 September 1867; Antonio Espinosa to the governor, 28 February 1871, in *LRdP*, 3 March 1871; Evaristo Esquivel to the governor, 11 February 1873, in *LRdP*, 14 February 1873; Roberto Erosa to the governor, 25 March 1873, in *LRdM*, 30 March 1873; Esquivel to the governor, 5 April 1873, in *LRdP*, 7 April 1873; José Díaz to the governor, 26 April 1873, in *LRdP*, 28 April 1873; "Izamal," *LRdM*, 2 May 1873; Nicolás Aguilar to the governor, 24 May 1873, in *LRdP*, 27 May 1873; Felipe Díaz to [the governor?], 29 July 1874, in *LRdP*, 5 August 1874; Rafael Pérez to the governor, 11 December 1874, in *LRdP*, 16 December 1874; Moreno Navarrete to the governor, 6 March 1875, in *LRdP*, 8 March 1875; Fernando Piña to the governor, 19 February 1875, in *LRdP*, 24 February 1875; General Palomino to the governor, 15 March 1875, AGEY Ejecutivo, Caja 73-A, Sección Gobernación; Sabino Piña to the governor, 11 March 1876, in *LRdP*, 17 March 1876; Nazario Novelo to the governor, 26 February 1879, in *LRdP*, 3 March 1879; N. Ramirez to Sub-inspector de las colonials militares del estado, 27 February 1879, in *LRdP*, 3 March 1879, p. 2–3; Novelo to the governor, 3 April 1879, in *LRdP*, 16 April 1879; Cortés to the governor, 11 April 1879, AGEY Ejecutivo, Caja 208, Sección Milicia; Novelo to the governor, 13 May 1879, in *LRdP*, 16 May 1879.

Sources which mention the prisoner distribution, but which speak only of personal service to a Maya officer (not necessarily service on a farm) include: "Statement of José de los Angeles Loesa," 26 August 1861, AB, R. 74; Nazario Novelo, "Noticias que emite el C. Anastasio Durán á esta jefatura, de su prisión en Tunkas por los indios bárbaros, conducción y permanencia en Santa Cruz ..." 26 August 1862, republished in *EP*, 12 September 1865; petition of Barbara and María Guadalupe Xuluc before Juez de la 1a instancia, Izamal, 6 September 1869, AGEY Justicia, Caja 86-C, 1869 (rolls 80, 81); "Declaration of Juan Lopez," contained in Benigno Lara to [the governor?], 18 September 1870, in *La Discusión*, 27 September 1870; José Díaz to the governor, 1 December 1871, in *LRdP*, 6 December 1871; Moreno Navarrete to the governor, 4 March 1873, AGEY Ejecutivo, Caja 185, Sección Gobernación.

Sources which mention captives engaged in work or errands that do not appear to have been public works, but rather work for an individual (probably an officer, though not specified) include: Francisco Córtes to the governor, 11 August 1864, in *NE*, 15 August 1864; Nazario Novelo to the governor, 12 December 1869, in *LRdP*, 17 December 1869.

Specifically concerning the fate of the Chinese who fled to rebel territory, see:

Edwin Adolphus to Thomas Graham, 4 December 1866, AB, R. 93; J. K. Longden to Governor Grant, 16 September 1869 (including Declaration of Luca Lat, Corozal, 1 September 1869), AB, R. 98, No. 105. The figure of 150 Chinese who escaped to the rebel Maya comes from Immigration Agent, Belize, to Colonial Secretary Mitchell, 23 October 1868, AB, R. 102.

11. For a fuller accounting of the ranches of Maya leaders and their use of captive labor, see my article "Para qué lucharon los mayas rebeldes?" in Paul Sullivan, *Para qué lucharon los mayas rebeldes, y Vida y Muerte de Bernardino Cen* (Chetumal, Quintana Roo: Universidad de Quintana Roo, 1998). Sources provide two names for the ranches of Bernardino Cen—Chan Cah Derepente and San Pedro. The latter may have been San Pedro Yoksas. Moreno Navarrete to the governor, 6 March 1875, in *LRdP,* 8 March 1875; Fernando Piña to the governor, 19 February 1875, in *LRdP,* 24 February 1875; General Palomino to the governor, 15 March 1875, AGEY Ejecutivo, Caja 73-A, Sección Gobernación, Serie Correspondencia. Captives who escaped from Poot's service gave three names for Poot's farms, though it is not clear whether these were in fact three places or two places (with two different names for one of them)—Nohcaan (seven leagues south of Santa Cruz), Chunyá (two leagues south of Santa Cruz), and San Isidro (four or five leagues south of Santa Cruz). Roberto Erosa to the governor, 25 March 1873, in *LRdM,* 30 March 1873; Untitled article published in *LRdM,* 30 April 1873, p. 2; "Al redactor de *LRdM,*" *LRdM,* 2 May 1873; Felipe Díaz to [the governor?], 29 July 1874, in *LRdP,* 5 August 1874; Nazario Novelo to the governor, 26 February 1879, in *LRdP,* 3 March 1879.

12. A Yucatecan military deserter who came under the control of the rebel Maya of Santa Cruz in the late 1860s reported, after his return to Yucatan many years later, that he had learned how to construct cane mills (*trapiches*) in Santa Cruz. "Declaration of José María Eduardo Solís," conveyed in Cisneros to the governor, 20 February 1885, AGEY Ejecutivo, Caja 232, 1885. At the beginning of the 1860s, alcohol was scarce in Santa Cruz, General Leandro Santos was the only seller there, and the price of a bottle of *aguardiente* was quite high. Venancio Puc may have tried to establish a distillery there in 1862, using equipment plundered from Tunkas. By 1864 there was a still in Santa Cruz that was considered the common property of all the Maya officials. And two years later Bernardino Cen attempted to acquire another by dunning and threatening debtors in northern British Honduras. By the 1880s an escapee reported there were several stills in the rebel capital. Nazario Novelo, "Noticias que emite el C. Anastasio Durán á esta jefatura, de su prisión en Tunkas por los indios bárbaros, conducción y permanencia en Santa Cruz . . ." 26 August 1862, republished in *EP,* 12 September 1865; Manuel A. Sierra de O'Relly and Pantaleon Barrera to Prefecto político del departamento de Yucatán, 13 June 1864, in *NE,* 24 June 1864; "Declaration of José Domingo Andrade," May 1866, AB, R. 93, p. 123. Cisneros to the governor, 20 February 1885, AGEY Ejecutivo, Caja 232, 1885. Concerning sales of Santa Cruz rum further afield, in Chun Pom/Tulum area, to Campeche allies, and in northern British Honduras, sources include: "Información practicada con Saturnino

Fernández [y otros] apresados en Tekax . . . Setiembre de 1886," AGEY Ejecutivo, Caja 241. "Declaration of José María Eduardo Solís," conveyed in Cisneros to the governor, 20 February 1885, AGEY Ejecutivo, Caja 232, 1885; John Carmichael to Lieutenant Governor Austin, 8 August 1867, AB, R. 96. James Plumridge to the lieutenant governor of British Honduras, 1 September 1869, AB, R. 105. These last two sources provide only indirect evidence, insofar as it contains a discussion of whether rebel Maya rum should be admitted duty free to British Honduras.

That there was a corn market in Santa Cruz is suggested by reports from captives citing the price of corn there: Nazario Novelo to the governor, 12 December 1869, in *LRdP*, 17 December 1869; "Flodoro. Correspondencia," *LRdP*, 5 August 1874; "Gacetilla, El campo enemigo," *LRdM*, 15 July 1884; John Carmichael to Lieutenant Governor Austin, 8 August 1867, AB, R. 96; James Plumridge to the lieutenant governor of British Honduras, 1 September 1869, AB, R. 105.

13. Concerning lengths of time captives spent assigned to public works, see:

Nazario Novelo, "Noticias que emite el C. Anastasio Durán á esta jefatura, de su prisión en Tunkas por los indios bárbaros, conducción y permanencia en Santa Cruz . . ." 26 August 1862, republished in *EP*, 12 September 1865. Regarding captives taken in 1861, whites were killed after eight days of public works, while Indians worked for five months before distribution.

Nazario Novelo to the governor, 17 May 1868, in *LRdP*, 20 May 1868. Captured in 1867, José Agustín Can spent his entire nine months of captivity on public works in the rebel capital.

José Díaz to the governor, 1 December 1871, in *LRdP*, 6 December 1871. Bernardino Cauich, captured in December 1870, spent only about three months on public works before being distributed.

Captives taken in a massive frontier raid in January 1873 did not spend more than two or three weeks in public works at Santa Cruz before being distributed to officers, as indicated by the fact that when a number escaped in early February and March, they had already been destined to the service of individual Maya officers. Evaristo Esquivel to the governor, 11 February 1873, in *LRdP*, 14 February 1873; Moreno Navarrete to the governor, 4 March 1873, AGEY Ejecutivo, Caja 185, Sección gobernación; Roberto Erosa to the governor, 25 March 1873, in *LRdM*, 30 March 1873; José Díaz to the governor, 26 April 1873, in *LRdP*, 28 April 1873. Four captives from those raids explicitly stated either that they labored fifteen days on public works at Santa Cruz, or that they were distributed after fifteen days: "Izamal," *LRdM*, 2 May 1873; and Evaristo Esquivel to the governor, 5 April 1873, in *LRdP*, 7 April 1873. One captive from those raids recalled that they were distributed right after having arrived in Santa Cruz: Fernando Piña to the governor, 19 February 1875, in *LRdP*, 24 February 1875. Another captive from that raid simply did not mention having been assigned to public works, only having been assigned to labor for Bernardino Cen: Moreno Navarrete to the governor, 6 March 1875, in LRdP, 8 March 1875.

Santos Escamilla, captured in 1875, had to work hammering away at rock on the plaza of Santa Cruz for three weeks before being assigned to labor on one of the farms of Crescencio Poot: Sabino Piña to the governor, 11 March 1876, in LRdP, 17 March 1876, p.1.

Juan Tilam and Esteban Cen, captured in 1879, had to labor fifteen days on public works before being assigned to serve Maya officers: Nazario Novelo to the governor, 13 May 1879, in LRdP, 16 May 1879; same to same, 3 April 1879, in LRdP, 16 April 1879.

One report, at least, would appear to contradict my assertion that the use of captives in private service to Maya officials increased at the expense of their use in public works, though that evidence is not very reliable. Luciano Cahum, captured in 1865, recalled that he was assigned as a slave of Crescencio Poot as soon as he arrived in Santa Cruz. But he made that report only after escaping his captivity fourteen years later. He may well have forgotten a few weeks or months spent in public works in the rebel capital fourteen years earlier, when he was only eleven or twelve years old. Or perhaps children of that age were not assigned public works labor: Nazario Novelo to the governor, 26 February 1879, in LRdP, 3 March 1879. Julian Euan, captured in 1862 and escaped after seventeen months of captivity, made no mention of having performed public works, only having labored for a Maya officer on his farm: I. Montalvo to the governor, 12 February 1864, included in M. Barbachano, "A última hora," NE, 15 February 1864.

That the church at Santa Cruz was unfinished and still walled with scaffolding is mentioned in a newspaper article accompanying the declarations of María Cocom, et. al., recently escaped from the rebel capital. "Declarations of María Cocom, et. al.," conveyed in Antonio Espinosa to the governor, 28 February 1871, in LRdP, 3 March 1871. That the church was still unfinished in 1874 was cited in "Correspondencia," Valladolid, LRdP, 5 August 1874, p. 4. Mayas in that region today assert that the church at what was Santa Cruz, now Felipe Carrillo Puerto, Quintana Roo, is still unfinished.

14. M. Barbachano, "La redacción: movimiento de los bárbaros—Su persecución. Derrota que sufrieron en Yaxcabá," El Constitucional, 9 September 1861; M. Barbachano, "La redacción: sobre la última correría de los bárbaros," El Constitucional, 11 September 1861. Newspapers reported that Manuel and the others actually caught the rear guard of the raiders and inflicted heavy casualties among them. However no scrap of evidence was ever offered to support that claim.

15. The first such request came in the petition of Manuel Rodríguez Solís and other citizens of Tunkas to the governor, 25 September 1861, El Constitucional, 30 September 1861, p. 3–4.

16. The rebellion of Rodríguez and Navarrete is recounted in Juan Francisco Molina Solís, *Historia de Yucatán desde la Independencia de España hasta la época actual,* vol. 2 (Merida, 1927), 364ff.

17. Rodríguez's march from Kampolkolche back north across Yucatan, and Navarrete's displeasure at his excesses, are mentioned in Rodríguez to Felipe Navarrete, 20 July 1864; Navarrete to Rodríguez, 21 July 1864; same to same [second dispatch], 21 July 1864, in *NE,* 22 July 1864. Concerning his final break with Navarrete, see Faulo Sánchez-Novelo, *Yucatán durante la intervención francesa, 1863–1867* (Merida, Maldonado Editores, 1983), 61–62.

18. One can calculate these ages and the approximate date of the union of Manuel Rodríguez and Jacinta Gómez, from information given in "Diligencias promovidas por Doña Manuela Canto, para justificar la patria potestad que ejerce sobre su nieta Eulalia Rodríguez, 1877," AGEY Justica, Caja 146-C, 1885.

19. I have not found a good count of prisoners taken at Tunkas in 1861, though contemporary sources estimated that there were hundreds. Reports from captives who escaped Santa Cruz after the fall of Tunkas reported that all the white men had been executed either on the road or shortly after arrival, and that only the lives of women had been spared. "Declaración de Pedro Hernández," in Felipe Pren to the governor, 14 February 1862, in *EN,* 19 February 1862. Concerning captives still alive a year later, see: "Relación de los vecinos que existen prisioneros en el campo de Chan Santa Cruz," Peto, 22 August 1862, included in Leocardio Espinosa to the governor, 24 August 1862, in *EN,* 27 August 1862. For the women of Tunkas accounted for in 1864, see: José María Martínez de Arredondo, "To Editor of the *Periódico Oficial,*" 14 March 1864, in *NE,* 19 March 1864.

20. Documents concerning the estate and estate proceedings up to the return of Josefa Romero, include: "Diligencias practicadas por el Juez 1 de lo civil Lic. Manuel Meneses en el intestado de D. Manuel Rodríguez Solís," Merida, 1873, AGEY Justicia, Caja 97, 1873; "Intestado de Manuel Rodríguez Solís," AGEY Justicia, Caja 99, 1873; "Inventarios, valúos, adjudicaciones é hijuela de partición de los bienes del finado D. Manuel Rodríguez Solís," 27 May 1875, AGEY Justicia, Caja 104, 1875.

21. The case involving the rights of this second child to a share in the estate of the deceased was not settled until 1885. Witnesses established that this second Eulalia, born in 1868, was his daughter and he treated her as such, but the evidence was inadmissible for various procedural reasons, and her claim to a share of the estate was denied. See: "Solicitud de Doña Manuela Canto reclamando la patria potesta de Eulalia Gómez, 1874," AGEY Justicia, Caja 102, 1874; "Diligencias promovidas por Doña Manuela Canto, para justificar la patria potestad que ejerce sobre su nieta Eulalia Rodríguez, 1877," AGEY Justica, Caja 146-C, 1885; "Juicio ordinario promovido por Doña Manuela Canto contra la Señora Josefa Romero de Rodríguez Solís y C. Esteban Rodríguez Solís, para que se declare que su nieta la menor Señorita Eulalia Rodríguez Solís se halla en posesion de los derechos de hija legítima de D. Manuel

Rodríguez Solís, Juzgado 2 de lo civil, 1880," AGEY Justicia, Caja 124, 1880; "1885, Juicio ordinario promovida por Doña Manuela Canto para que se declare que su nieta Eulalia Rodríguez Solís se halla en posesion de los derechos de hija legítima de D. Manuel Rodríguez Solís; y diligencias promovidas por la representación de dicha Señora sobre intervención de varias fincas," AGEY Justicia, Caja 146-C, 1885.

22. Since she was taken captive in 1861 and died at the age of eleven, Eulalia must have died sometime before 1872. She could have died as early as 1868 or 1869, had she been born, say, a year after Josefa's marriage in 1856. Her death would then have occurred, by the way, around the time Bernardino Cen was reported to be mourning the death of a favorite daughter. Eulalia's age at death is given in the "Will and Inventory of the Estate of Josefa Rodríguez Romero," AGEY Justicia, Caja 130-A, 1881.

23. The only basis for estimating Encarnación's age is evidence later provided by her husband that they married in January 1846. Assuming she was, at the youngest, sixteen years old at that time, that would make her about ten years older than Josefa. "Diligencias promovidas por el C. Francisco Avila en representación de su esposa Doña Encarnación Rodríguez para que se le entregue una cantidad de pesos ... , Juzgado 20 de lo civil, Iniciaron el 3 de febrero de 1882," AGEY Justicia, Caja 130-A, 1881.

24. That Josefa and Encarnación were servants in the household of Zapata comes from "Declaración de Buenaventura Naal y otros," in Felipe Díaz to the governor, 29 July 1874, in LRdP, 5 August 1874. This report comes after Zapata's assassination, so it is not certain that the two women were assigned to that household while Zapata still lived. But once assigned to an officer, captives were rarely, if ever, reassigned to another officer at Santa Cruz, though some might be given to allies in Campeche, freed, or allowed to marry and make their own lives among the rebel Maya.

25. The issue of Josefa having been taken as the wife of one of the Maya leaders of Santa Cruz and having borne a child by him only came out in the Yucatecan press after the death of her true husband and after her release from captivity. Even then, the subject was handled gingerly and to no great extent, leaving the matter somewhat obscure to posterity. The sources concerning the wives of Crescencio Poot and his son include: "Declaration of José Luciano Cahun in N. Ramírez to Sub-inspector de las colonias militares del Estado, 27 February 1879, in LRdP, 3 March 1879; "Declarations of Buenaventura Naal, Pedro Chan, María Benita Chan, and María Naal," in Felipe Díaz to the governor, 29 July 1874, in LRdP, 5 August 1874.

That Josefa was taken as the wife of a Maya leader was mentioned first in a Mexico City newspaper in an article subsequently reprinted in Yucatan: José Patricio Nicoli, "Yucatán y los Ingleses," LRdM, 18 November 1875. Nicoli also claimed that Josefa could no longer speak Spanish, that she refused to provide much information about the rebel Maya, and that she appeared profoundly affected by her captivity. The editor of La Revista de Mérida, Nestor Rubio Alpuche, after having spent much time conversing with Josefa, wrote to refute those claims. He did not, however, refute—he did not even mention—Nicoli's assertion that Josefa had had an Indian "husband" and a child by the man; had those assertions been false, Alpuche certainly would have trounced them. He did have occasion in that article to refer to Josefa's late husband as "el único y legítimo esposo," that is to say, "the one and legitimate spouse" of Josefa, which verbal exertion makes one further suspect that he knew the rumor about an Indian mate was true. Nestor Rubio Alpuche, "La Señora de Rodríguez Solís," *LRdM*, 21 November 1875.

No document with whose preparation Josefa was involved ever mentioned her having a child other than Eulalia.

Who was the "principal chief" who took Josefa for his mate? It could have been Dionisio Zapata, since after Zapata's death Josefa was still attending to his widow. But his wife would not likely have put up with bigamy (documents do not reveal that any Maya woman among the rebels tolerated such). It is true that, while preparing to flee his assassins, Zapata was betrayed by his wife. She told the killers that he had commenced his flight from Santa Cruz, which allowed them to catch him and kill him. Perhaps, after all, she was upset about the "other woman"? Still, in 1864, several years into the captivity of Josefa, a good record of prisoners at Santa Cruz listed her as being there only with one child, Eulalia, not with another by a Maya husband. Josefa could have been the concubine of other top Maya leaders like Bonifacio Novelo, Crescencio Poot, or General Canché. Novelo was already rather old, and he died in 1869. Canché would also have been elderly. Crescencio Poot in 1874 had already taken another Tunkas captive to be his wife, Pastora Rean. Had Josefa also been the wife or concubine of Crescencio Poot, historian Serapio Baqueiro would have known that, since he was, as he himself wrote, a friend of the husband of Josefa's captive sister, Encarnación. Baqueiro, in his mini-biography of Crescencio Poot, did write that Poot took a young captive to be his wife, and had two children by her, but he was certainly referring to Pastora Rean. Most of the principals involved in the ransom of Josefa, and later attempted ransom of Encarnación, were dead by the time Baqueiro wrote, so the delicacy of the situation should no longer have inhibited Baqueiro from writing what he knew of the matter. Serapio Baqueiro, "Crescencio Poot," 1887, republished by Luis Millet Cámara in "Un estudio biográfico de Crescencio Poot por el Lic. Serapio Baqueiro," *Boletín de la E.C.A.U.D.Y.*, 16(96), 15–33 (1989). That leaves Bernardino Cen as the most likely candidate among the "principal chiefs."

26. Trumbach had been a sugar planter as recently as 1870: "The Memorial of John Carmichael, Andrew Hall, Stewart Carter, William Jones, and others, . . . to His Excellency Charles Buller Hugh Mitchell Esquire, Administrator of the Government of British Honduras and the Honorable the Executive Committee of said Colony," (parts of which memorial are dated May 1870, while other parts are undated), AB, R. 106.

27. Or so one assumes was the fate of countless captives who were never heard from again. That their servitude could last many years, at least, and presumably then

until the end of their lives, is suggested by the story of María Cocom (who spent six to eight years in captivity until her escape), "Declarations of María Cocom, et. al.," in Antonio Espinosa to the governor, 28 February 1871, in *LRdP*, 3 March 1871; Pedro Uc (who spent six years serving his master, until his master's death and his escape), "Declaration of Pedro Uc," contained within Rafael Pérez to the governor, 11 December 1874, in *LRdP*, 16 December 1874; Josefa Romero (who spent thirteen years serving her mistress, until her ransom from captivity) and her sister (who died in captivity after about twenty years), as I discuss in chapter 9, and Luciano Cahun (who spent fourteen years in captivity serving on one of Crescencio Poot's farms), in Nazario Novelo to the governor, 26 February 1879, in *LRdP*, 3 March 1879. Escapees reported in 1873 that captives taken in raids against Hacienda Tzalam still labored on one of Poot's farms. Tzalam had been raided eleven years earlier and again four years earlier. See Evaristo Esquivel to the governor, 11 February 1873, in *LRdP*, 14 February 1873. Reports of captives or defectors being killed for attempting to escape or for otherwise attempting to leave their service to a Maya officer include: Edwin Adolphus to Thomas Graham, 4 December 1866, AB, R. 93 (killing of Chinese); Declaration of Luca Lat, 1 September 1869, in J. K. Longden to Governor Grant, 16 September 1869, AB, R. 98, No. 105 (killing and death threats against Chinese); News commentary, "La guerra de castas y la última excurción," accompanying "Declaración de María Cocom y otros," *LRdP*, 29 March 1871 (killing of two who tried to escape); Esquivel, 11 February 1873, cited earlier in this note (public execution of a captive who tried to escape); José Díaz to the governor, 26 April 1873, in *LRdP*, 28 April 1873 Díaz (knowing that all who are caught trying to escape, three who flee Santa Cruz fight to the death against their pursuers); "Izamal," *LRdM*, 2 May 1873 (two escapees report they were constantly threatened with death); José Díaz to the governor, 1 December 1871 in *LRdP*, 6 December 1871 (Crescencio Poot gave captive Bernardino Cauich to a rebel officer in Campeche); "Declaración de Pablo Encalada," 12 August 1867, in *EP*, 24 and 27 September 1867 (Pablo Encalada was captured and had to serve the early rebel leader Jacinto Pat; when Venancio Pec assassinated Pat, Encalada had to serve Pec, until a year or so later, when Pec freed him); Pérez 11 December 1874, cited earlier in this note (Pedro Uc was "freed" after his master was assassinated); General Palomino to the governor, 15 March 1875, AGEY Ejecutivo, Caja 73-A, Sección Gobernación, Serie Correspondencia (Narciso Cutiz had to serve Bernardino Cen only six months before he was "freed," though subject to vigilance).

28. Between 1860 and the end of the century, of the one thousand or so people who stumbled down forest trails into captivity, only seventy-eight adults managed to walk out again, bringing with them just seven children. There were probably others who returned home and never came to the attention of authorities, though their number was likely small. The arrival of someone from the enemy camp prompted talk in a settlement and such talk, on more than one occasion, resulted in authorities calling someone in for a debriefing. The total I give does not include a handful of "de-

fectors"—people who joined the rebel Maya or who were born in Santa Cruz and who later sought to return to Yucatan. Of those who made it out, only one in three had spent more than a year in captivity. Only one in ten had spent more than two years. Men were far more likely to escape than women. A scant eighteen women managed to flee captivity after 1860, and most of them were following their husbands. Juana Cob organized the only escape by women without men. She invited her *comadre*, María Cocom, a captive already for more than six years to join her, and three other women went along as well. They wandered through the forest for fifteen days before reaching the safety of their homes in Yucatan. See "Declaración de Maria Cocom y otros," *LRdP*, 29 March 1871.

29. Rosado's brief memoir of his captivity and ransom was written in 1915 and published many years later as Richard Buhler, *A Refugee of the War of the Castes Makes Belize His Home. The Memoirs of J. M. Rosado*, (Belize: Belize Institute for Social Research and Action, 1975). The relevant parts of that memoir have been republished in Terry Rugeley, editor, *Maya Wars: Ethnographic Accounts from Nineteenth-Century Yucatan* (Norman: University of Oklahoma Press, 2001), 68–78.

30. That upon her return to Yucatan Josefa could only speak Maya was taken by some as a symptom of her captivity (see discussion of Nicoli article in note 25 to this chapter). But it may be that is the only language she ever spoke, it then being not unusual, as Nestor Rubio Alpuche reasoned in his article about Josefa, that white people living in small rural settlements or on rural estates only learned the language of the common people, i.e., the Indians. Alpuche praised Josefa's command of Maya, noting, "This rich language acquires in her lips greater beauty still, as she speaks it with fluency and purity." Nestor Rubio Alpuche, "La Señora de Rodríguez Solís," *LRdM*, 21 November 1875.

31. As it turned out, the weather was too rough to permit them traveling far. They put in at a small fishing village on the coast and continued on later to Belize City.

32. Adolphus actually wrote: "The Indian Commandant who leaves directly for Bacalar informed me on my handing him the letter for the Chiefs that Bernabel Cen, their Second General, is at present in that place awaiting the result of his mission to Corozal, and that, if satisfied with the letter addressed to him and the other chiefs, he may at once take action relative to the same. Cen, I think, it right to observe, has the reputation of being the most impetuous and unrelenting of all the Indian Chiefs." It seems very likely that Adolphus miswrote, and that he meant to write "dissatisfied" rather than "satisfied." Adolphus to acting colonial secretary, 28 December 1874 [second dispatch], AB, R. 114.

33. Such bare fragments of what transpired back in Santa Cruz in January and February are communicated in the reports of two captives who in that period escaped from Cen's service, and from a report of the trader Andrade upon his return to Santa Cruz. Nazario Cutis fled Cen's farm on 4 February, and reported that Cen was opposed to Josefa's ransom and that there was dissension between Cen on the one hand,

and Crescencio Poot and Alonso Chablé on the other. Cutis reported that Cen had struck Poot over the matter. "Declaration of Nazario Cutis," contained in Fernando Piña, Jefatura política de Sotuta to the governor, 19 February 1875, *LRdP*, 24 February 1875; some additional detail in General Palomino to the governor, 15 March 1875, AGEY Ejecutivo, Caja 73-A, Sección Gobernación. Marcos Balam fled from Cen's service (while he and others were carrying fish back from the coast, on or around 21 February). He too reported the disagreement involving Cen, who evidently was still in the area at that time. "Declaration of Marcos Balam," communicated in Moreno Navarrete to the governor, 6 March 1875, in *LRdP*, 8 March 1875.

34. A defector who had worked on Aké's ranch escaped in November 1874 and reported that Aké had been assassinated about a year earlier. He alleged that Aké had been murdered because he had planned to surrender himself to Yucatan. That seems unlikely (unless he knew there was a conspiracy against him), though it is very possible that rivals accused him of that offense punishable by death: "Declaration of Pedro Uc," contained within Rafael Pérez to the governor, 11 December 1874, in *LRdP*, 16 December 1874. Alvino Aké is mentioned in a list of rebel Maya leaders who came to power after the assassination of Venancio Puc back in 1864. He is listed as a member of the level of leaders immediately below Bonifacio Novelo, Bernardino Cen, and Crescencio Poot: Manuel A. Sierra de O'Relly and Pantaleon Barrera to Prefecto político del departamento de Yucatán, 13 June 1864, in *NE*, 24 June 1864. Aké was Commandant of Bacalar as early as late 1866. The 23 December 1866 declaration of a frequent trader to the rebel Maya, José María Trejo, mentions that Aké was then the new commandant there: "Declaration of José María Trejo," Corozal, 23 December 1866, AB, R. 89. Also mentioning that Alvino Aké was commander of Bacalar are: John Carmichael to Austin, Belize City, 29 January 1867, AB, R. 89; Adolphus to Longden, 1 December 1869, AB, R. 105; Adolphus to Longden, 30 September 1869, AB, R. 105. That Alonso Chablé was a "captain" of Alvino Aké is mentioned in Adolphus to Austin, 24 August 1868, AB, R. 102.

35. The open letter to the president was Ramón Aznar, et. al., "Exposicion dirigida por los vecinos de esta capital al Supremo Gobierno de la Nación," 10 July 1873, published twice in *LRdP*, 25 July 1873 and 30 July 1873. The request of Yucatan's federal deputies, dated 23 September 1873, and the report of the minister of war are found in *Dictamen de las comisiones primera de guerra y de defensa contra los bárbaros sobre la pacificación de Yucatán* (Mexico, Imprenta del Gobierno, 1873).

36. "Datos interesantes," *LRdP*, 10 March 1875.

37. The panic is detailed in Roberto Erosa to the governor, 15 March 1875, and again on 16 March 1875; Juan Aguilar to Roberto Erosa, 18 March 1875; all in *LRdP*, 19 March 1875. Also see: Augustus Le Plongeon, "Pánico en Tizimin," *LRdM*, 6 May 1875.

38. Only one source reports that there was actually a battle in Santa Cruz. That is José Patricio Nicoli, "Yucatán y los Ingleses," *LRdM*, 18 November 1875. Nicoli

claimed that there were people who assured him that six hundred died in the battle. A report in July suggested that because of the dissension among the leaders at Santa Cruz, hundreds of Indians were heading from rebel territory to British Honduras, a report, if true, consistent with serious fighting in Santa Cruz: "Los indios," *LRdM*, 25 July 1875. That there was a fight in Santa Cruz appears to be confirmed by a bit of Maya oral history recorded by researcher Charlotte Zimmerman in 1961. Interested in the religious life of former Maya rebels, she tape-recorded a lengthy oral recitation of the "Divine Commandments" given by the aged secretary of the shrine village of Chun Pom, Juan Bautista Vega. In that recitation Vega twice declared (without any prompting from Zimmerman, who would not have known who Cen was nor what it was that Vega was obscurely referring to) that it was 12 April when Bernardino Cen "fought on earth." In one of those mentions, Vega states that it was "Monday, the twelfth of April." Between Cen's rise to power in Santa Cruz and his death, the only year in which 12 April was a Monday was 1875, which leads me to conclude that the fight to which Vega was referring was Cen's struggle with Poot in Santa Cruz. Vega's recitation is discussed by Zimmerman in "The Hermeneutics of the Maya Cult of the Holy Cross," *Numen: International Review for the History of Religions*, 7(2), 139–59 (April 1965). I am grateful to Zimmerman for having provided me with a copy of her recording of Vega's recitation.

On the other hand, the account of Cen's conflict with Poot that derives from reports of prisoners taken at Xuxub mentions no battle between the two, only that Cen fled because he learned he was to be assassinated. The only eyewitness for that report, however, was an admittedly terrified twelve-year-old boy. Reports of a fight and of a plot to kill Cen are not necessarily contradictory. See Baltazar Montilla to the governor, 15 October 1875, and "La invasión de Xuxub," both from *LRdP*, 20 October 1875 (additional information about these sources is discussed in note 40 of this chapter).

39. "Los indios," *LRdM*, 25 July 1875. That report indicated that because of the division at Santa Cruz, large bodies of Indians were emigrating to Corozal, and that at least one group of about six hundred might be trying to cross to safety in Yucatan itself. The report itself expressed uncertainty about that last movement, and I haven't found any evidence to suggest it actually happened.

40. The details of Cen's flight from Santa Cruz to Tulum and thence northward derive from the interrogation of two men and a boy captured after Cen's raid on Xuxub. Only the boy, aged twelve, the orphaned child of slaves of Cen, accompanied Cen all the way from Santa Cruz. The only accounts I have ever found of what those prisoners had to say are provided in: Baltazar Montilla to the governor, 15 October 1875; and "La invasión de Xuxub," *LRdP*, 20 October 1875. (Though published on the same date, the two accounts evidently derive from two different interrogations of the prisoners, one near the point of their capture, the other in Merida.)

41. How many men actually went along with Pat and Cen? One source estimated those who raided Xuxub may have numbered 150: Montilla to the governor, 15 Octo-

ber 1875, *LRdP*, 20 October 1875. Another source numbered the raiders about 90: "La invasión de Xuxub," *LRdP*, 20 October 1875. The final, and probably accurate estimate, deriving as it did from a count given by three of the captured raiders, is Domingo Evia, "Causa seguida por el C. Jefe político de Merida, contra Encarnación Cahum, Perfecto Chimal y José Chan, por los delitos de robo, plagio, asesinatos . . . , verificados en el rancho Xuxub," 29 May 1876, in *LRdP*, 2 June 1876.

42. The route taken from Muyil is detailed in Montilla to the governor, 15 October 1875, *LRdP*, 20 October 1875. My description of the conditions they would have encountered derives from the description provided by Nicolás Urcelay when in August 1872 he traversed much of the same route in reverse. Nicolás Urcelay, Dolores, Isla Mujeres, "Itinerario de la marcha de las tropas sobre los indios bárbaros," 19 August 1871, in *LRdP*, 26 August 1872. That at least part of the route was flooded is indicated in the source recounting the massacre of the Xuxub captives. Montilla to the governor, 15 October 1875, *LRdP*, 20 October 1875; and Joseph Byrne to Ramón Aznar, 18 October 1875, Claims.

43. That the raiders arrived early on 11 October, a day before their assault of Xuxub, was evidenced by fisherman Ramón Gasca, who found their tracks on that morning. Affidavit of Ramón Gasca, Holbox, 18 January 1876, Misc. Letters, roll 462. That the raiders had arrived on 11 October, not 12 October, was a point greatly relevant to subsequent evaluations of the government's response to the invasion. Also important was the impression the raiders gave that they would encounter no opposition from government forces—a point discussed further in the chapters that follow.

CHAPTER 7: UNNATURAL CRUELTY

1. Mary Stephens to Ulysses S. Grant, 3 December 1875, Misc. Letters, roll 453.

2. "Assassination of an American Citizen in Yucatan—Wholesale Butcheries by the Indians," *NYH*, 12 December 1875.

3. Catherine Stephens Vila to Fish, 9 November 1875, Misc. Letters, roll 451.

4. Fish to Stephens Vila, 12 November 1875, Dom. Letters, roll 80.

5. Fish to Daniel L. Richardson, 29 November 1875, Instructions, vol. 19, roll 115.

6. John L. Cadwalader to Mary Stephens, 24 December 1875, Dom. Letters, roll 80.

7. Fish Diaries, entry for 23 December 1875.

8. Mauricio Tejero, Escribano del Tribunal de Circuito de Yucatan, Campeche, Tabasco y Chiapas, 13 December 1875, in *LRdP*, 17 December 1875, pp. 1–2.

9. Tribunal Superior de Justicia, Yucatan, "Fallo en las diligencias practicadas en comision del H. Tribunal Superior de Justicia contra el C. Baltazar Montilla," 30 December 1875, AGEY Justicia, Caja 110. There was one moment when the court hesitated in clearing Montilla. On 20 December 1875 the court secretary observed to the Governor Ancona that when Montilla undertook his controversial explorations he was acting as Comandante Militar. Ancona responded two days later explaining that that could not have been the case, since his selection as Comandante Militar was only

approved in Merida on 15 May 1875, and given the considerable distance out to Puntachen, news of that approval could not have been received before Montilla undertook at least the first of his incursions. Instead, Ancona educated the court, Montilla had been acting in accordance with municipal regulations and was inspired "by no other motive than his patriotic zeal excited truly by the natural desire of self defense." As Olegario Molina of the Governor's Council observed two days later, that nicely resolved a problem of jurisdiction, since had Montilla been acting as Comandante Militar, then the complaint against him would have to have been heard by a military tribunal. All of these communications are filed with the "Diligencias," cited above.

10. Lespinasse to Skilton, 4 December 1875, Mlr, vol. 1870–1876.

11. Testimony was taken and recorded in Spanish. As the testimony was recorded, sometimes Aquilino referred to himself in the first person—"I was an eyewitness"—other times in the third person—"He saw when Mr. Stephens was taken." To avoid confusion I have altered third-person statements back to first-person statements. Affidavit of Aquilino Bautista, Merida, 7 December 1875, Misc. Letters, roll 462.

12. Tribunal Superior de Justicia, Yucatan. "Fallo en las diligencias practicadas en comision del H. Tribunal Superior de Justicia contra el C. Baltazar Montilla," 30 December 1875, AGEY Justicia, Caja 110.

13. Affidavit of Ceferino Guevara, Merida, 7 December 1875, Misc. Letters, roll 462. I have altered one point of Guevara's deposition. It was recorded that he said "the laborers of Kantunil and peaceful Indians of Kantunil," when he surely said "the laborers of Solferino and peaceful Indians of Kantunil."

14. Concerning the escape of Hernández, see D. S. Osorio to the governor, 20 November 1875, in LRdP, 22 November 1875; affidavit of Francisco Hernández, Merida, 7 December 1875, Misc. Letters, roll 462.

15. Reporting right after the attack on Xuxub, Montilla stated that fourteen men and boys and two women had survived (not counting Byrne and another member of the estate's management). Baltazar Montilla to the governor, 15 October 1875, LRdP, 20 October 1875. Byrne wrote to Mary Stephens that nineteen from Xuxub had survived (including adults and children). Joseph Byrne to Mary Ann Stephens, 21 October 1875, Misc. Letters, roll 451. Subsequent documents mention by name nine male workers who survived the Xuxub attack. Only four—those mentioned earlier in this chapter—were ever deposed by Aznar and Lespinasse. The other workers are identified in: D. S. Osorio to the governor, 20 November 1875, LRdP, 22 November 1875; Tribunal de Circuito, Fallo of 9 December 1975 (mentioning other workers who Aznar wanted deposed at that time), communicated in Mauricio Tejero, Tribunal de Circuito, 13 December 1875, LRdP, 17 December 1875; and Tribunal Superior de Justicia, Yucatan, "Fallo en las diligencias practicadas en comision del H. Tribunal Superior de Justicia contra el C. Baltazar Montilla," 30 December 1875, AGEY Justicia, Caja 110.

16. "La invasión de Xuxub," *LRdP*, 20 October 1875.

17. A prisoner taken in the retaliatory raid that Nicolás Urcelay led against San Antonio Muyil named Domingo Cauich, a fugitive from Isla Mujeres, with Encarnación Cahum and three "companion fugitive workers" from Dzaptun as those who had guided invaders to Kantunilkin. "Declaration of Juan Chan," in Nicolás Urcelay to General en jefe de la brigada de operaciones sobre Yucatán, 19 August 1872, *LRdP*, 26 August 1872.

18. "Decreto de 12 de mayo de 1847 puesto en observancia por el de la junta gobernativa del estado, de fecha 18 del que finaliza [August 1863]," in *NE*, 31 August 1863.

19. "Acto de compromiso del C. José Aragon con su amo D. Ramón Aznar a prestarle su servicio personal en su hacienda de Chablé," and "Compromiso del C. Francisco González . . . ," both from AGEY Justicia, roll 92.

20. "Juicio verbal seguido por el C. Benito Pérez, contra el C. Ramón Aznar, por suma de pesos," Juzgado 4 de Paz, Inicio el 29 de Octubre 1879, AGEY Justicia, Caja 121-A. Six years later Aznar let Cardos go to another employer for only twenty-eight pesos and a few cents. Cardos had probably not worked off that much debt. Aznar simply had little investment in him to begin with. In any event, Urcelay soon caught up with Cardos, who wound up laboring off his original debt back at Solferino. The average amount owed by laborers at Solferino in 1883 was seventy pesos.

21. "1866 Juzgado 3 de Paz, Juicio que sigue Don Andrés Urcelay contra Estanislao Tzek de Papacal," AGEY Justicia, roll 68.

22. "Juicio de revision intentado por el Lic. D. Julian Carrillo con poder de Vicente Yam contra su amo D. Andrés Urcelay," AGEY Justicia, Caja 71, 1863.

23. "Ley para el servicio en los establecimientos de campo," 3 November 1868, in *EP*, 6 November 1868. The Yucatan law did not say employers could punish workers. The law in Campeche did, and practice in Yucatan was no different.

24. I have not found any legal code that expressly permitted such a measure of corporal punishment. But estate owners or others accused of abusing their workers did successfully defend themselves in court by claiming, among other things, that the punishments they meted out did not exceed a presumably permissible limit of, for example, twelve lashings. Concerning the common use of the lash against the Indians and peasants of Yucatan, see Terry Rugeley, *Yucatán's Maya Peasantry and the Origins of the Caste War* (Austin: University of Texas Press, 1996), 86–87.

25. "Inventarios, valúos, adjudicaciones é hijuela de partición de los bienes del finado D. Manuel Rodríguez Solís," 27 May 1875, AGEY Justicia, Caja 104. All my information concerning what was going on at Kancabchen comes from:"Causa seguida á Don Manuel Rodríguez Solís por servicia y fuerza, Juzgado 2 de lo criminal del departamento, Juicio el 1 de Mayo 1869," AGEY Justicia, Caja 86-B, 1869.

26. Apolinar Garcia y Garcia, "Los sirvientes en Yucatan," *LRdM*, 11 October 1871.

27. The mean debt of laborers on Kancabchen in 1875 was 117 pesos, which sum would represent what such a laborer could earn in about seven hundred days—if he

was paid, that is. The median debt was 115, with some laborers owing as little as 14 pesos, and others as much as 153 pesos. "Inventarios, valúos, adjudicaciones é hijuela de partición de los bienes del finado D. Manuel Rodríguez Solís, 27 May 1875, AGEY Justicia, Caja 104.

28. The principal sources concerning the murder of Manuel Rodríguez Solís are "Causa seguida á Justo Cocom, Juan Catzim, Juan Tuyim, Juan y Santiago Nahuat, Estevan Gamboa, Juan Tuyim Yam, Cesario Cocom, José Chan, José Domingo Canché y Tomás Nahuat por homicidio calificado," AGEY Justicia, Caja 97; and "Causa á Justo y Canuto Cocom y socios por homicidio calificado," AGEY Justicia, Caja 102-A, 1874.

29. For the initial characterization of the incident as an Indian uprising, and the subsequent determination that it was a simple crime, see: Yanuario Manzanilla to the governor, 14 May 1873, in LRdP, 15 May 1873, and "Noticia grave," LRdM, 14 May 1873.

30. The literature concerning debt servitude, social control, and brutality on Yucatan's henequen plantations runs the gamut from the inflammatory exposé of John Kenneth Turner, Barbarous Mexico (Chicago: Charles Kerr, 1911), which shocked American readers when serialized in magazines, to a host of scholarly treatments like Moises González Navarro, Raza y tierra: la guerra de castas y el henequén (Mexico: El Colegio de México, 1970); Lawrence Remmers, "Henequen, the Caste War, and the Economy of Yucatan, 1846–1883: The Roots of Dependence in a Mexican Region," (Ph.D. diss., University of California, Los Angeles, 1981), chapter 6; and, most recently, Allen Wells and Gilbert M. Joseph, Summer of Discontent, Seasons of Upheaval: Elite Politics and Rural Insurgency in Yucatan, 1876–1915 (Palo Alto: Stanford University Press, 1996). One of the few studies of peonage as it was in Yucatan just prior to the rise of henequen—the time, in other words, when Manuel Solís was beating his workers—is Pedro Bracamonte Sosa, Amos y Sirvientes: Las haciendas de Yucatán, 1789–1860 (Mérida: Ediciones de la Universidad Autónoma de Yucatán, 1993). For an overview of the scholarly debate about the nature of Yucatecan debt peonage, see Gilbert M. Joseph, Rediscovering the Past at Mexico's Periphery: Essays on the History of Modern Yucatán (University, Alabama: University of Alabama Press, 1986), 59–81.

31. A widely known planters' manual from the period stated that haciendas with five thousand mecates planted in henequen would require about seventy laborers (Remmers, "Henequen," 459). At the time of his death, Manuel Solís had fifty-five hundred mecates of henequen at Kancabchen. How many laborers did he have? Thirty complained against him or were otherwise mentioned during the proceedings in 1869. (The defense noted that this group included almost all of Solís's laborers.) Seven more individuals are mentioned in the case involving Solís's murder four years later. Eight more are listed in the records inventorying the dead man's estate in 1873. That makes for a total of forty-five individuals identified as being laborers at Kancabchen. Some of those named in records from 1873, however, were clearly still children back in 1869. Some of the adults mentioned in the 1869 records were likely dead

or gone by 1873. Hence, my estimate is that at any given moment Solís had about forty adult male laborers at Kancabchen.

32. Concerning the paradoxical effect of mechanization on henequen plantations, see Allen Wells, "From Hacienda to Plantation: The Transformation of Santo Domingo Xcuyum," in Jeffery T. Brannon and Gilbert M. Joseph, eds., *Land, Labor, and Capital in Modern Yucatán: Essays in Regional History and Political Economy* (Tuscaloosa : University of Alabama Press, 1991). Wells observes that while henequen planters mechanized the rasping of fiber and aspects of henequen transport, they failed to make any technological advances in the planting or care of henequen fields. New machines drove the demand for more leaves, but having more henequen leaves depended entirely upon increasing manual labor. For a continued discussion of the increasing rigor of henequen labor regimes after mechanization, see Allen Wells and Gilbert M. Joseph, *Summer of Discontent, Seasons of Upheaval: Elite Politics and Rural Insurgency in Yucatan, 1876–1915* (Palo Alto: Stanford University Press, 1996), 145ff.

CHAPTER 8: SUITABLE MEASURES

a. The firsthand account that alludes to Cosme Cob's demise is the affidavit of Francisco Hernández, Merida, 7 December 1875, Misc. Letters, roll 462. Hernández also reported that the Indians believed it could only have been the peaceful Indians of Kantunilkin who attacked them at Xuxub. Reports of the slaughter of captives in a flooded savanna came presumably from the few captives that escaped, and those reports were conveyed in: Baltazar Montilla to the governor, 15 October 1875, *LRdP*, 20 October 1875; and Byrne to Aznar, 18 October 1875, accompanying Foster to Fish, 10 November 1875, Min. Mexico, roll 53, dispatch 350. Two of those captives who escaped, boys it seems, reported that they saw General Pat dead of a gunshot wound, which was also reported in Montilla to the governor, 15 October 1875. Though two newspapers reported that Pat's body was found by an exploratory party in a savanna a short distance from Xuxub, that was probably a mistake. See "La invasión de Xuxub," *LRdP*, 20 October 1875; and Nestor Rubio Alpuche, "Invasión de Xuxub," *LRdM*, 21 October 1875. Montilla mentioned no fighting beyond the plaza of Xuxub, nor did he mention having found Pat's body. When Montilla reported that the boys had seen Pat's body, he mentioned only that they had seen it along the path they had taken. Byrne, the only other person, besides Encarnación Cahum, Perfecto Chimal, and José Chan, who would have recognized General Pat, was quite specific that Pat had left Xuxub hours before Montilla and his men arrived. This mystery would appear to have only two solutions: Either for some reason Pat returned to Xuxub and was shot by Montilla's men, or Pat was shot by his own men, either accidentally or in a mutiny (e.g., they did not want to follow him back to Xuxub to fight there).

1. The only source that spoke of the workers having been required to declare their grievances against Stephens and strike him was Joseph Byrne, "To the Editor of *La*

Unión Liberal," 22 October 1875, found with dispatch 19, 13 November 1875, vol. 2, consular dispatches from Merida. (Microfilm copies of the Merida dispatches do not include the complete copy of this article.) Byrne did not repeat this story in any of his other tellings of what transpired at Xuxub, I assume because it raised a question he and Aznar did not want raised—i.e., whether the workers did have grievances against Stephens. Sources that indicate that Stephens was taken to his execution by General Pat and four Indians include Byrne to Aznar, 18 October 1875, Min. Mexico to Mexico, roll 53; Byrne, "To the Editor . . . ," cited above; and affidavit of Francisco Hernández, 7 December 1875, Misc. Letters, roll 462. The affidavit of Aquilino Bautista, Merida, 7 December 1875, Misc. Letters, roll 462, indicates that Pat called for two of his men to accompany him. "La invasión de Xuxub," *LRdP,* 20 October 1875, indicates that Cosme Cob was one of those who accompanied Stephens's executioners and that he shouted insults at Stephens. That Cahum accompanied them is stated in the affidavit of Francisco Hernández, cited above, and in the final findings of the trial of Cahum (Domingo Evia, "Causa seguida por el C. Jefe político de esta capital contra Encarnación Cahum, Perfecto Chimal y José Chan," 29 May 1876, in *LRdP,* 2 June 1876). From this I conclude that the four men whom Byrne said accompanied Pat and Stephens included the two soldiers Pat called for and Cosme Cob and Encarnación Cahum.

2. Baltazar Montilla, "Letter to the Editor," 8 October 1875, in *LRdM,* 17 October 1875.

3. There are two versions of Byrne's letter to his employer, Ramón Aznar. One is dated 18 October 1875, the other, 1 November 1875. They are substantially the same letter, and each was intended to be read as Byrne's first communication with Aznar. That is to say, the 1 November letter was to replace the 18 October one. The 1 November letter is identical to the 18 October letter, except for: changes in spelling (e.g., Cen instead of Kemh, Pat instead of Paht); shifts in temporal reference ("I have just arrived from Jolvos [Holbox]," became, "I arrived here from Holbox on the 18th of October last" and "Nov 1st—I was summoned as a witness" became "A few days ago I was summoned as a witness"; trivial changes ("a flooded savanah" to "a savannah," and "a portion of the Indians" to "the Indians"); and the one significant change I have cited about "harsh treatment." The letters are: Byrne to Aznar, 18 October 1875, Min. Mexico, roll 53, accompanied by Foster to Fish, 10 November 1875. Byrne to Aznar, Merida, 1 November 1875, Con. Merida, roll 1.

4. "D. Roberto Stephens," *UL,* 23 October 1875.

5. Rafael de Portas, *Tratado sobre el cultivo de la caña y elaboración de azuar, y, Bases de economía rural y gobierno para los establecimientos de azúcar y para toda finca de campo de Yucatán, con instrucciones relativas al cultivo del henequen* (Mérida, Imprenta del Gobierno, 1872).

6. Two workers—Aquilino Bautista and Ceferino Santos, told a judge that the invaders had come across the savanna. See: Tribunal Superior de Justicia, Yucatan.

"Fallo en las diligencias practicadas en comision del H. Tribunal Superior de Justicia centra el C. Baltazar Montilla," 30 December 1875, AGEY Justicia, Caja 110. Lespinasse and Aznar could not come up with any workers—the only eyewitnesses, after all—who would swear that the Indians had come down Montilla's road.

7. However, executions could still not be carried out until the state governor or other state authority had decided whether to pardon the criminals.

8. It is not entirely obvious from the text of the law that this should happen. See "Ley de Salteadores y Plagiarios" of 3 May 1873, renewed for one year on 28 April 1875, in Manuel Dublan and José María Lozano, eds., *Legislación Mexicana. Colección completa de las disposiciones legislativas expedidas desde la independencia de la república*, vol. 12 (Mexico, 1882), 443–44, item 7169. Evidently authorities so construed their obligation in practice. The chief of the Merida District who tried the prisoners from Xuxub explained it so. See Domingo Evia "Causa seguida por el C. Jefe político de esta capital contra Encarnación Cahum, Perfecto Chimal y José Chan," 29 May 1876, in *LRdP*, 2 June 1876.

9. The reasoning of the court in referring the matter back to the district chief is given in Yanuario Manzanilla, "To the Editor of *La Revista de Mérida*," in *LRdM*, 18 November 1875, which included "Juzgado de Distrito del Estado de Yucatan—Merida 4 November 1875."

10. Ramón Aldana and Perfecto Solís, "To the Editor of *La Revista de Mérida*," 10 November 1875, in *LRdM*, 11 November 1875.

11. *LRdP*, 10 November 1875.

12. Urcelay to Ancona, 18 November 1875, in *LRdP*, 22 November 1875.

13. Concerning Chan, see: Nestor Rubio Alpuche, "La invasión de Xuxub," *LRdM*, 21 October 1875; Rogenio Aguilar Andrade to the governor, 30 May 1876, AGEY Ejecutivo, Caja 74, Sección Gobernación; Domingo Evia, "Causa seguida por el C. Jefe político de esta capital contra Encarnación Cahum, Perfecto Chimal y José Chan," 29 May 1876, in *LRdP*, 2 June 1876. Concerning Chimal, see: Nestor Rubio Alpuche, "La invasión," cited above; and Evia, "Causa seguida," cited above; Nestor Rubio Alpuche to the governor, n.d. (sometime in May 1876), AGEY Ejecutivo, Caja 74, Sección Gobernación. For sources concerning Cahum, see: Evia, "Causa seguida . . . ," cited above; "Declaration of Juan Chan," in Nicolás Urcelay to General en jefe de la brigada de operaciones sobre Yucatán, 19 August 1872, *LRdP*, 26 August 1872, and Nestor Rubio Alpuche, "La invasión," cited above.

14. Mention of the publication in *La Revista Universal* of Mexico City was made in "Prensa Nacional," *LRdP*, 20 December 1875.

15. Fish Diaries, entry for 6 January 1876.

16. Fish Diaries, entries for 27 and 28 January, 17 February, and 9 March 1876.

17. Fish to Foster, 8 January 1876, Instructions.

18. Foster to Juan de Dios Arias, 7 February 1876, Min. Mexico, roll 54.

19. Arias to Foster, 12 February 1876, Min. Mexico to Mexico, roll 54.

20. Arias to Ancona, 12 February 1876, Con. Merida, roll 1.

21. Lespinasse to Hunter, 10 March 1876, Con. Merida, roll 1.

22. Hunter to Lespinasse, 31 March 1876, State-Consuls, vol. 81, pp. 570–71.

23. Corte Suprema de Justicia de los Estados Unidos Mexicanos, 1a Sala, Decree of 24 January 1876, Claims, Mexican Reply Memorial, Annex 31.

24. D. S. Osorio to the governor, 21 February 1876, and same to same, 22 February 1876, in *LRdP*, 25 February 1876. Concerning the beginnings of the revolt in Yucatan, see Albino Acereto, "Historia política desde el descubrimiento europeo hasta 1920," in *Enciclopedia yucatanense*, vol. 3 (Mexico, 1947), 331–32.

25. I have not been able to find out why Urcelay was replaced, nor what became of him. He would have been completing his second year as Jefe Político, so his replacement was likely routine. (A district chief could serve more than one two-year term, but not in immediate succession.) There is no indication that he was removed because of the Xuxub affair.

26. Mary Stephens, affidavit and claim of 4 March 1876, Misc. Letters, roll 459. Ramón Aznar, affidavit of 6 April 1876, Misc. Letters, roll 462. That Mary Stephens had little hand in the drafting of her claim is indicated not only by the language—it contrasts radically with the language of Mary Stephens to John J. Cadwalader, 24 February 1876, Misc. Letters, roll 458, and is in many parts verbatim with Ramón Aznar's claim—but also from something Aznar wrote to Mary Stephens: "Inasmuch as with the untimely death of your husband, you and your family have remained without funds, a protest has been made under the direction of the American lawyer, Mr. G. F. Ford, which I enclose and which please sign and return. This claim has been made for $30,000, in view of the verbal instructions you gave me." Ramón Aznar to Mary Stephens, 3 March 1876, File of Evidence Not Used, Claims.

27. Things were not quite that simple. The individual was slowly acquiring a standing in international law. American and Mexican commissioners to the Claims Commission of 1868 disagreed on this very point; the American commissioner asserted the more traditional view that claims submitted were the claims of one government against another, while the Mexican commissioner argued that the claims were the claims of individuals, not governments. See Frederick Dunn, *The Diplomatic Protection of Americans in Mexico* (New York: Columbia University Press, 1933), 97.

28. This is one of the basic findings in Frederick Dunn, *The Diplomatic Protection of Americans in Mexico* (New York: Columbia University Press, 1933). See, for example, pp. 7–8, and pp. 102–3.

29. Mary Stephens to John J. Cadwalader, 24 February 1876, Misc. Letters, roll 458. Cadwalader was assistant secretary of state. I have found no evidence that he ever responded to this letter. Mary Stephens wrote directly to Fish on 8 June 1876, and Fish in response made reference to "voluminous documents" that he had on file concerning the case. Hence my reasoning that he would also have seen Mary's 24 February missive. Mary Stephens to Hamilton Fish, n.d, Misc. Letters, roll 466. Fish to Mary Stephens, 8 June 1876, Dom. Letters, roll 82.

30. When an American was injured in Mexico, he or she could forward a protest

directly to the U.S. Legation in Mexico City. Claims seeking monetary damages, however, had first to be reviewed by the State Department in Washington, before being acted upon in any way by American diplomats in Mexico. That is why the Stephens and Aznar claims went first to Washington and then on to the U.S. Legation in Mexico City.

31. Fish to Foster, 29 May 1876, Instructions, roll 115.

32. In his brief discussion of the standing, or non-standing, of the individual alien under international law, A. H. Feller observes that the right of the state to espouse a claim against another state for harm done to one of its nationals "on the one hand ... springs from a primitive feeling of clannishness, the necessity of protecting a member of the clan and of avenging him when he is injured." His subsequent argument that vengeance, rather than restitution, was the motive behind much such claim-seeking and diplomatic intervention rings true for the years and cases I deal with in this book. A. H. Feller, *The Mexican Claims Commissions, 1923–1934, A Study in the Law and Procedure of International Tribunals* (New York, The MacMillan Company, 1935), 83–85

33. Domingo Evia, "Causa seguida por el C. Jefe político de esta capital contra Encarnación Cahum, Perfecto Chimal y José Chan," 29 May 1876, in *LRdP*, 2 June 1876. I have not actually found copies of the defense submissions, but their content can be inferred from Evia's refutations of the arguments that had been raised.

34. Ancona to Ministro de Estado, México, "Desacuerdos entre los propietarios del rancho 'Xuxub' y las autoridades locales de 'Puntachen'" 4 November 1875, Claims, Mexican Reply Memorial, Annex 1.

35. Petition for mercy for Encarnación Cahum, Perfecto Chimal, and José Chan, 29 May 1876, AGEY Ejecutivo, Caja 74, Sección Gobernacion, Correspondencia/Instrumentos Legales.

36. Rogenio Aguilar Andrade to the governor, 30 May 1876, AGEY Ejecutivo, Caja 74, Sección Gobernación.

37. Nestor Rubio Alpuche to the governor, n.d., AGEY Ejecutivo, Caja 74, Sección Gobernación.

38. Juan J. Molina Solís to the governor, 30 May 1876, AGEY Ejecutivo, Caja 74, Sección Gobernación.

39. Encarnación Cahum to H. Tribunal Superior de Justicia del Estado, 31 May 1876, AGEY Justicia, Caja 112.

40. "Ejecucion de Justicia," *LRdP*, 2 June 1876.

41. Ancona to C. Oficial Mayor encargado del Ministerio de Relaciones Exteriores, Mexico, 22 June 1876, Annex 32, Mexican Reply Memorial, Claims; Arias to Foster, 28 June 1876, NfMFO, vol. 27; Foster to Fish, Min. Mexico, roll 54.

CHAPTER 9: WORLDLY SATISFACTION

a. Baltazar Montilla once estimated that under Maricio Palmero Xuxub was home to about thirty families. Baltazar Montilla, "Letter to the Editor," 8 October 1875, LRdM, 17 October 1875. I assume that a few years later, with Xuxub supposedly growing more prosperous every year, there still were some thirty families living there under Robert Stephens. That would make, conservatively, for about a hundred people. At most only twenty—Joseph Byrne and nineteen others—were ever reported as having been "saved" (see note 15 to chapter 7). Byrne once reported that of the thirty-seven Xuxub residents killed (including Robert Stephens), thirty were killed in the savanna. Joseph Byrne to Ramón Aznar, 18 October 1875, Min. Mexico, roll 53. Later he revised that number upwards, claiming that thirty-seven were killed out in the savanna. Joseph Byrne to the editor of La Union Liberal, 22 October 1875, a copy of which was found in Con. Merida. One of the workers who managed to avoid the massacre and escape his captors reported (though how could he know?) that precisely four women and one child from Xuxub were living in captivity, or, as the source put it, "in enemy territory suffering the horrors of a true slavery." D. S. Osorio to the governor, 20 November 1875, LRdP, 22 November 1875.

b. The plundering of Xuxub by Montilla is alleged in the affidavits of Adolfo Correa, 11 December 1875, and Ramón Gasca, 18 January 1876, and seemingly corroborated by Juan Alvarez, 30 January 1876. The first two affidavits are found in National Archives, Misc. Letters, roll 462 (accompanying Ramón Aznar's claim of 6 April 1876), the last in National Archives, Con. Merida, roll 1.

1. The incident in southern Yucatan was reported in Rafael A. Pérez to the governor, 12 October 1875, in LRdP, 15 October 1875; same to same, 18 October 1875, in LRdP, 20 October 1875; and Various residents of Peto to the editor, 16 October 1875, in LRdM, 21 October 1875. That the party had come from Santa Cruz is suggested by the report of the male captive who fled Santa Cruz months later: "Declaration of Santos Escamilla," in Ancona to Ministry of Foreign Relations, Mexico City, 18 March 1876, in LRdP, 3 May 1876. Word of the arms shipment—including 360 firearms—and information concerning the planned invasion of Yucatan came from escaped captive Santos Escamilla, whose declaration is cited above.

2. I discuss and document the many twists and turns of the peace process in "The Search for Peace in Yucatan, 1876–1886," Saastun: Revista de Cultura Maya, 0.3 (December 1997): 3–46. For a somewhat different account of the process, see Don Dumond, The Machete and the Cross: Campesino Rebellion in Yucatán (Lincoln: University of Nebraska Press, 1997), 325–31.

3. The quoted passage comes from a postscript to the written commandments, known to scholars as the Proclamation of Juan de la Cruz or Sermons of the Talking Cross. The postscript was dated 15 August 1887. The postscript is included in versions of the text published in Victoria Bricker, The Indian Christ, the Indian King: The Historical Substrate of Maya Myth and Ritual (Austin: University of Texas Press, 1981). 206–7, and Alfonso Villa Rojas, The Maya of East Central Quintana Roo (Washington, D.C.:

Carnegie Institution of Washington, 1945), 163–64. Relying upon the Maya text provided in Bricker, I've deviated from the English translation a bit. This postscript was penned very near the second anniversary of Poot's fall, and hence may have inspired it (that was the biggest thing that had happened since the fall of Cen a decade earlier still). The forces that overthrew Poot occupied Santa Cruz and killed Poot's main general, Juan Chuc, on 23 August 1885, according to the text of the Sermon of the Talking Cross as published by Villa, cited above. (Villa transcribed the name as "Chi" though the person referred to was clearly Juan Chuc. Poot himself, it seems, was assassinated within days after that.

4. That Attorney Hijuelos handled all of Josefa's affairs and that Josefa lived otherwise isolated from the world is stated by her uncle, Genaro Rodríguez, in his 26 April 1881 petition to the Juez 2 de lo Civil, contained in the "Will and Inventory of the Estate of Josefa Rodríguez," AGEY Justicia, Caja 130-A, 1881. Records of the long fight to disinherit the daughter of the mistress of Manuel Solís include: "Solicitud de Doña Manuel Canto reclamando la patria potesta de Eulalia Gómez, 1874," AGEY Justicia, Caja 102; "Diligencias promovidas por Doña Manuela Canto para justificar la patria potestad que ejerce sobre su nieta Eulalia Rodríguez, 1877," AGEY Justicia, Caja 146-C; "Juicio ordinario promovido por Doña Manuela Canto contra la Señora Josefa Romero de Rodríguez Solís y C. Esteban Rodríguez Solís, para que se declare que su nieta la menor Señorita Eulalia Rodríguez Solís se halla en posesion de los derechos de hija legítima de D. Manuel Rodríguez Solís, Juzgado 2 de lo civil, 1880," AGEY Justicia, Caja 124; "1885, Juicio ordinario promovida por Doña Manuela Canto para que se declare que su nieta Eulalia Rodríguez Solís se halla en posesion de los derechos de hija legítima de D. Manuel Rodríguez Solís"; and "Diligencias promovidas por la representación de dicha Señora sobre intervención de varias fincas," AGEY Justicia Caja 146-C. Court actions against the freed killers of Josefa's husband are indicated in Expediente without title page, AGEY Justicia, Caja 121, 1879; "Juicio verbal seguido por el apoderado de la Señora Josefa Rodríguez contra el C. Santiago Nahuat, Juzgado 4 de paz," AGEY Justicia, Caja 121-B; and "Juicio verbal seguido por el apoderado de la Señora Doña Josefa Rodríguez de Solís, contra el C. José Chan por deuda, Juzgado 4 de paz," AGEY Justicia, Caja 121-B. The men are still listed as debtors to Josefa in the inventory of her estate made after her death. The estate Josefa inherited upon the death of her husband was valued at $61,000. When Josefa died, her estate was valued only at $11,000. Her property had not depreciated in value—what she still held in property inherited from her husband had actually increased in value. Rather, property had been sold and the money spent or misdirected.

5. "Diligencias promovidas por el C. Francisco Avila en representación de su esposa Doña Encarnación Rodríguez para que se le entregue una cantidad de pesos en cuenta de su haber en la testamentaria de su hermana Doña Josefa del mismo apellido," AGEY Justicia, Caja 130-A, 1881.

6. Aznar to Mary Stephens, 3 March 1876, File of Evidence Not Used, Claims.

To his credit, Aznar did propose to split his award with Mary Stephens fifty-fifty, since that award would represent, in effect, the liquidation of the Xuxub property. Mary Stephens also hoped to receive an award for the death of her husband.

7. Foster to Fish, 7 July 1876, Min. Mexico, roll 54; Richardson to Arias, 30 July 1876, NtMFO, vol. 9; Romero Rubio to Richardson, 30 September 1876, NfMFO, vol. 27.

8. Richardson to Fish, 5 October 1876, Min. Mexico, roll 55.

9. Mary Stephens to Fish, 6 January 1877, Misc. Letters, roll 477.

10. Fish to Mary Stephens, 12 January 1877, Dom. Letters, roll 83. Concerning the scramble to raise funds to make the first claims payment, due that same month, see Daniel Cosío Villegas, *The United States Versus Porfirio Díaz*, trans. Nettie Lee Benson (Lincoln: University of Nebraska Press, 1963), 15ff.

11. Mary Stephens to William Evarts, 4 April 1877, Misc. Letters, roll 483. Evarts to Stephens, 19 April 1877, Dom. Letters, roll 84. That Evarts would not involve himself in careful study of such matters is also suggested by John Foster's observation of him years later: "A brilliant lawyer, an orator of a high order, and a vigorous writer, he was without method in his office and left the routine business of the Department to his subordinates." Foster, *Diplomatic Memoirs*, vol. 2, 261.

12. Stephens to Evarts, 10 January 1878, Misc. Letters, roll 501. Evarts to Stephens, 16 January 1878, Dom. Letters, roll 85.

13. Foster prepared a lengthy memorandum reviewing the history of the anti-claims policy when he was asked in 1889 to write an opinion of yet another American citizen's claim against Mexico. John W. Foster, Opinion in Baldwin case, 8 May 1889, Misc. Letters, roll 772. That aggrieved foreigners should seek local redress was the well-accepted premise under international law. The United States and the Latin American Republics would for decades contest, however, whether diplomatic intervention could ever be justified. The Latin American Republics sought by various means to have diplomatic intervention categorically excluded from the remedies aggrieved foreigners might seek. The United States defended the practice of diplomatic intervention on various grounds and always in the case of serious violations of international law. In that regard, long memorandums like Foster's cited above, while stating non-controversial positions (i.e., individuals should seek local redress), left unexplored such key issues as: Has a claimant truly had equal access to local courts? Has justice been denied or delayed? Do the standards of justice in the country in question meet the minimum standards of "civilized nations"? For a cogent discussion of these and other issues that the U.S. and the Latin American Republics disputed for decades, see Donald Shea, *The Calvo Clause: A Problem of Inter-American and International Law and Diplomacy* (Minneapolis, University of Minnesota Press, 1955). Concerning Foster's high opinion of Porfirio Díaz, Foster's efforts (eventually successful) to obtain U.S. recognition for Díaz's government, Foster's friendship with Díaz (Foster's wife introduced the new president to the woman he would marry), and the threat

of war with Mexico, see Michael J. Devine, *John W. Foster: Politics and Diplomacy in the Imperial Era, 1873–1917* (Athens: Ohio University Press, 1981) 20–24. Mexican historian Daniel Cosío Villegas explores in detail this tense period of U.S.-Mexican Relations in *The United States Versus Porfirio Díaz*, trans. Nettie Lee Benson (Lincoln: University of Nebraska Press, 1963). Foster appears never to have reported acting upon the instructions he received in the matter of Mary Stephens, and in subsequent stages of this claims process State Department officials reported they had no records indicating that the proofs had in fact been requested by Foster or anyone else. See, for example, Hunter to Mary Stephens, 9 June 1879, Dom. Letters, roll 89.

14. Records of the Hudson and Bergen County Catholic Cemeteries indicate that Robert Stephens is buried there, in grave number block B-I-16, 24 Jan. 1882. That can hardly be the case. His remains would have been interred on Holbox Island. That the grave holds the remains of Mary Ann Stephens is indicated by a letter dated 10 June 1935 from the Office of the Hudson and Bergen County Catholic Cemeteries, Claims, File of Evidence not Used. Concerning Mary Stephens's household around that time, see National Archives, 1880 Census, Schedule 1, "Inhabitants in the Township of West Hoboken," p. 437 of roll T-9, 785. Mary Stephens did once more, in 1886, communicate with the State Department about her claim, prompted to do so by something she had read in local newspapers, "that this country and Mexico have had a little trouble on account of bad treatment to an American citizen." It was a brief letter referring to her claim still on file. I find no response to her letter, and she never wrote again. Mary Stephens to Bayard, Secretary of State, 9 August 1886, Misc. Letters, roll 708.

15. Affidavits of Manuel Alvarez and Adolfo Correa, 11 December 1875, Misc. Letters, roll 562.

EPILOGUE: TRUTH, GUILT, AND NARRATIVE

1. The mention of Chun Ox is a telling, probably accurate little detail. Chun Ox is a small village in the vicinity of Chun Pom and (before it was abandoned) San Antonio Muyil.

2. "Gacetilla. Otro incendio," *LRdM*, 16 May 1880. I have no direct evidence that Aznar at that point gave up on Xuxub. The above-cited article noted, "intelligent people are of the opinion that . . . that establishment cannot produce sufficient benefits to recompense the work and capital invested in it." After this date I find no further mention of Xuxub as a functioning sugar farm. Hence, I conclude that Aznar quit the place to focus on his other estates. While Aznar's operations at Chablé generated much paper that wound up in archives, concerning his two henequen estates I have found only advertisements for their sale: one, north of Valladolid, had evidently only recently planted in henequen, and was advertised in *LRdM*, 22 November 1883, p. 1; the other, with cattle and henequen, three leagues east of Merida, was advertised in

LRdP, 28 June 1880, p. 4. That Aznar was selling the estates does not mean he ever operated them. He may simply have acquired them through foreclosure on bad debts.

3. The petition of the residents of Puntachen and Holbox for land around Santa Cruz Majas, three leagues south of the coast from Puntachen, is discussed in: L. Yrigoyen to the governor, 26 July 1878 (dispatch 119); and M. Romero Ancona and Juan Esquivel to the president of the Council of Government, 17 July 1878, both in AGEY Ejecutivo, Caja 203, Sección Gobernación. The petition was expected to be declined because federal law prohibited granting land to a corporation, which the group of petitioners was considered to be by virtue of its "groupness." A report of an official visit to Puntachen in 1881 indicated that Puntachen had remained largely abandoned after the attack on Xuxub, and that only 52 men, women, and children lived there. The official supposed that all were indebted laborers working for a daily wage in logwood cutting. The 150 residents of Holbox were reportedly engaged in the same kind of work under the same conditions. Antonio Cisneros Cámera to the governor, 8 September 1881, in *LRdP,* 21 September 1881. A census completed six years later found only 38 people at Puntachen over the age of fifteen, all of them reported to be laborers. "Partido de Progreso—Municipalidad de Isla Mujeres, Padrón general de los vecinos que habitan en el puerto de Puntachen . . . ," AGEY Ejecutivo, Caja 246, Poblacíon.

4. When the attacks occurred in July of 1882, first reports were that the barbarous Indians had invaded. The entire frontier went on alert, troops sallied out of Valladolid in pursuit of the invaders, and the state government quickly shipped weapons to Holbox Island so that men there could respond to the Indian menace along the coast. Once the panic had passed, however, more sober minds concluded that only a couple of dozen or so men had staged the attack. The bizarre little episode generated many dispatches but little reliable information. A report in the 15 August 1882 edition of *LRdM,* to the effect that there may have been as few as fifteen "invaders," seems plausible, though even that newspaper added that perhaps there were several such groups, bringing the total closer to sixty.

5. The assets of the late Manuel Urcelay totaled about 50,000 pesos, not including the value of two life insurance policies. His debts totaled 32,300 pesos. The balance was actually bleaker, however. Assets put up for auction garnered only two-thirds of their assessed value. If the entire saleable estate had been liquidated at that rate (which it could not be), the estate would have had a negative balance. "Autos de juicio de intestado del C. Manuel Urcelay, 1883," AGEY Justicia, Caja 138, 1883. As for the estate of Nicolás Urcelay, one of his properties, Majas, was valued by the assessor as worth some 11,000 pesos. But that was a fantasy. Without laborers, management, and energy to apply, it was worth next to nothing, and the tax man assessed Majas and another property, Axnal, combined as worth only 500 pesos in November 1889. "Testamentaria de Nicolás Urcelay," AGEY Justicia, Caja 161-D. That Ramón

Aznar was an agent for New York Mutual Life comes from an announcement he placed in the paper: "Seguros de vida," *LRdM*, 13 May 1884.

6. The subsequent history of competition and consolidation of properties and concessions in the northeast of the Yucatan Peninsula is detailed in Antonio Higuera Bonfil, *Quintana Roo Entre Tiempos: Política, poblamiento, y explotación forestal, 1872–1925* (Chetumal, Quintana Roo: La Universidad de Quintana Roo, 1997); Martha H. Villalobos González, "Las concesiones forestales en Quintana Roo a fines del porfiriato," *Relaciones: Estudios de História y Sociedad*, 14(53), 87–112, 1993; Herman Konrad, "Capitalism on the tropical-forest frontier: Quintana Roo, 1880s to 1930," in Brannon and Joseph, eds. *Land, Labor and Capital*, 143–71. As for the late petitions for land around Kantunilkin, Chiquila, and other spots, I consulted reports of the Secretary of the Agrarian Reform, Mexico City, Expedientes 23:24228 (Chiquila), 23:8542 (Kantunilkin), 23:17504 (Solferino). It was the petitioners of Solferino who wrote of how "when we installed ourselves here slavery predominated in this region." The lands of Xuxub were given to the agrarian community of Chiquila in a grant made in 1979.

7. I have discussed the present-day prophetic and apocalyptic proclivities of the descendants of Maya rebels in: Paul Sullivan, "Contemporary Maya Apocalyptic Prophecy: The Ethnographic and Historical Context," (Ph.D. diss., The Johns Hopkins University, 1984); and Paul Sullivan, *Unfinished Conversations: Mayas and Foreigners Between Two Wars* (New York: Alfred A. Knopf, 1989). More complete ethnographies of those postwar Maya are: Alfonso Villa Rojas, *The Maya of East Central Quintana Roo* (Washington, D.C.: Carnegie Institution of Washington, 1945), and Ueli Hostettler, "Milpa Agriculture and Economic Diversification: Socioeconomic Change in a Maya Peasant Society of Central Quintana Roo, 1900–1990s" (Ph.D. diss., Institut für Ethnologie, University of Berne, 1996).

8. Baqueiro's article about Poot was published in issues of *El Eco del Comercio* on 18, 21, 25, and 27 June 1887, and that article was republished by Luis Millet Cámara as "Un estudio biográfico de Crescencio Poot por el Lic. Serapio Baqueiro," *Boletín de la Escuela de Ciencias Antropológicas de la Universidad de Yucatán* 16(96), 15–33 (May–June 1989).

9. Ibid., 27.

10. Ibid., 22.

11. Ibid., 26–27. Baqueiro did not name Avila and Josefa, but there is no mistaking to whom he was referring when he wrote: "Here [what I was told] by a good friend, resident of Tunkas. . . . He had written ahead of time [to Poot] asking permission to come looking for his wife, who for twenty years he [Poot] had held captive." Baqueiro goes on to relate Avila's first encounter with Poot, and how Poot then had Avila's wife brought and allowed Avila to have her back, implying that she was thus freed. Of course everyone at the time could read in newspapers how things actually turned out, and Baqueiro knew even more, having signed as witness to the judicial transaction in which Avila received 3,500 pesos from his wife's estate in order to

secure the release of Encarnación Rodríguez."Diligencias promovidas por el C. Francisco Avila en representación de su esposa Doña Encarnación Rodríguez . . . ," AGEY Justicia, Caja 130-A, 1881.

12. For what sketchy details are available about Baqueiro's difficulties with the first volume of his grand work, I rely upon Hernan Menéndez, *Iglesia y poder: Proyectos sociales, alianzas políticas y económicas en Yucatán, 1857–1917* (Mexico City: Editorial Nuestra América and Consejo Nacional para la Cultura y las Artes, 1995), 54–56; and Alan Wells, "Forgotten Chapters of Yucatan's Past: Nineteenth-century Politics in Historiographical Perspective," *Mexican Studies/Estudios Mexicanos* 12:2 (Summer 1996): 191–229.

13. Ramón Aznar to Grover Cleveland, 30 May 1890, Misc. Letters, roll 828.

14. Edward Thompson to Thomas R. Ryan, 25 September 1890 (enclosed with Ryan's 20 October 1890 dispatch to James Blaine), Min. Mexico, roll 100.

15. Aznar's troubles at Chablé are detailed in:"Juicio verbal promovido por María Victoriana Tus, contra el C. Ramón Aznar Pérez, por suma de pesos," AGEY Justicia, Caja 121-B, 1879;"Complaint of Prospero Patron, et. al., against Julian Pech, et. al., 1884," AGEY Justicia, Caja 145, 1885;"Representación del C. Don Ramón Aznar, pidiendo que su hacienda Chablé y anexa San Francisco, del municipio de Chocholá, pasen al municipio de esta capital," Indice de expedientes del fondo Congreso del Estado, Sección Comisión de gobernación, Serie dictamenes, vol. 5, exp. 7; Camilo Solís to the governor, 10 November 1885; and Arturo Patron to the governor of Yucatán, 12 November 1885, both from AGEY Ejecutivo, Caja 233; protest of Ramón Aznar, 17 May 1890, with Miscellaneous Affidavits; and Aznar to Cleveland, 30 May 1890, both from Misc. Letters, roll 828; Edward Thompson to Thomas R. Ryan, 25 September 1890 (enclosed with Ryan's 20 October 1890 dispatch to James Blaine), Min. Mexico, roll 100; Blaine to Ryan, 5 November 1890, Instructions, roll 118; Ryan to Ignacio Mariscal, Mexico, 21 November 1890 (enclosed with Ryan to Blaine, 21 November 1890), Min. Mexico, roll 101; Miscellaneous Affidavits, Misc. Letters, roll 828 (mistakenly filed with J. R. Duff, 4 November 1891, regarding Mary Stephens against Mexico); Mr. Azpiroz to Ryan, 23 February 1891, Min. Mexico, roll 102; Aznar to Cleveland, 19 January 1891, Cleveland Papers, roll 68; Aznar to Duff, New York, 17 April 1891, Misc. Letters, roll 828 (filed with J. R. Duff, 4 November 1891).

16. Ramón Aznar, affidavit, January 1892, Misc. Letters, roll 832 (enclosed with Duff to Blaine, 28 January 1892).

17. Duff to Foster, 26 July 1892, Misc. Letters, roll 844.

18. FCP [Partridge?], Department of State, to Duff, 5 August 1892, Misc. Letters, roll 844. Concerning Foster's fee-generating work for foreign governments, see Michael J. Devine, *John W. Foster: Politics and Diplomacy in the Imperial Era, 1873–1917* (Athens: Ohio University Press, 1981), 34–35, 49–50. (*NYT* quote comes from page 50 of Devine.) That Foster would have, if paid enough, done what he could for Mary Stephens despite the long passage of time is suggested, at least, by his support in 1890

for the claim of an American client who alleged losses from a riot in Panama back in 1856. See Foster to secretary of state, 19 March 1890, Misc. Letters, roll 791. In any event Foster was clearly one of America's first revolving-door officials, serving alternately (and at the same time?) public and private, foreign and domestic interests, and a more thorough study of his career in that regard is merited.

19. Duff to Cleveland, 22 November 1893, Misc. Letters, roll 877.

20. Edwin F. Uhl to Duff, 4 December 1893, Dom. Letters, roll 122.

21. Affidavit of John McCauley [former police chief of West Hoboken], 6 June 1835, Claims. "Mrs. Joseph R. Duff, Ex-Health Commissioner of West Hoboken a Suffrage Leader," [obit.], NYT, 28 November 1845. John J. Haynes to the secretary of state, 26 September 1904, Misc. Letters, roll 1224. F. B. Loomis to John J. Haynes, New York, 30 September 1904, Dom. Letters, roll 163. Loomis to Mrs. Joseph Duff, 7 February 1905, Dom. Letters, roll 164 [this mentions Evangeline having written to the president on 1 February 1905; I have not found her letter, however]. Henry Goldfogle to Elihu Root, 15 February 1906, Misc. Letters, roll 1284. Root to Goldfogle, Dom. Letters, roll 169. Certificate and Record of Death, State of New Jersey, Bureau of Vital Statistics, Mary A. Stevens, 20 September 1907. Mary Stephens was seventy-nine years old.

22. The agreements establishing the U.S.-Mexican Claims Commissions, as well as their procedures and practices, are discussed in considerable detail in A. H. Feller, The Mexican Claims Commissions, 1923–1934: A Study in the Law and Procedure of International Tribunals (New York: The MacMillan Company, 1935). My characterization of the work of the commissions pertains especially to the General, rather than Special, Claims Commission, as it was the General Claims Commission that considered the Xuxub claim.

23. Memorandum of Claim, United States of America on behalf of Ramón Aznar vs. United Mexican States, 29 August 1925, Claims. Memorandum Relative to a Claim Submitted by Ramón Aznar, Julian Aznar G., 22 December 1926, Claims. Ramón Aznar died in New York City in 1896.

24. U.S. Agency to Mrs. Joseph Duff, 22 October 1826, Claims. For the tally of the slim accomplishments of the General Claims Commission, see A. H. Feller, The Mexican Claims Commissions, 1923–1934: A Study in the Law and Procedure of International Tribunals (New York: The MacMillan Company, 1935), 60. The commission made eighty-nine awards in favor of the United States amounting to 4.6 million dollars, and five in favor of Mexico amounting to only 39 thousand dollars. In addition some fifty-four claims, mostly American, were disallowed or dismissed. The achievements of the Special Claims Commission were even more meager.

25. Policy Statement of the U.S. Agency, 10 December 1934, Claims. In the estimation of A. H. Feller, one of the reasons for the virtual failure of the prior U.S.-Mexican General and Special Claims Commissions was that the diplomatic offices of each nation simply dumped into the lap of the commissions every scrap of a possible

claim they could find, rather than carefully selecting beforehand to present only those claims that might truly have merit. A. H. Feller, *The Mexican Claims Commissions, 1923–1934: A Study in the Law and Procedure of International Tribunals* (New York: The MacMillan Company, 1935), 57.

26. In each of their subsequent reviews of what transpired, American lawyers would contend that authorities promised to protect Stephens. That promise was oblique, at best, and was contained only in an editorial published in the official newspaper, "La Cuestion Stephens," *La Razón del Pueblo*, 15 October 1875, 3–4. In that editorial was written: "Sr. Stephens should not complain because the activity of the authorities of Puntachen guarantees him that in the case of an invasion of the rebels, there are those who with their lives will defend his property." The American lawyers writing decades later overlooked that when that public "promise" was made, Stephens was already dead.

27. Memorial, Preliminary Statement, Claims. The American Agency had hoped to present this claim on behalf of still other descendants of Robert and Mary Stephens, namely the children and grandchildren of the other sister, Catherine. The others, however, were unable to assemble proofs of descent and citizenship before the memorial was filed with the claims commission, and Mexico argued insistently (and successfully) that no other claimants could be added after the filing had occurred.

28. "Contestación," [Mexican response to United States Agency Brief and Memorial] c. October 1935, Claims.

29. That Mexico was at the same time before the Special Claims Commission agreeing to pay for damages resulting from just such acts was not a contradiction. The U.S.-Mexican convention that established the Special Claims Commission stipulated that Mexico would entertain such claims for damages inflicted by revolutionary armies and bands during the Mexican Revolution not because it was obliged to under international law, but, rather, only because it felt "morally bound to make full indemnification." It did so, in other words, as part of a policy designed to improve international relations (and secure recognition for its government), not because international law required it. For a discussion of this issue, see A. H. Feller, *The Mexican Claims Commissions: 1923–1934: A Study in the Law and Procedure of International Tribunals* (New York: The MacMillan Company, 1935).

30. Secretary of State to James Slattery, 19 November 1937, Claims.

31. Mary Stephens to Ulysses Grant, 3 Dec. 1875, Misc. Letters, roll 453.

Index